A 17th CENTURY SCOUNDREL: THE LIFE AND TIMES OF THOMAS SPIGURNELL, ATTORNEY, CLERK OF TAUNTON CASTLE, CONFEDERATE, FATHER, GENTLEMAN, PETTYFOGGER, STEWARD AND SURVEYOR OF TAUNTON, WILTON, CLEMENT'S INN AND LONG SUTTON, 1630-1663

Long Sutton church where Thomas Spigurnell's first wife was
buried in 1657. Then, after his second marriage to Elizabeth
Browne, their youngest child Elizabeth was baptised in 1661.
Thomas was buried there in 1663 in a 'very meane manner'.
(Author's photograph)

A 17th CENTURY SCOUNDREL: THE LIFE AND TIMES OF THOMAS SPIGURNELL, ATTORNEY, CLERK OF TAUNTON CASTLE, CONFEDERATE, FATHER, GENTLEMAN, PETTYFOGGER, STEWARD AND SURVEYOR OF TAUNTON, WILTON, CLEMENT'S INN AND LONG SUTTON, 1630-1663

Adrian James Webb

HARRY GALLOWAY PUBLISHING

A 17th century scoundrel: the life and times of Thomas Spigurnell, attorney, clerk of Taunton Castle, confederate, father, gentleman, pettyfogger, steward and surveyor of Taunton, Wilton, Clement's Inn and Long Sutton, 1630-1663

This series contains new research based upon primary records held in archives, libraries and private collections. These volumes provide new perspectives on aspects of Somerset's rich and diverse archival heritage. Each volume contains a mixture of research and transcripts of original records.

Privately published in a limited edition print run by the author
c/o 19 Kirke Grove, Taunton, Somerset, TA2 8SB

Typeset in Garamond by the author

Cover design by the author. The front cover is a photograph of Sherford House where Thomas Spigurnell lived for a short time (courtesy of Mr Rodney Pepperell). The back cover is a print of the Exchequer rooms at Taunton Castle and (below) is Court Farm, or Court House, at Long Sutton (photographed by the author)

I.S.B.N 1-86241-047-3
© Adrian James Webb, 2023

CONTENTS

ACKNOWLEDGEMENTS

I am grateful to acknowledge the help given to me by David Bromwich, Charles Doble, Emma Down, William Hancock, Susan Moore, Sandra Ogborne and the late Margaret Webb in researching, checking and helping in some capacity in producing this text for a wider audience. My biggest debts go to William Hancock for sharing his knowledge of 17th century legal matters and for many hours of support. Also to Sandra Ogborne for typing the majority of the transcripts, particularly the depositions, the subject index and discussing the life and times of Thomas Spigurnell over numerous cups of coffee in Edgell Building.

EDITORIAL

Dates are shown from the 1st of January until the 25th of March as 1661/2 to reflect the calendar in use before 1754. Text shown in single quotes is taken from contemporary documents, e.g. 'pricked'. Text in square brackets has been added by myself e.g. edit[or]. Text that is missing from contemporary documents is shown as full stops e.g. docu...ts. A section of a document that has been omitted is shown as three dots together e.g. ... Latin text if untranslated is shown in italics. Words that are crossed through in the original are shown thus ~~crossed through~~. Words that are interlined are shown within angular brackets e.g. <interlined>. Numbers shown in bold in square brackets, e.g. [7] refer to transcripts printed in this volume; a list of these appears on pages 1-2.

INTRODUCTION

At the heart of the main dispute brought to light in this volume was the office of clerk of Taunton Castle and an Interregnum attorney of dubious intent. This important office was held by a patent from the bishop of Winchester who for centuries was lord of the manor of Taunton and Taunton Deane. A contemporary in the 1660s described the main duties of that office within the bishop of Winchester's 'great manor of Taunton Deane':

> by himself or his deputy in that behalf to take and enter all surrenders both absolute surrenders mortgage surrenders and others and all other acts for the passing and conveying of the said copyhold lands and tenements from one person to another and also to enter all admittances of tenants to their tenements parcel of the said manor.

These were important financial undertakings for the bishop of Winchester and his tenants involving numerous property transactions every year, including mortgage surrenders 'made of lands or tenements within the said manor for the use of the mortgagees'. The clerk had use of a 'certain place called the Castle of Taunton a house or office commonly called or known by the name of the Exchequer' which contained all the court rolls, court books, account books 'and entries and other writings evidences of and concerning the lands and tenements of the said manor'. This was where the clerk or his deputy usually did 'all things relating to that office and to receive such money as aforesaid there payable'. This official and the exchequer were 'very well known unto the tenants of the said manor'.[1]

However, it is worth pointing out how the patent holders did not exclusively undertake the day-to-day duties of an office clerk ranging from copying documents to holding courts. They employed men learned in the law, like John Porter (c. 1591-c. 31 March 1663),[2] to run the administrative and legal side of the bishop's local business. The mass of records that were generated from the castle needed to be kept in good order and indexed, especially as they were regularly consulted for many different reasons. Inevitably some patent holders were more closely involved with matters in the castle's exchequer than others, not only because they had a vested interest but they lived in or near to the castle, such as the Browne family. As the manor of Taunton and Taunton Deane was large and prosperous, so the profits of certain offices were highly prized. The patent of clerk was worth £120 per annum, which could have paid for the purchase of 18 horses in 1660, or the equivalent of 1,714 days labour by a skilled craftsman.[3] If you use the figure of 1,714 and multiply it by £200 per day, then the office has a worth in 2022 of about £342,800 per year! This is why the office of clerk attracted some wealthy landed families like bees round a honey pot.

The principal parties involved in the main controversy brought to light in this volume can thank two men, Sir Henry Portman I baronet (*c.* 1530-1591) of Orchard Portman and Sir John Browne I (*c.* 1558-1627) of Frampton, Dorset esquire for their involvement; see pedigree 1. Through the marriage of Sir Henry's daughter Jane Portman to Sir John Browne I so the two landed families united. As was the way with landed families many sons studied law in London and entered an inn of court. Thus three of Sir John's sons, John II (*c.* 1582-1659), George I (1583-1631) and Robert I (1587-1648) I became lawyers. All three studied at the Middle Temple. Two of these men, George I and Robert I, who were also Sir Henry Portman's grandsons, obtained the patent of clerk of the castle of Taunton, along with Sir Henry Portman II (d. 1621), on 4 June 1618 from Bishop James Mountague.[4] George I and Robert I were born in Dorset and obtaining the patent for the clerkship of Taunton Castle was not an obvious acquisition. It fitted in with their legal careers and was, most likely, thanks to the Portmans long association with Taunton and the manor of Taunton Deane.

After the death of George I in 1631, on 14 May 1633 the patent was then granted to his brother, Robert Browne I armiger, and his nephew, John Browne III (*c.* 1608-1670/1), deputy lieutenant of Dorset, who also held the office of Porter or Keeper of the Gate of Taunton Castle.[5] After serving as M.P. for Bridport, Dorset in 1624,[6] Robert took up residence in Taunton Castle by 1632 and following his death in 1648 his wife Elizabeth took over the office until her death in 1661. On 7 February 1661/2 the patent was granted to George Browne III (Robert I's son) and John Gollop armiger (George Browne III's brother-in-law).[7] George and John held the patent until 1679 and 1680 respectively, so ensuring that the ancient house of Browne, including descendants of Sir Henry Portman I, were involved with the administration at Taunton Castle for just over 60 years. During those years the officers witnessed the most turbulent period of the history of the office of clerk. Not only did they survive the civil war and a change in ownership of the manor, but they had to deal with the nefarious activities of one Thomas Spigurnell I (*c.* 1630-1663). His activities during the 1650s for Parliament in the great land grab earned him a reputation as 'A creature then in fashion well becomming and complying with those tymes'.[8]

During the period the patent was held by the Portmans, Brownes, and Gollopps the day-to-day clerical duties were undertaken by Walter Underwood until 1622, John Porter from 1626 until 1662, Thomas Harvey from 1662 and

Bishop James Mountague (1568-1618) who granted the patent of Clerk of the Castle of Taunton in 1618 appointing Sir Henry Portman of Orchard Portman and John Browne of Frampton, Dorset (Courtesy of Wells Cathedral)

William Harvey from 1674 until after 1680. The description of these men is sometimes confusing as they are referred to as clerks, deputy clerks and they served as stewards, particularly of the manorial court for the borough of Taunton. Sometimes they were referred to as deputy stewards. Nevertheless these were men who like the vast majority of their employers also had a good knowledge of the law. They served both the bishop and the patent holder to good effect ensuring all was well with the busy world of admissions, surrenders, loans and mortgages on the bishop's satellite estate and its administrative headquarters at Taunton Castle. This was until two events of totally different proportions occurred. The first had been building up for years and was of national proportions. It saw a rift between King and Parliament that affected Taunton in both dramatic and subtle ways. It saw the manor of Taunton Deane pass out of the hands of the Bishop of Winchester, not for the first time, and sold to Brampton Gurdon and Roger Hill, a change in clergy in the parishes of St James and St Mary Magdalene, the town placed under siege, which became a garrison town and military stronghold, an unknown number of resident civilians and soldiers were forced into poverty and, subsequently, at the Restoration a community that was definitely not going to easily forget the sufferings of the 1640s.

Whilst all this turmoil was underway a teenager by the name of Thomas Spigurnell, a servant of Dr John Palmer (*c.* 1609-1659/60), entered the scene in

Taunton. Spigurnell came from the Berkshire town of Maidenhead and by a chain of events found himself in Taunton looking after the good doctor's horses. From relatively humble beginnings Spigurnell progressed to All Soul's College, Oxford, thanks to the patronage of Palmer. From Oxford he went to Clement's Inn (one of the inns of Chancery) where he learnt and practised law, taking advantage of the sequestration and sale of both Church and Royalists' estates in Somerset. After being appointed surveyor of the former Stawell estate by a group of influential men in Taunton, known as confederates, he married Ann Godwin from a wealthy Catholic family of Wells. The couple lived at Long Sutton but the marriage was short lived. He subsequently arranged a new marriage portion and married again which brought him into the world of the Browne family of Taunton Castle and Wilton. It also brought him into the higher echelons of Taunton society and to some extent a degree of respectability. Spigurnell was thus given the opportunity to get even more fingers in even more pies had only his £1,000 marriage portion been handed over. He obtained the patent of the office of clerk of the Castle of Taunton and the fees and financial opportunities it presented. But, as the evidence in this volume shows, Spigurnell was a pettyfogger whose dubious financial and legal engagements, combined with being a Parliamentarian in the Royalist world of the 1660s, resulted in one dispute after another.

As a result of the marriage portion dispute between Spigurnell and his wife's family the matter was brought before the High Court of Chancery. This was a court of great antiquity that dealt with cases relating to money. The simple fact that Browne v Spigurnell was a dispute over equity is not in question here. Throughout the case there is a clear theme of a different type of dispute, not about money but concerning politics, *i.e.* Roundhead versus Cavalier, which after 1660 involved a degree of retribution [**10**]. For a short time Robert III's cousin, George Browne II of Frampton (*c.* 1623-1677) served the King but in 1644 changed his allegiance to Parliament.[9] Whereas the Taunton branch held on to their pre-war appointment by the bishop of Winchester until it was taken over by Spigurnell. George III was also a Royalist supporter but his kinsmen John Browne esquire was instrumental in securing the Dorset militia for Parliament in 1642[10] and Robert of Godmanston was also of the Parliamentary party.[11] The question of the Brownes precise allegiance is not clear but it is one that manifested itself in several court cases. Numerous court papers reveal a deep-seated hatred between two different groups of society. The Brownes of Wilton were from landed gentry stock, whereas Spigurnell had no such obvious standing in Somerset but was definitely a Parliamentarian. If the Chancery depositions in this volume are correct then Spigurnell, a servant to a member of parliament who tended his horses, by his own description claimed to be a gentleman, which suggests he had something in his background to justify this claim but exactly what is not known.

How the Brownes came into contact with Spigurnell and then came to be at odds with each other is borne out in the documents required by the High Court of Chancery. The main document of wider interest from a local history perspective is a roll of depositions. This contains evidence given in answer to a series of two sets of questions, or interrogatories, drawn up by the person (or persons) who brought the case, known as the complainant (or complainants), and those by the person (or persons) who were being brought to court, or the defendant (or defendants). These statements, or more properly answers, are firsthand accounts of people who lived through the English Civil Wars, the Interregnum and into the early years of the Restoration. This has left us with a unique insight into relationships and activities at Taunton Castle, within the borough of Taunton, neighbouring Wilton and further afield [10]. Technical details about the principal documents in the disputes between the Brownes and Spigurnells can be found in Appendix 1.

The life of Thomas Spigurnell

The main character in this story is Thomas Spigurnell. His was probably born in Maidenhead in 1630 as, according to his own deposition, he was 24 years old in 1654. He thought of himself as a gentleman when he lived in Taunton. Two years later whilst at Clement's Inn, London he gave his age as 26 confirming the date of 1630. Thomas had two siblings, James III (baptised in 1634) who appears at the beginning of the story and George, a gentleman, who lived in Wells in the 1660s[12] and married Mary West at Wells St Cuthbert in 1666, but later disappears from local records.[13] After their father's death, Thomas I was placed under the tuition of a relative by marriage Sir Henry Sambourne (c. 1570-1665) [5]. Exactly how they were related was through one of Sir Henry's sisters who married a man with the surnames Holmes.[14] Fortunately, a record of an Ann Homes marrying James Spickernell on 21 August 1623 at Burnham, Buckinghamshire has survived.[15] It was the same James Spigurnell II (d. 1641), a mercer of Maidenhead, who was the father of Thomas I, and probably the son of James I (c. 1558-1627) a clerk of the same town.[16] A James Spigurnell witnessed the will of James Rixeman, a gentleman of Maidenhead in 1620, who can be classed as someone the family were associated with.[17] The date of the mercer's death fits in with the evidence Thomas gave in a Chancery case of 1661 that mentions being placed under the tuition of Sir Henry [5].

Undoubtedly the Spigurnells were of some standing. In Bray in 1296 John Spignell (probably a mis-reading) paid 3s 8d for a fishery[18] and Nicholas and his wife Alice are recorded there in 1324.[19] James Spigurnell I was appointed as 'minister' of the chapel of St Andrew and St Mary Magdalene, Maidenhead in 1606.[20] However, James does not appear to have attended Oxford or Cambridge universities, neither does he appear to have held any living within the Church of

England.[21] His appointment was by the gift of the Corporation of Maidenhead.[22] His probate inventory, of 21 August 1627, reveals how he lived a middling sort of life, with only 'Books and a deske in the studdy' and his wearing apparel each valued at £3, out of a total of £84 9s consisting mainly of furniture and domestic goods.[23] James II and Ann, who married in 1623, also had a son James III baptised at Cookham (just north of Maidenhead) in 1634. James Spigurnell II drew up his will on 13 December 1640, when he was weak in body, but only mentioned two sons, Thomas and James. He bequeathed his 'temporall estate in Lands and Tenements ... and all my freehould Lands and Tenements in Maydenhead' to his wife, then after her death to his two sons equally and then to their heirs. He did not list all of the lands he was in possession of,[24] but they included a messuage or inn called the White Hart in Maidenhead, a piece of ground (54 x 16 feet) extending from the south end of Thomas Terry's property unto a parcel of ground belonging to Windsor Castle lately in the occupation of John Egham, another piece of ground about one acre named Picked Acre in Brayfield, four acres of arable land in Maidenhead field in the parish of Cookham, an acre of meadow in a meadow called West Meade, as well as a message called the Quart Potte in Cookham.[25] Collectively a goodly inheritance for his wife and two sons.

An extract from John Speed's map of Berkshire showing 'Madenhead' and its location on the boundary with Buckinghamshire on the River Thames where in 1296 John Spignell leased a fishery.

After Thomas's mother became a widow, she was able to redeem the lands her husband mortgaged with John Andrewes gentleman of Hurley, Berkshire. But shortly afterwards she died leaving young Thomas without his mother, just before 1644. Having lost both of his parents within the space of four years so Sir Henry Sambourne had to take control of young Spigurnell's inheritance. But to do so the documents of title to the properties had to be reclaimed from Andrewes. But Andrewes refused to hand them over. So in order to obtain them Spigurnell had to enter a bill of complaint in the High Court of Chancery against Andrewes and Thomas Lane of Burnham Abbey, Buckinghamshire in May 1644. Thomas did not know where the documents were and felt he was in 'dainger to loose all the premisses'. But there was a problem. As Thomas was under age, Lane, who held the six parchment documents, refused to hand them over to young Thomas Spigurnell. So, on the 6 July 1644 at Maidenhead, Andrewes and Lane gave their answer to Thomas's complaint. Lane declared that he would hand over the documents to whoever the court decided because the defendant was under 21 and was 'therefore uncapeable' to give Lane 'any Lawfull discharge upon his receipt thereof'.[26]

The timing of this event in 1644 is an interesting one as Thomas was described as a gentleman of Maidenhead. An entry in a rental of 1650 for Maidenhead shows a payment from the heirs of 'Sir Pickernell' which may have been a transcription error for Spickernell.[27] If this was the same Thomas Spigurnell of our story, who was born in 1630,[28] then he would only have been about 14 in 1644 but 20 when the rental was drawn up. If he inherited the lands James II bequeathed in 1640 then why is he not listed in the rental of 1650, or was he one of the heirs of Spickernell? Interestingly, Thomas made no mention in later life of any of the lands in Berkshire, which suggests he may have been forced to sell them, thus they passed out of the family's ownership.

Apart from the 1644 Chancery dispute very little is known about the time Thomas spent under the tuition of Sir Henry Sambourne. Something is known of Sir Henry. He was born around 1570, so he would have been in his late sixties or early seventies when he entered into the role of guardian for Thomas. He was a man of some standing as he was knighted by King James I in 1608 when he served as High Sheriff of Oxfordshire. He later served as High Sheriff of Berkshire in 1632, was an owner of a significant amount of land and held patents for the manufacture of saltpetre from the Crown. Something is also known about his personality. Whilst High Sheriff of Oxfordshire, some of his activities concerning drunkenness and local bread were published in the form of a ballad.[29] During the Civil War, Maidenhead witnessed many interactions, and in November 1642 the royal court was based there.[30] Much later, Sambourne tried to conceal his true worth when it was alleged by Parliamentary officials that he was 'not to be trusted, After the war turned in Parliament's favour for he never dealt honestly with anybody',[31] thus as a Royalist he was committed to the Upper Bench prison on 29 May 1646.[32] His sharp practice may have rubbed off on his young charge, a factor which may have influenced Spigurnell's transactions, as will be seen. Spigurnell claimed to be a gentleman and perhaps it was his connection with 'Uncle' Henry that helped him make such a claim. The Spigurnell family name means sealer of writs and the arms of one branch was argent, fretty gules, on a chief or lion passant guardant gules,[33] although it is not known on what authority they could claim to use them. There were families of the Spigurnell name of some standing in Warwickshire[34] and Nottinghamshire,[35] one was a judge and another constable of Dover.[36] Nearer to Bray and Cookham was the manor of Dagnal and Spigurnell (in Hertfordshire) where Sir Henry Spigurnell was lord of the manor in 1323[37] but how, or if, Thomas was descended from them is unclear.[38]

All this happened before Thomas was known to William Wellman, parish clerk of Drayton, sometime around 1648 or 1649.[39] Nevertheless it was thanks to his uncle Henry that he was encouraged to study 'the profescion of Phisick' under Doctor John Palmer [5] which resulted in an association that lasted for at least a decade.[40] However, perhaps it was his involvement with the High Court of Chancery in 1644 that influenced young Thomas towards a career in the law, not medicine.[41] Thanks to Sambourne's association with Doctor Palmer whilst the latter was warden of All Souls College, Oxford he appointed Spigurnell as 'Steward and Surveyor of all the lands' belonging to the college. Subsequently Spigurnell was 'imployed by severall other persons of great worth and authority in matters of the like nature'. This enabled him, in his own words, by his 'industrie therein made a fair addicion to a Competent estate left this defendant by his father' [5].

From Oxford Spigurnell went to Clement's Inn, one of the inns of Chancery, where he was educated in the law. Exactly when this was is not clear, or when he qualified as an attorney but both occurred before 1656.[42] As well as keeping his rooms at Clement's Inn he moved to Long Sutton and married Ann Godwin at St Clement Danes, Middlesex[43] on 18 May 1657. Spigurnell married well as his wife was the daughter of James Godwin II esquire (*c.* 1600-d.bef. 1644) of Wells[44] 'a person of great worth and reputation and qualitie'. Through this union and a substantial marriage settlement he came into a 'considerable estate' [5]. Ann's brother was the third generation of men named James Godwin in Wells. Her father James II was admitted to the Inner Temple in 1619 and called to the Bar in 1632. James II was the son and heir of James Godwin I (*c.* 1564-1616) and Maud who were Recusants.[45] James I represented Wells in parliament and with his wife Maud had five children, two sons and three daughters.[46] Ann's father, James II, married Sarah Clarke of Worminster (in Wells) in the 1630s and they had a son James III baptised at St Cuthbert's church on 23 March 1640/1. After James II died Sarah married John Morgan of Wells, gentleman (before 1644)[47] and they appear in Chancery proceedings in 1666 as one of the surviving names on the lease of Long Sutton Farm.[48] Pedigree 3 contains more information about the Godwin family connection.

The Godwin family were devout Catholics, who were part of a group of recusants in Wells[49] that were very well known to the local authorities. This family set up a charity in Wells in 1617 named "James Godwin's Gift", based on the rent from a mansion house at the west end of St Cuthbert's Street in the city. The rent of £10 per year was to be used by the mayor, masters and burgesses of the city for the benefit of the poor of the almshouse and the city. It was planned to turn the house into a workhouse but the property was knocked down.[50] James Godwin II had a sister Elizabeth who lived in Wells before becoming a nun at St Monica's, Louvain[51] and he was at Douai on 10 July 1620.[52] Mrs Margery Godwyn and Mrs Mary Godwyn appear as recusants in both the 1641 subsidy[53] and in a list of those excommunicated in October 1639.[54] But why did Spigurnell marry into a Catholic family when it appears he held no openly obvious Catholic tendencies?

It is very unlikely that Spigurnell held any Catholic beliefs, especially as Catholocism was so hated by the Parliamentarian masses in the 1640s and 1650s that he sided with. However, the choice of his place of marriage was obvious as at that time he was practising at Clement's Inn but why did they not get married in the bride's home parish? Perhaps as her father was deceased she was free to marry where she pleased but whether her brother had any say in the matter is not recorded. However, when her brother, who was buried on 13 March 1676/7 at St Cuthberts,[55] made his will he made no mention of any of his Godwin blood relatives, or the Spigurnell or Chard families, only his wife Edith.[56] Perhaps there were no relatives left to leave his vast estate, hence why Edith inherited it all. The Godwins, Clarkes and Morgans were all families who appear in the visitation of Somerset, who bore the right to bear arms whereas the Spigurnells do not.

But like many aspects of Spigurnell's life there are many twists and turns. Following Ann's father's death, her mother's second marriage was to a local man, John Morgan, from an important family who lived at Worminster in Wells. It is likely that Ann lived with her mother, step father, her siblings James and Sarah during those difficult years of the 1640s. Ann's step father, John Morgan, due to his rank in society served as a major in the King's Army. One story of his service has survived from 1643:

> As Major John Morgan of Wells, was marching with the King's army into the west, he fell sick of a malignant fever at Salisbury, and was brought dangerously ill to my father's at Broad-Chalk, where he was lodged secretly in a garret. There came a sparrow to the chamber window, which pecked the lead of a certain pannel only, and only one side of the lead of the lozenge, and made one small hole in it. He continued this pecking

and biting the lead, during the whole time of his sickness; (which was not less than a month) when the major went away, the sparrow desisted, and came thither no more. Two of the servants that attended the Major, and sober persons, declared this for a certainty.[57]

Following his military service for the King in Colonel Robert Phelips' Regiment of Foot,[58] in August 1645 he decided to swop sides. To do this he went to the Somerset Committee at Axbridge and took the National League and Covenmant and Negative Oath, thus swopping sides and becoming a turncoat in the process.[59] His reason for doing so may have been because the outcome of the war was not going to be favourable for the Royalist party. A few weeks before he would have known about the defeat of the Royalists at the Battle of Langport. It was an astute move and one that would have put him on the same side as his future step son-in-law Thomas Spigurnell and his confederates.

Sadly Spigurnell's first marriage to Ann Godwin was a short one as she was buried at Long Sutton in 1657 and a floor slab commemorating this fact remains there to this day. It reads: 'Under this stone / resteth the body / of Anne SPIGURNEL / wife of Thomas Spigurnel / of the parish of Long / Sutton, gentleman / and daughter of James / GODWIN, of Wels, in the / county of Somerset / Esquier'.[60] It is unlikely Thomas and Ann had any children as none appear in the Long Sutton parish register either as being baptised or buried. What promised so much resulted in so little for him. Ann's brother James, who owned substantial lands and property in Wells, Taunton, Mark, Blackford, Heathouse, Wedmore and Butleigh lived on until 1676 but does not obviously appear again in Thomas's story.[61] Spigurnell gained financially from this marriage and in the following year completed some substantial modifications to Court House in Long Sutton. Thomas had a small plaque inscribed 'THOMAS SPIGVRNEL, GENT, 1658' (carved on four lines) inserted on the outside of the house.[62] Perhaps it was due to this lack of familial ties with the Godwins that Spigurnell wasted no time in finding another wife.

An artist's impression of the wording, situated high up next to the main road and suffering from over 350 years of weathering, recording the renovations to Court House in 1658 (Author)

How Spigurnell came across his second wife Elizabeth Browne of Wilton is not totally clear. She was probably born around 1635 when her parents lived in Taunton Castle. Spigurnell claimed that he lived near Elizabeth when he served Dr Palmer, which means he either lived near the castle or in Sherford (in the adjacent parish of Wilton). Or he may have lived with Dr Palmer's father when in Taunton [5]. Spigurnell spent some time in Taunton before 1644 [10], possibly in 1645 when Dr Palmer was elected member of parliament for the town, then again in the 1650s. As her father was involved in the legal side of activities centred on Taunton Castle the possibilities for them meeting are many and varied.

A match between two families of the gentry class was not unusual but the two families held very different feelings towards King and Parliament. On the one hand was Spigurnell's involvement with Taunton's MP and his own efforts on behalf of Parliament to sell off Royalist's estates during the 1650s. He also had personal dealings with men in Taunton who were very much anti-Royalists, one of whom had been incarcerated in Taunton Castle. He fell in with the 'usurped authority' under Palmer and according to his brother-in-law 'appeared as if hee had bene a person of some quality'. So when Spigurnell approached his future mother-in-law 'to bee admitted a suitor for marriage' (some time before April 1658) it caused a bit of controversy in the Browne family. According to George Browne III his mother only agreed to it because it was 'more out of feare then for any affeccion' towards Thomas, as she was of a 'contrary Judgment to him and very much abhorringe the accions hee was dayly guilty of in adhering to those in that Rebellion against his sacred Majestie' [4]. Thus a Parliamentarian creature of the times married the daughter of a suffering Royalist's widow.

The Browne family of Wilton were predominantly Royalist supporters, something that the testimonies of those that knew Spigurnell and/or the Brownes were happy to profess [10]. Other evidence supports this. For example, George Browne III and his wife Ann's first child was born at Netherbury, Dorset on 20 April 1655 and baptised there on the 18th of May and not at Wilton. Was it safer for them to be living away from the radicals in Taunton? With such a difference in allegiances was this the reason Spigurnell married Elizabeth Browne at St Clement Danes, Westminster on 20 April 1658 and not at Wilton over one hundred miles away where she was living with her mother, and possibly with her brother George and his wife Ann? It may simply have been more expedient for Spigurnell to get married at the parish church where he was practising as an attorney, but unusual the ceremony not o have been conducted in the wife's parish. It is likely that after some sort of reconciliation the couple returned to Wilton where their first child, Thomas Spigurnell II, was baptised at the parish church on 14 January 1658/9, followed by a daughter Elizabeth on 8 November 1659. The Spigurnells did not have to wait very long from the date they married to the birth of their first child, then the birth of their second, before there were two children aged under two at Sherford House. Although the newly weds may initially have got on well with old Mrs Browne at Sherford, Elizabeth's brother George did not like his Parliamentarian brother-in-law. It was alleged that whilst they lived there George III threatened his sister that if she did not leave Sherford House, and take her husband with her, 'hee would prick her against the wall like a Toade' [10].

The house where the Brownes lived has survived to this day, although part of it where the original kitchen was situated was extensively renovated in the Victorian period. It still retains many features that were there in the mid 17th century, including a plaster overmantle in one of the upstairs bedrooms. It was a substantial house in Spigurnell's day, with a hall containing a table big enough to accomodate six chairs, a sideboard, fireplace and clock. In the parlour there was enough room for twice as many chairs, two 'Fare Pictures' and a landscape painting, a table, sideboard, two carpets and a viol. The kitchen was extensive with a large fireplace and settle, a sideboard, a large number of brass, pewter, bell metal and copper weights, pans, kettles, dishes, plates, a salt seller, a custard pan, pie plates as well as latine ware. A larder near the kitchen was big enough to house a trestle table and a buttery contained at least four and a half hogsheads and two tubs. The brewhouse may have only been small as it housed a kettle, a dressing board and a tub. The bedrooms or chambers were many and included ones named after the kitchen, dairy, entry, hall, parlour, and new buttery. There were also garrets over the new buttery chamber and the kitchen chamber. Outside there was some sort of stable or barn for horses, pigs, a cow, hay and barley.[63] This was not your average farmhouse but a more fitting residence for a gentry family.

The family moved to Long Sutton and their third child Mary was baptised in the parish on 17 December 1661. Known today as Court House, in Spigurnell's day it was called Long Sutton Farm which extended into two parishes[64] and it was described as a mansion house.[65] Nevertheless it was and still is a substantial and fine dwelling that shows a record of Spigurnell's vanity. In his day it contained a hall, buttery, milkhouse, kitchen, brewhouse, gallery, kitchen chamber, long chamber and hall chamber;[66] outside there was a dove house.[67] All the rooms were stocked with eveyday items. Some items of note include a livery cupboard in the hall, two pie plates in the kitchen that might hint at the owner's taste for pies, a rug in the hall chamber; such items reveal a very ordinary selection of goods and no opulency that was found at the Browne's house at Sherford. The farm and other agricultural interests included a harness for ploughing but no plough, two saddles and bridles, a colt and a lame mare could be found along with hay, wheat, reed and barley. The estate was worth, before the lord's rent was paid and any national taxes accounted for, the princely sum of £70 per annum. Spigurnell leased the property from Mr Bourne on his life and that of Sarah Morgan of Wells his mother-in-law (from his first marriage).

(Above) Court House, or Long Sutton Farm, home of the Spigurnells for a brief time in the 1660s. (Below) The inside of the dove house that has seen little significant change since Spigurnell's day (Author).

Spigurnell was no farmer and practised as an attorney in Taunton and Clement's Inn while his wife and children remained at Long Sutton. He leased Drayton Wood that was considered a good investment, where he owned 120 hurdles, a quantity of Hardwood faggots, 1,000 Wallet faggots, 56 oaks and 100 oak poles; in all the value of these commodities was £55 3s 5d.[68] He leased the wood from 30 November 1660 from James Symes esquire one of His Majesties auditors and William Firmin who held it by letters patent, but by 1663 Spigurnell was three years behind on his rent payments totalling a debt of £24.[69] Other sources of income included a lease of the tithes of Barton St David.[70] He also rented out numerous closes of lands from which he received a reasonable income on Lady Day, after paying his taxes, although this amount varied from year to year, possibly depending upon the yields from the land (see Appendix 7 for a list); in 1666 this amounted to £91 6s 10d before taxes. However, there were costs incurred by the landlord in the 1660s as well as unexpected income, such as 5s received from William Wallis for pigeon dung.

The estate needed maintaining and payments were made to his tenants, such as 3s 4d to Joseph Bull, tenant of Higher Ablack, for 'throwing the Coare in the River at the ground called Hamocks and stoping of Shades'. This maintenance of the banks of a waterway with wooden boards (or shides) was a proactive way of helping flood prevention and drainage. Joseph Bull, John Creason, Robert Thomas and Robert Richards were paid for 'dickeing the dich' and 'widening and scoureing the reynes'. Other men were paid for more specialist tasks, such as John Culliford for making posts and bars needed in the Eastern Hamocks. Other payments include 1s 2d for the carpenter and smith to mend the barn door, as well as 9d for 300 'twiggs for sewers' and 6s 3½d for spars.[71] Such were some of the expenses that were needed to maintain the estate. Spigurnell may have consciously avoided paying for this maintenance as these payments were made after he died.

The growing Spigurnell family also benefitted from the lease of 20 acres in the common fields for a term of 80 years from the Earl of Northampton. Thomas entered into this on 30 November 1661 for the lives of his children in return for a rent of 20s a year. But, during one of his numerous financial scrapes, he assigned the lease less than a week after he acquired it (on 5 December 1661) to Francis Naylor of Staple Inn. In return Naylor loaned him £26 10s with the clause that it had to be repaid by 7 December 1662. Spigurnell did not repay this money, and although being in debt was not uncommon in seventeenth century England, the writing was on the wall concerning his financial situation.[72] Other unusual or dubious monetary matters came to light after his death, such as the time he used some money from a client for his own purposes that should have been used for financing a lease.[73] One example, of which there were many, of recovering moneys he owed occurred when a case was brought against him in the Court of Kings Bench by Thomas White of Wells for a debt of £200. This was the tip of a much bigger iceberg as Spigurnell failed to pay his rent to the Earl of Northampton of 20s per annum. It was not all bad news as White eventually received £100 of the £200 he was owed. However, Mary Sampson of Taunton, widow, brought an action against him for debt, as did Thomas Chapple of Barton St David. On another occassion Richard Dewdney had to go to the Court of Common Pleas to recover his debt. Dorothy Over used the same mechanism to recover £200 of which £100 was outstanding at the time of Thomas's death. Richard Heywood of London went down the Kings Bench route to recover £80 in 1659. Spigurnell had also entered into a bond with a man named Parkins for £300 which needed repaying. Other debts he owed involved two men from Langport (John Weech a mercer and John Mitchell)[74] who Spigurnell had purchased goods and 'divers wares and merchandizes' from,[75] an apothecary Henry Jacques and a merchant Jerom Churchill both from Somerton, William Sutton of Long Sutton, Thomas Cox, William Haberfield, as well as John Paddocke. In 1663, there were even some others he owed money to but his wife, Elizabeth, did not know their names![76] After his death she knew that her husband was heavily in debt and shared this fact with her servants.[77] She was soon to feel the effects of her late husband's irresponsible financial activities.

Not only had Thomas amassed considerable debts but it also came to light that he was capable of sharp practice. This can be seen in the case of the impropriate tithes of the parish of Barton St David. The tithes had been sequestered before 1660 and appear to have belonged to Spigurnell who employed Thomas Chapple (or Chappell) of Barton St David, yeoman to gather them in for him. Spigurnell 'oftentymes' promised Chapple that he should 'not bee a penny looter' when he collected the tithes and our pettyfogger promised to pay him £10 in return.[78] Following the Restoration, about the beginning of June 1660, Dr Emanuel Ewtey, minister of Stepney, was made prebendary of the prebend of Barton St David (of the church of Wells). He 'suffered much misery by the late troubles, but was allsoe undone and ruined for his loyalty and obedience to his mate Majestie Kinge Charles the first of blessed memory'.[79]

However, it is not clear whether Chapple knew that Spigurnell no longer had the right to claim the benefit of them[80] and Ewtey authorised Chapple to gather them for the year 1660. It came to light that the tithes were not just for Ewtey's benefit as some of them were used to pay for the repair of St Pauls. Ewtey dutifully paid his 'Contribution money rates and all other taxes in 1660' due to the state. At this time Chapple was described as tenant to the impropriate tithes and subsequently the £30 and 'upwards' he collected was delivered to Spigurnell, who then gave security to Chapple 'for to keepe and save harmlesse and indempnified the said Complainant against the said Doctor Ewtey'. Spigurnell did not give Ewtey any money but events soon changed the situation.[81]

On 14 June 1661, Ewtey leased the tithes to John Whorrow of St Mary Le Savoy for £315, with a yearly rent of £3 10s to the Prebendary and £16 to the vicar of Barton,[82] described in 1662 as an 'Orthodox minister'. The good doctor died in August and was buried shortly after on 2 September 1661 at St. Dunstan, Stepney, leaving his wife, as executrix, to administer his estate. She wasted no time in taking Chapple to court, seeking redress at the assizes. Unfortunately the £9 she tried to recover meant bringing her witnesses from London to Somerset at a cost of £9 but she appears to have been successful. Hence Chapple then took her to Chancery which she thought was to cause 'meere vexation and to barr or hinder her of the said judgement of eighteene pounds'. Spigurnell, acting as legal adviser to Chapple, according to Ewtey's widow 'doth not only countenance the Complainant in thus vexing and troublinge of this defendant here in this honourable court but doth alose ... maintayne the same suite with his owne proper money and uppon his only Costs'.[83] Chapple ended up having to pay £22 and an additional £3 10s to defend the case.

This was not the only time Chapple and Spigurnell had been involved in a court case. Spigurnell brought a case in Chancery on Chapple's behalf that ended up costing the latter £5 10s. Chapple should have known Spigurnell was not reliable when he failed to pay him £4 for 20 bushells of beans which he purchased from him. Spigurnell's involvement with Chapple and Barton St David's tithe money was shortlived but typically problematic for those involved with him.

Despite being married for a relatively short time, he fathered three children before he died about the time of the Assizes[84] in August 1663, probably on the same day he made his last will and testament.[85] Thus Spigurnell's last days were spent in Taunton where he was working as an attorney. It is likely that he had been practising law since the early 1650s,[86] certainly since 1656,[87] and definitely since at least 1660[88] in either Fore Street or High Street, Taunton. As an attorney at law he was rated at £3 in the subsidy taxation but he refused to pay this to the new administration.[89] Why Spigurnell refused to pay may have been due to his dislike for the new Royalist regime and the return to the old world of kings and bishops, or that he may have paid elsewhere? In his last days at Taunton he was attended in his illness by a local physician, George Glasbrooke, who received 10s from Thomas for his pains.[90] Glasbrooke, like Spigurnell, had served Parliament during the 1650s but as muster master of the Somerset Militia under Richard Bovett, possibly with his brother Peter Glasbrooke.[91] George lived with his wife and five children[92] in a five hearth house in East Street, Taunton[93] in one of the better sorts of houses that had a parlour, hall, kitchen, buttery, forechamber, gallery, parlour chamber, hall chamber and his kitchen contained 93lbs of pewter. As an educated man Glasbroke owned £6 worth of books.[94] Around the time of his death Mary Mantle, a local widow in her late sixties, also attended Spigurnell in the house of Mr Thomas Stone.[95]

After he died £4 in a purse he kept under his pillow was given by Mr John Herring,[96] a Taunton innholder,[97] of Fore Street,[98] to one of his executors John Dryer of Long Sutton, as well as a pocket book and some other writings belonging to his wife.[99] Stone and Herring both promised to send his possessions, books, papers and writings to Long Sutton after his death.[100] Dryer arranged for his corpse to be transported from Taunton to Long Sutton at a cost of 20s and for his coffin to be built at a cost of 6s 8d.[101] Herring claimed he arranged the transportation of Spigurnell's body from Taunton to Long Sutton and paid for the funeral, all of which cost £6 3s 4d.[102] Spigurnell's body had arrived at his home at Long Sutton by 31 August 1663,[103] but there was no grandious funeral as he was buried in a 'very meane manner'. No bell was rung at his funeral and the wake was held at his house where mourners consumed meat and beer.[104] In London, after he died, a lock was put on his door at Clement's Inn to avoid his estate being tampered with,[105] until John Adams (a fellow Taunton lawyer) and Dryer had access to his study and chamber.[106] Adams and Dryer found that he kept his wife's fine linnen in a great trunk in his chambers, as well as a gown and a 'mantle of very good value'.[107]

Spigurnell's legacy was like his finances and legal affairs very complicated. His will drawn up on the 27th of August possibly hours before his death did not help matters. He claimed he was 'sick of body' but of sound and perfect memory. He left what he described as Long Sutton Farm to his children, with instructions to his executors to sell it and place it in trust for his three youngsters. His 20 acres on Brent Hill and his personal estate was also left to them. John Pyne the elder of Curry Mallet esquire and Dryer were appointed executors 'in trust' but nothing was left to his wife! No mention was made of any of his debts, or other property interests, indicating the haste in which his will was drawn up. However, after he drew up this will he was 'asked about his wife and what he intended to give her', to which he replied 'I leave unto her her portion which is In her brothers hands', that was the hands of George Browne III of Wilton. This clause was a somewhat bitter reflection of his dislike for his brother-in-law for not handing over the money when he married and, possibly, some resentment of his wife. It was well known that his marriage portion had been an issue for Thomas since his betrothel. In fact it had become such an issue by the time of his death that his will makes it appear he had washed his hands of the issue, being content to leave his estate to his children and his wife to her own devices. His will and codicil of sorts were both witnessed by Richard Bovett senior and junior, and Herring the innholder.[108] His choice of the Bovetts was not only through his connection to Palmer's family (as Richard senior was married to one of Palmer's daughters), but also due to being one of the Taunton confederates.

At the time of his death Spigurnell was in debt to fifteen different people. This may have been one reason Elizabeth remained a widow for two years but she was able to hold on to their house for six months after his death.[109] However, with three small children to look after and no husband she clearly found things difficult. One report described how the children 'were almost naked for want of clothes'[110] and the family were 'reduced to a perishing condicion for want', it was alleged that this was because Dryer, instead of acting in their best interests, 'wholly endeavoured the utter ruine and prejudice of them to destroy that small estate which was intended them'.[111] Elizabeth had to rely on the 'Charitable ayd and assistance of her kindred friends and relations' or they would have become chargable to the parish. Elizabeth claimed Dryer tried to 'circumvent and deceave the said Infants of what rightly belonged to them'.[112] To help them in their time of need Mr Joseph King, her solicitor from Yeovil, not only 'apparelled' the children but also paid rates and taxes for Elizabeth that were due.

Some of the responsibility for the welfare of the children fell on Thomas's executors and friends. One of them, John Pyne, stalwart of the Parliamentary party in Somerset against the late King, took Spigurnell's son into his own household. He was there for about 21 months when Pyne gave him 'educacion and maintenance, clothinge food and Rayment' at Pyne's own cost.[113] But all was far from well with this arrangement as Elizabeth had to retrieve her son from Pyne's household and something was very wrong with the 'trust' element of her husband's will. As for the other executors, John West, a carpenter from Drayton, threshed wheat in her barn and knew Dryer provided her with five pecks of malt for brewing. He also knew Elizabeth took two or three bushells of apples from the orchard.[114] Both of these events ocurred during a time when Elizabeth held great concern that the income from her late husband's estate was being witheld by his executors, particularly Dryer.[115]

Dryer had been a client of Spigurnell's legal business,[116] so as he was a farmer and neighbour it made sense for Thomas to have made him one of the executors. It therefore appears he undertook the lion's share of matters relating to matters in Long Sutton. He claimed the estate was worth £70 per annum but this was contested by Elizabeth.[117] He sold 'certaine parcells' of hay belonging to Spigurnell worth £4 or £5 to three local men (Richard Burt, John Pinkard and Thomas Hurd) and a colt worth £10 or £11 to a man from Ilchester. It was alleged that Dryer did not hand over the money to Elizabeth, although some reed cut from his land was used to repair her house. Elizabeth became desperate. She wanted to 'better provide and take care' of her children and asked Dryer some twenty times to discharge his executorship to her, or in the words of her servant Sarah Pellett 'yield upp such pretended trust'. Things became so desperate for Elizabeth that she sent Sarah with one of her children 'in a very meane condition' to the Dryer's house to try and obtain some maintenance. Mrs Dryer was having none of it and refused to let them in and said "the parish must keepe them", meaning thy were chargeable to the parish overseers of the poor. Despite this

Sarah left the child at the house and returned to her mistress. The matter did not end there as shortly afterwards Dryer's maid brought the child back to Court House, or Long Sutton farm. On another occassion Elizabeth was so hungry that she begged John Dryer for a cheese but his wife would not let her have it unless she paid for it.[118] The dire financial position Elizabeth found herself in was a long way from the lifestyle she enjoyed at Taunton Castle and Sherford House.

The Spigurnell estate, apart from the house where Elizabeth and the children lived, along with the garden, came into the possession of Dryer. A miller from Yeovilton, Philip Bursey, described Dryer as leading a 'very civill life and conversacion' who was 'very skilled in all sorts of husbandry' and carefully managed the 'Farme and Lands unto the best advantage'. He also knew that Dryer provided Elizabeth with corn. How did he know this? Answer: because Bursey had ground it for him.[119] The estate later came into the possession of Timothy Cotten who decided to 'lett and dispose of severall partes' to Edward Hill, John Westlake, Edith Roberts, William Gee, Edward and Henry Clasey.[120] Cotten knew that the estate had to continue to function if it was to generate any income for both landlord and tenant. Therefore Thomas Chappell who had fallen foul of Spigurnell's dubious legal activities was employed to cut the grass and hay at Hammocks in 1667 and Cotten personally offered John Richards (a yeoman from Long Sutton) the chance of renting the same plot. But when Richards and his two sons tried to cut the hay they were arrested by order of the widow Elizabeth and her lawyer. Some of the hay ended up going to Court House but the hay cut in the Western Hammocks went to Dryer. Cotten used Dryer and Joseph Bull as his agents for collecting rents on the former Spigurnell estate.[121]

Faced with all of these problems the widow Elizabeth decided to re-marry. It looks as if her precarious financial position may have been one of the reasons she chose Edward Chard, a bachelor aged about 26. On 29 June 1665, Chard took out a marriage allegation when he was living at St Martin in the Fields, Middlesex. They were allowed to be married in St Peters and Pauls Wharf or Bridewell Precinct, London[122] but not in Somerset. This was an interesting match as she was from a much higher ranking family in society than her new husband. Even more interesting is the fact that her only sibling, George Browne III, later claimed he knew nothing about the marriage! [14] The couple appear not to have had any children baptised at Long Sutton, nor are any mentioned in the numerous transactions Edward and Elizabeth were involved with after their marriage. Does this suggest she married for money rather than love? Perhaps her first unpaid marriage portion attracted Edward into this union.

Legal life

When Spigurnell first came to Taunton, possibly as early as 1640, he had been seen by James King, a Taunton carpenter, in the town working as a groom to

Palmer. Spigurnell lived with Palmer as his servant and King thought he was 'but a very meane person'. Spigurnell dressed, saddled, watered and ordered Palmer's horses and cleaned out the stables, a job that King had undertaken before Spigurnell's appointment. Spigurnell was also seen riding the horses whilst wearing a canvas frock. From Taunton he went to Oxford and then to Clement's Inn that was all thanks to Palmer. When Spigurnell was at All Souls, Oxford, he did not undertake those sorts of duties of a groom to Palmer as these were undertaken by John Prew [10]. Notably while at Oxford he had easy access to a range of law books and could well have started learning aspects of the profession at that time. But when he first started studying the law at Clement's Inn may now be lost but was certainly before 1656.[123]

However, shortly after he arrived at Oxford (where he lived at All Souls College under Palmer's patronage) by September 1651 his involvement in a legal capacity with the Parliamentary party is well documented. It is therefore highly likely that Spigurnell may have started reading law at Oxford, as well as serving as surveyor of college lands belonging to All Souls. So Spigurnell became involved in the biggest land grab since the Reformation by taking full advantage of the sale of Royalists' estates and the opportunities it presented. Parliament passed an act for the sale of Royalists', or delinquents' estates, and on 22 September 1651 Spigurnell wrote to the 'Right Honourable the Trustees appoynted by Parliament for the sale of Delinquents estates' from All Souls College, Oxford. In this letter he gave his consent for his 'Welbeloved' friend Henry Cotton of 'Clement Danes' to act as his attorney when dealing with any financial matters Spigurnell needed handling in London. Spigurnell described himself as a trustee for the sale of delinquents estates and how he was involved 'surveying the said lands'. His seal on this document is not heraldic and appears to be his initials 'TS'.[124] Spigurnell was on his way to acquiring a sizable share of delinquents' estates mainly in the county of Somerset. His professional career was truly underway.

While in Taunton in January 1651/2, he wrote to the Committee for Compounding begging for payment of his fifths as discoverer of an estate of £62 8d belonging to Alexander Middleton, a yeoman of Drayton, which Spigurnell undervalued in his particular. Middleton had compounded as a delinquent and because Spigurnell had discovered this estate he was entitled to one fifth of the yearly profits. The commissioners for Somerset were ordered to look into the matter.[125] Spigurnell continued to work from Taunton where, on 24 June 1652, he became possessed of 'all those lands or tenements called Oldhouse and Strangs tenements lying in Tintinhull'. These were held for a term of six years but the estate had fallen in hand upon the death of Joan Hopkins, widow. The estate generated a yearly rent of £25 and the information was approved by a fellow Tauntonian Samuel Whetcombe.[126] Other duties he undertook for Parliament at that time saw him keeping an account (entered in the Exchequer) that showed Mr John Glasbroke, minister of Stocklinch Ottersey (from 1652 to 1656), was owed £53 6s 8d.[127] Spigurnell also served as a surveyor of lands for the Taunton compensation scheme that was established to provide money to those in the town who suffered losses during the wars.[128]

Although the evidence in the records for Spigurnell is either lacking or unclear, there was a well established way into the legal profession. One man who attended grammar school then went to Cambridge University for three years, after which he was admitted to Clifford's Inn, appears to have generically followed a similar path to Spigurnell. During his time at university he may have only been exposed to the subject of law through conversation, or reading the odd legal volume that he may have come across. He most likely attended assizes at Norwich and would have witnessed how the law was applied to the cases being dealt with. As Spigurnell accompanied Palmer it is likely that he too witnessed many legal interactions. Indeed it is well documented that although there may have been no legal education available in a formal sense when Spigurnell was at Clement's Inn, there would have been other opportunities. As Spigurnell was no pauper and had wealthy connections with the Sambournes and Palmers, as well as a small estate of his own, he would have been able to fund a type of apprenticeship with an attorney of Clement's Inn. Working as a clerk in an inn of Chancery would have given him the knowledge of conveyancing, assignments, grants, and preparing papers for Chancery suits; this type of work was something that he was definitely involved with in later life, as is evidenced in the numerous cases he was involved in, as well as his work as a surveyor. In addition to this many 'senior members of an inn of court could be particularly valuable teachers' of the law. Being in London Spigurnell had access to many courts where he could have increased his legal knowledge simply by listening to the arguments in open court.[129] Spigurnell is known to have made many friends in the legal world that also would have provided him with useful knowledge.[130]

Possibly in the late 1640s, Spigurnell would have started studying the law but it is not clear where he did this. The obvious location would have been at Clement's Inn that he entered in the 1650s. The date of his entry into the legal world may now be lost but was certainly before 1656.[131] An education, or training, at Clement's Inn in the late 1640s and early 1650s is a bit of a mystery as Sir John Baker's research found that 'in the 1640s the educational routines of all the inns collapsed suddenly and completely when they were vacated by reason of war'.[132] Another source claims 'the practice of training barristers at the Inns of Chancery had died out by 1642, and the Inns instead became dedicated associations and offices for solicitors'.[133] Indeed, reforms proposed in 1646 were not put in place at the time Spigurnell was known to be at Clement's Inn.[134] Also, as a subordinate inn to the Inner Temple, Clement's Inn was able to use the reader of its parent body. It is well documented that one reader, Philip Wyott, did not undertake his duties as a bencher from 1642 to 1649 at the Inner Temple. He continued to be chosen until 1655 but it is unclear if he undertook any teaching duties, or actually deliver any type of education that Spigurnell could have benefitted from?[135]

Spigurnell's time at Clement's Inn, possibly as an apprentice, but later as a member, is described in the wonderfully titled book *Pettyfoggers and Vipers of the Commonwealth*. The time Spigurnell spent as a clerk was the most commonly used method which led to entry into Clement's Inn. However, Brooks stated that 'clerkship to a country attorney was probably the most typical avenue into the profession, but there are examples of men who served as clerks to judges, serjeants at law, town clerks, and town court attorneys'. Any one of those might apply to Spigurnell and one man spent nearly nine years in an apprenticeship before becoming an attorney of the Common Pleas. In Spigurnell's case, as both his parents were dead, his apprenticeship would have been arranged by Dr Palmer. Apprentices were required to undertake different duties in addition to those of a clerk. One apprentice was required to rise at 5 every day, wait on their master's table, keep an eye on the stable and horses, brush any clothing that was required, cut wood, teach his master's children and do the gardening.

Most apprentices joined an inn after completing their apprenticeship and were able to practice on their own. After entering Clement's Inn as an attorney, he was required to pay for commons for a whole term even if he only used it for a week. Subsequently some men took a room in a nearby inn at Holborn but Spigurnell chose to have his own room at Clement's Inn. Such a decision suggests that he had enough money, or affluent clients, to support this lifestyle, but on the other hand he may have been living beyond his means. Whilst there the statutes, or regulations, prohibited its members having a beard, staying out late at night, bringing women back to the inn, using bad manners at meals in commons, and gaming. The advantages of life at Clement's Inn were the ability to mix with like-minded professionals, as well as the opportunity to discuss cases to obtain a greater knowledge of the law.[136]

Spigurnell was an attorney, well at least a tax collector thought so in Taunton,[137] but as there was no defined training which he could benefit from his entry into the legal world is intriguing. Indeed it may be that he was more of a solicitor as the division between that occupation and an attorney had become blurred by the 1650s. But his later associations with Clement's Inn point to him being an attorney. A general rule of thumb was a requirement to be 'brought up in the courts or otherwise well practised in soliciting causes and proved by their dealings to be skilful and honest'.[138] Brooks and Herber state that 'those wishing to become attorneys or solicitors obtained most of their legal education from articles rather than lectures or 'moots' at the Inns of Chancery'.[139] After entering Clement's Inn, Spigurnell kept his rooms until his death.[140]

Thanks to his connections to the Palmer family, he also became involved with the office of bailiff of the manor of Taunton and Taunton Deane, also known as the Liberty of Taunton Deane. He was one of a group of 'confederates' who by October 1654 included Walter Cliffe gentleman who was living in Exeter, John Palmer late of Taunton 'Doctor of Phisicke' (who from 1645 until 1653 had served as the town's member of parliament), Edward Theare of Taunton a yeoman (Palmer's brother-in-law) and John Herring of Taunton a shoemaker. Spigurnell was referred to as a yeoman of Taunton being an inaccurate description of his occupation, suggesting his late inclusion into the group of confederates. The owners of the manor were concerned enough about the activities of the bailiff (of the same manor) that they ended up taking the confederates to court. The key issues were the rights of the bailiff and what happened to the money they collected, part of which was owed to the new lords Brampton Gurdon of Letton Hall, Norfolk esquire and John Hill of Taunton, gentleman.[141]

Gurdon and Hill bought the manor on 15 March 1647/8[142] but by October 1654 had not received any money from the men who held the office of bailiff. The lords expected to receive money principally from rents, castle rents, greenwax money, woodward money, 'Hockdays waight', yearly fairs, courts, fines, millers, deodands goods, fugitives, outlawed persons, customs, rights, franchises, as well as the money collected by their bailiff from felons, sealing leather, weights and measures, hundred pence, tithing money, and from free suitors. The lords claimed that Spigurnell and his confederates, including the town's MP, held the office by a pretended patent. Cliffe claimed he obtained a patent from a bishop of Winchester that allowed him to be bailiff for life, thanks to a grant that was made to him and John Palmer (father of the MP). Palmer senior died in 1647 and Cliffe claimed the right to keep all the profits whereas Dr Palmer held them by descent.[143]

The lords knew that the confederates, including Spigurnell, had, allegedly, collected moneys in Taunton, Taunton St James, Lydeard St Lawrence, Otterford and Bagborough, and from fairs held elsewhere, as well as from the sealing of leather, from fees collected at manorial courts, as coroners and money relating to deodands. Among the allegations made by the lords was that the confederates had collected and divided the money amongst themselves, as well as taken possession of the castle and 'houses thereunto adjoyning and have taken the whole issues rents and profits thereof ever since the garrison there kept for the Parliament was discharged'. These buildings, or what was left of them, had been converted into a notorious common alehouse that had become a 'receptucle for all manner of persons of all behavior drunkenes wantones & idlenes'. In reply to the allegations, Cliffe claimed the confederates had a legitimate right to live in the houses and edifices of the castle rent free thanks to a grant from Bishop Neile in 1631. As for Palmer he gave his evidence while at All Souls on 21 April 1655, mirroring that given by Cliffe and he also refused to show his patent of office.

He also pointed out that the profits of the office were 'now of little or now value ever since the Complainants have beene in possession', mainly due to the cost of collecting them.

When Edward Theare gave his account of moneys collected from 1648 until 1654 he included the costs of repairs he was involved with because the hall and the houses were 'very ruinous'. Theare was more helpful than his fellow confederates as he left the original patent in the hands of Thomas Rogers, servant to Roger Hill the elder uncle to the complainant Roger Hill, to copy. He was of the view that Cliffe and Palmer, as holders of the patent, were the only men who were 'to have the benefitt and use of Two roomes Called the Exchequer to keepe the records of the said mannor', as well as 'the use of the greate hall there to keepe lawdayes and Courts and touchinge the reparacion thereof the Defendants were never denyed by this defendant or any other ... to doe it'.

But where did this leave Spigurnell? Incorrectly described in the case papers as a yeoman may reflect his minor role in the affair. He was undoubtedly one of the confederates but he did not hold the patent, which points to his role as one of a bailiff's lacky, probably used to collect rents and other fees. So he was most likely under Theare's supervision, who was under the careful eye of John Porter, steward of Taunton Deane.[144] The result does not appear to have survived.[145]

Possibly in 1652, or 1653, Spigurnell was at Ashill at a commission supervised by Colonel Edward Ceely, Major Sansum and Mr Robert Hunt[146] (a relative of the Browne's of Wilton).[147] This case between two minor landowners (Cotten and Chaffey) concerned the disputed ownership of Gilberts Hill in Tintinhull and a tenement in Martock.[148] Spigurnell's involvement was probably in some legal capacity but he held two tenements in the parish[149] and five years later he leased an estate which fell in the parishes of Martock and Long Sutton.[150] While at Ashill Spigurnell saw Thomas Browne leave the chamber where he was examined by the commissioners. Browne then entered into a conversation with Spigurnell about the business in hand. Browne with 'much sadnesse and trouble of spiritt', started to weep. Spigurnell thought ths was due to the lies Browne had spoken to the commissioners and subsequently had a very bad attack of his conscience. The next day the two men rode towards Ilchester together during which time Browne wept again and clearly had a very troubled conscience. He even asked Spigurnell to 'end the business' so he would not have to hear any more about it. Because of this alleged instance of giving false evidence, a subsequent Chancery case was brought. So, on 7 April 1654, Spigurnell, who was still living in Taunton, was at Montacute before George Raymond, Richard Bovett, Robert Hunt and William Strode who were given authority on 25 February 1653/4 to examine witnesses on behalf of Timothy Cotten by his guardians, plaintiff and on behalf of John Chaffey, defendant. This time Spigurnell gave his deposition about his experience with Thomas Browne. He also gave evidence about the value of the estate of John Lye that he thought was worth at least £2,800 but he could not find out how Lye was related to the Chaffeys who claimed ownership.[151] The case was resolved in 1657 in the High Court of Chancery[152] but in the mean time Spigurnell had been busy elsewhere.

In September of 1656, after entering his legal chambers at Clement's Inn, he found himself back in Taunton giving evidence in a case involving the attorney general against John Pyne and his confederates. Depositions were taken at Bishops Hull and Taunton in September and October 1656 when the inhabitants took on the ruling elite of John Pyne, Richard Bovett, George Searle and Samuel Whetcombe 'as to whether there was a garrison in Taunton under the command of the Parliament'. There was also the question of the alleged burning of the town 'by reason that the inhabitants opposed the late King's party in the late Warre'. Spigurnell gave his deposition along with 43 local merchants, gentlemen and artisans describing himself as a gentleman of Clement's Inn. Spigurnell confirmed the facts that inhabitants of both Taunton parishes were involved in the allotment compensation scheme who were entitled to receive money from the rents of Lord Stawell's sequestered estate. The money used to fund the scheme needed to be managed and Spigurnell's role involved surveying the demesnes and manors of Cothelstone and Cushuish, and familiarising himself with the manor of Prestleigh. He reported to the most important and powerful men in Taunton, namely John Pyne, George Searle, Richard Bovett and Samuel Whetcombe, two of whom had served as mayor of Taunton; James Aish and Colonel Alexander Popham were also involved. Spigurnell gave evidence how he examined the allotment accounts and how they showed the four men had served Parliament faithfully since 1647.

This case also brought to light the actions of Robert Hucker who Spigurnell knew very well. Before the wars Hucker was a butcher and a man of a 'very meane estate' but due to the changing times he was trusted with the receipt of the rents of Stawell's sequestered lands. But there were problems with the rents Hucker had to collect from the lands due to two factors. The first factor was seen first-hand by Spigurnell during his survey work. He stated how 'havinge beene frequentlie upon the said Lands did never see anie of the same Lands plowed or sowed or improved by Lime and soyle or otherwise'. This suggests that the lands may have been left fallow, or had not generated anything of significant value, because they were not fertilized, only being used for grazing. The second factor was the collection of the rents by Hucker. Matters came a head on 26 March 1656 when Spigurnell, as steward of the manor of Cothelstone and Cushuish, held court there. In front of Hucker, Whetcome 'did in the name of himselfe and the rest of the Trustees demaund from the said Hucker an accompt of the rents and proffitts of the said Lands soe by him received'. In reply Hucker refused to pay the money and claimed the trustees had no right to hold any court there. There was also an issue about tenants' rights to the use of timber. Here Spigurnell stated how he had surveyed the lands and examined the leases issued by Sir John Stawell and found them not to contain clauses about the free use of any timber. Despite these issues Spigurnell was not out of pocket. His work in stewarding and surveying the lands for the gang of four (Pyne, Searle, Bovett and Whetcombe) saw him receive £40 by 1656 with the expectation of a further £150 for his 'expences and disbursements'.[153]

Spigurnell returned to Clement's Inn as by 4 March 1656/7 he acquired land in South Brent and the rectory and parsonage of Berrow. He then assigned one acre of arable land in Little Oatgretton and half an acre of arable in Great Rawcroft (in South Brent), the rectory and parsonage of Berrow, as well as 3½ acres of meadow in Longhuish to Gerard Wood of East Dearham, Norfolk, clerk in consideration for £80.[154] Then, on 6 August 1657, he entered into a bond of £1,000 to be paid before the 1st of December with Richard Jeane, a lawyer from Taunton, who had to pay Spigurnell 100 marks for his costs and charges in the common dining hall at Clement's Inn. And it is lively that Jeane, Spigurnell and Thomas Latham were at the Blue Boars Head Inn, Westminster on 30 November 1658.[155] Other associates of Spigurnell in London included William Firmyn an apothecary of High Holborne, and James Symes of Gray's Inn, both of whom he borrowed money from. When in London he was able to utilise his friend Henry Cotton's house. Spigurnell kept his books there, that were not worth more than 50 shillings, as well as old items of clothes, stockings, table cloths, a coat, shoes, sheets, cuffs, a cloak, doublet, breeches, hats and the like. His interest in land holding and surveying accounts for the mathematical instruments in his possession worth 15 shillings, all of which were valued at £10 5s 10d.[156] Cotton continued to live at Clement's Inn[157] until 1698.[158]

During his time at Clement's Inn Spigurnell made many friends and clients, as well as a few enemies. Similarly his work in Taunton increased that number of contacts. One of those contacts, Richard Jeane, a gentleman and attorney at law, found himself embroiled with Spigurnell in 1658. Thanks to Spigurnell's role with 'courts of survey' for Parliament he became associated with Jeane (who also lived at West Monkton) who, allegedly, 'in a most Malitious manner [did] Blemish the Reputation of Thomas Spigurnell'. Jeane allegedly tried to prevent Spigurnell from recovering a sum of his own money, something the latter's friends warned him about. They thought Jeane's 'secrett and private Actinge [was] in order to undermine and utterly ruine' Spigurnell. It also came to Spigurnell's attention, some time before June 1659, how Jeane had spread rumours in London, Westminster and Somerset that Spigurnell was a 'Complotter with the Kings Party', and had a hand in the late insurrection at Salisbury.[159] If he was involved in the Penruddock Uprising in March 1655 his name is not in Desborow's list of suspects,[160] but it may have been the case of where there is smoke there is fire.

Shortly after the case between Spigurnell and Jeane was entered into, another case asked specific questions whether Spigurnell's loyalties were towards King or Parliament. At this later date it appeared he had not fought for Parliament although he had been seen wearing a sword during the wars [10], which suggests he may not have been so driven to die for his cause. However, he certainly used the pen (or quill) to undertake his battles for Parliament following the demise of the Royalist cause.

There may have been some truth to the doubts concerning Spigurnell's loyalty. There may also have been some jealousy on Jeane's part as Spigurnell thought the former was after his estate. In order for Spigurnell's estate to be forfeited Jeane engineered a plan. He needed to show Spigurnell was an opponent of the State. If he could then Spigurnell's estate, which included leases of many sequestered properties[161] and possibly the properties in Berkshire inherited from his father,[162] would be forfeited to the State, hence the rumour that he was involved in the Penruddock uprising. But there was more to come. Spigurnell was taken prisoner during the election for knights of the shire at Wells in 1656.[163] This was an important event in the county's calendar that attracted many of the leading figures in both society and local government, plus an array of traders and ordinary folk. Normally, in pre-Interregnum days, two men were elected to represent the county. However, in 1656, John Desborow, John Buckland, Alexander Popham, Robert Long, John Gorges, Francis Luttrell, John Ash, John Harrington, Lisleborn Long, William Wyndham and Francis Rolle were all elected.[164]

Jeane boasted about his success in getting Spigurnell incarcerated. Poor Spigurnell was guarded by a troop of horse and 'carryed the same darke night by the said Troopers over the mynes and cole pitts of Myndeep hill' to Ilchester gaol. Co-ordinating this activity was Major Desborow,[165] the man who married Cromwell's sister and was appointed in 1655 to the important role of major-general commanding the south west of England, making him the highest ranking official in the county.[166] He officiated over the Quarter Sessions held at Wells on 8 January 1655/6[167] and his title was not merely window dressing. After Desborow locked Spigurnell up, our pettyfogger was unable to undertake any legal business, which he claimed was to his great loss. But once again his friends were able to help him and encouraged him to be 'rouzed upp from his dejection of Spiritt' and enter into a suit against Jeane. Subsequently he prepared a suit to be heard at Taunton assizes, but Jeane backed out at the eleventh hour. Avoiding confrontation the pair agreed on a course of mediation before Thomas Latham, counsellor at law. After entering into a bond of £1,000 Latham heard the evidence and awarded Spigurnell £100 (to be paid by Jeane), as compensation for his role in a 'scandall of a very high nature'. But Jeane failed to pay the money and Spigurnell entered into a suit in Chancery. Their evidence was presented before Philip Lissant, Samuel Whetcombe and Thomas Harvey in Taunton.[168]

Sequestered estates

Many details are known of Spigurnell's interactions with sequestered estates (in addition to those already mentioned). In 1653, he leased a property known as Lake House or Lake House Farm in East Brent from Wadham Wyndham,[169] a fellow lawyer, who became a prominent judge, whose portrait still hangs at his ancestral home Orchard Wyndham. The reversion of the tenements had been sold to Wyndham whilst he was at Lincoln's Inn;[170] in 1663 this 20 acre property was described as being on Brent Hill,[171] but it is not quite on the hill, just to the west of it. The property had, allegedly, been burnt down and before Spigurnell leased it he knew that he had to rebuild it (as was stipulated in the terms of his lease).[172] Spigurnell's involvement with the estate reflected his attitude towards other holdings, as he got behind with his rent payments. Whether this was a conscious move or not is lost to history, nevertheless Wyndham instructed his bailiffs to obtain property belonging to Spigurnell to recover the amount he was owed and subsequently they detained two geldings and a colt. However, Spigurnell thought the two geldings and a colt had been stolen from Lake House Farm in November 1656. He alleged that the theft was undertaken by John Burrowe and Thomas Younger who were bailiffs of Wadham Wyndham. Subsequently he brought an action against them in the High Court of Chancery during Hillary Term 1657 using his attorney, Henry Plucknett. The complaint stated that Spigurnell had lost 'one mare one Geldinge and twenty sheepe' but this was changed. He attempted to claim £20 in damages. On the other side to contra this Burrowe and Younger were represented by their attorney John Jeffery. Burrowe and Younger denied the allegation that the animals had been stolen, stating they had been seized due to a default in the rents owing to the landowner, Wadham Wyndham. At the end of the day Wyndham was owed £5 17s in unpaid rents.[173]

Brent Knoll photographed from the Lake House area of East Brent (Author)

The matter did not end there. John Stibbens of Bristol, iremonger was involved in the ownership of Lake House with Spigurnell and they brought a case in Chancery, this time against Nathaniel Jones clerk and his wife Elizabeth. The lands were worth £16 per year and held a rent of 16s. A house was described as a 'causualtie of ffire burned downe and flatted'. Jones was allegedly a 'Traytor of this Commonwealth' and as such his lands had been sequestered.[174] Jones was certainly a supporter of bishops and episcopacy while he was rector of Christon in 1641.[175] Unfortunately Jones did not compound in time and Stibbens was owed money by Jones, so the property passed to Stibbens for 'security and imdempnity'. Stibbens purchased the estate and Spigurnell 'possessed the said Terme and hath ever since enjoyed the same'. Spigurnell claimed he was owed the rent and yearly profits. But Wyndham claimed the reversion and refused to accept Spigurnell's rent. The matter became legally very complicated. Stibbens and Spigurnell could not establish when the rent should be paid to Wyndham, and despite Wyndham having a counterpart of the lease he refused to produce it in evidence. Therefore Stibbens and Spigurnell had to result to the law.[176]

Wyndham answered Spigurnell's complaint in Chancery on 10 July 1658 confirming that Jones was seised of the tenement that he leased to him. The lease required the lessee to undertake any repairs and fulfill any suits of court required by the lord of the manor. Wyndham thought Jones had 'willfully' caused the property to be burnt down and subsequently sued him so he would have to rebuild the house. But Jones was a Royalist and the State sold his estate to Spigurnell who managed to purchase it at a 'verie lowe and inconsiderable rate'. It was alleged that Spigurnell should have rebuilt the house. Wyndham claimed that Spigurnell had not paid any rent for the property, attended any manorial courts, or rebuilt the house as was required by a lease of 23 November 1653. Wyndham did not want to go to law over the matter and tried to get his fellow lawyer to fulfill his obligations but failed to do so.[177] Interestingly there is some eidence to show Spigurnell did actually pay some of his rent. An entry in Wadham's account book shows that on 24 February 1657[/8] he received of 'Mr Thomas Spigurnel for rent due at Michaelmas 1656 and for capons and cost of ... the some of six pounds ten shillings for Lake house in edingworth' totalling £7 10s. However, this is the only entry in his account book covering the 1650s to show Spigurnell did pay anything.[178] Nevertheless this is yet another example of how Spigurnell benefitted from the spoils of war. It is also a good example of how the sequestration of Royalist estates was not without its complexities.

One of the greatest prizes in the great sell off of Royalists' estates in Somerset was the estate of Sir John Stawell. Such was the extent of his estate and the level of Stawell's dislike for everything that Parliament stood for, that an act of Parliament had to be passed to deal with the matter. This act was described in the early Restoration period as 'being made by the late usurped powers, or by the long Parliament or pretended Parliament in the late unhappie warrs'. The estate was sold for the use of the Commonwealth, or 'pretended Commonwealth, or otherwise disposed of as forfeited for Treason'. A very large sum of £7,000 resulting from the sale was granted to the people of Taunton by Parliament as compensation and was dealt with by a local committee of men that included Dr John Palmer,[179] Spigurnell's patron.[180] Subsequently Spigurnell was appointed as surveyor of the lands that were sold to benefit Taunton and became embroiled in numerous disputes relating to Stawell's former estate, including the Cushuish problem (described above). He also held leases in his own right of former Stawell lands. The outcome of the disputes is not always clear but the evidence given reveals much of Spigurnell's life and times.

One dispute occurred on 11 July 1660, whilst Spigurnell was living at Wilton. He was involved in a Chancery case against Taunton's bookseller, George Treagle. Spigurnell took Treagle to court over money matters when it was claimed the bookseller owed money to different people, including £100 to Roger Hill esquire of Taunton that was conditioned for the payment of £50. Treagle claimed he was in great distress and was threatened with the law in order to recover the money and he asked Spigurnell to supply him with money to repay the £100. Treagle offered to enter into a bond as security using his property on Quantock Hill as collatteral. Thus Treagle was another Tauntonian who benefitted from the sale of Stawell's lands and was prepared to convey the same to Spigurnell. Subsequently Spigurnell trusted Treagle and loaned him £35 in a 'faire and friendly manner' but the security was not handed over. Spigurnell felt this was done to 'defraude and decive' him and Treagle pretended he did not have the deed to the land on Quantock, all of which was done to avoid conveying the land to him. As Spigurnell had no loan documentation and could find no way in the common law to recover the money, he resorted to the High Court of Chancery to recover his loss.

Whereas Treagle put forward a very different version of events. He claimed that he never received the £35 or possessed the land on Quantock, so Spigurnell had no right to the land. Treagle revealed that when Parliament appointed Spigurnell for arranging the dividends for the people of Taunton from the sale of the Stawell estate, the bookseller was given £100. Spigurnell arranged for Richard Bovett (one of the Taunton commissioners) to give Treagle £10 to cover his immediate needs. On another occasion, about August 1659 when 'Sir George Booth was risen in the north', Spigurnell went to Treagle's house where the bookseller paid the lawyer £35 for Mr Roger Hill's loan. Treagle denied any claim that he tried to defraud Spigurnell. The outcome is not known but there was no political aggenda in this case as it involved Roger Hill esquire of Taunton, the trustees of Sir John Stawell's sequestrated lands, Spigurnell and Treagle who were all Parliamentarians. It appears Treagle had borrowed various sums of money claiming that he was possessed of certain land on Quantock Hill. As Spigurnell was acting in his capacity as steward, or surveyor, for the trustees it may have been a case of sharp practice by our attorney.[181]

One parcel of former Stawell lands Spigurnell found himself involved with as a leaseholder was referred to as Griggs tenement. It was, with others, 'disposed of to and amongst the late Souldiers and pretended sufferinge people of the saide Towne of Taunton'. Spigurnell, with the consent of Parliament, purchased the tenement from Richard Grigg of Staple Fitzpaine, through Roger Hurley of Taunton. Shortly after the agreement was made between Grigg and Spigurnell 'the Kinges Majestie being happily restored and by the influence thereof' Sir John Stawell was returned unto his 'Lands and Possessions'. Sir John demanded the arrears of rent. He also refused to acknowledge the right of Parliament to take such rent and subsequently he sued Grigg and Spigurnell for it.

Grigg thought that about 1647 and 1648 'in the heate of Warr' Stawell's estate was sold for the soldiers and people of Taunton 'as were in armes for the then Parliament'. Grigg's tenement and 60 acres was sold to George Treagle mercer at a very low rate, like other properties and then, on 27 August 1659, it was granted to Roger Hurley for the use of Spigurnell who was then living at Wilton. It did not take long for Spigurnell to start boasting about his latest purchase. In October he pretended to be the 'true and lawfull owner' and Grigg entered into a bond with Spigurnell for him to repay £30 to Grigg in case Stawell reclaimed his estate. The writing was on the wall for Parliamentarians and clearly people in Taunton thought Charles would soon return and reign over them as his father had done before him. When this actually happened both King Charles the Second and Parliament disabled Spigurnell from performing his contract with Grigg. Subsequently Grigg accused Hurley and Spigurnell of confederacy. In Spigurnell's defence he alleged Grigg declared our attorney had 'beene mistaken for a Cavoleere but now he should prove otherwise and that the Gentleman Souldiers had fought and suffered for itt and yt was fitt they should have it'.[182]

The next step in this saga occurred two year's later, almost to the day, when Spigurnell took Grigg to court. Spigurnell had been busy looking into the ownership of the property. It came to light that Samuel Chesterdam was Grigg's under tenant and Stawell had actually leased the property to Philip Granfield, gentleman. Grigg had leased the property on 28 September 1651 but after Spigurnell took possession Chesterdam defaulted on his rent. To seek redress Spigurnell turned to George How of Bishops Lydeard, husbandman, 'a man of very evil life' who was ordered to distrain Chesterdam's cattle to recover the sum of £6. Grigg tried to remedy the matter by involving Samuel Whetcombe of Taunton in some sort of mediation, along with Mr John Clarke. However, Spigurnell claimed that the ground 'taken in and inclosed' by Granfield 'from the Hill called Quantocke Hill beinge very poore ground' meant Sir John would never receive any rent until it was cultivated enough to be of any value.[183]

It was decreed in the High Court of Chancery that 'George Treagle together with the Trustees for the said souldiers and sufferinge people' of Taunton did convey the reversion in fee of the property to Hurley in trust for Spigurnell. The inheritance belonged to Stawell but Spigurnell 'pretendinge himselfe to bee [the] lawfull owner' contracted with Grigg for the fee simple for £70, of which Grigg only paid £30. It was found that Spigurnell had promised to pay back the money, with interest, if Stawell came into possession of the property. However, once again, Spigurnell did not keep to his word and hence the case came to court. After the depositions were taken the court decreed, on 18 May 1663, that Grigg should pay Spigurnell £40 without damages or costs at his house in Long Sutton 'on Michaelmas day next'. Grigg also had to deliver up the said bond to Spigurnell to be cancelled.[184] The problem with this ruling is that Spigurnell died before Michaelmas 1663. Add to this the problem that Richard Grigg may also have died shortly afterwards as his will was written on 25 August 1663, in which his daughter Charity, if she reached the age of 21, was to be his executor.[185] Subsequently Charity, as executrix of Richard, had to take Spigurnell to Assizes twice to recover the £140 he owed Richard, and was still owed £40 after Spigurnell died.[186]

The matter did not end there for the Spigurnell family. Four years after Spigurnell had passed away Hurley and Dryer took Spigurnell's children to court. As the kingdom was back in the hands of the House of Stuart in 1667 it was claimed the Stawell estate was sold for the 'pretended' suffering people of Taunton, that was a complete change of rhetoric. Charity Grigg had found her father's bond for £140 against Spigurnell and Hurley. Subsequently she brought a suit against Dryer and Hurley, resulting in an attempt being made to arrest Hurley as he was insolvent.[187] The outcome of the case is not recorded. In the 1660s there was an dislike between opposing sides during the wars of the 1640s some twenty years earlier. These claims and counter claims, changes of government, lost documents and bringing children to account for their deceased father's actions was all very unfortunate, but it was also a way of making money for those in the legal profession.

Another example of how Spigurnell benefitted from the demise of the Royalist party occurred some time before 1656. Henry Bragg, a yeoman of Crewkerne, possessed a long lease of a meadow and pasture in Crewkerne. Due to his loyalty to the late king 'of ever blessed memory' the land was sequestered from his father who was classed as a delinquent. The land was offered for sale and Spigurnell 'A creature then in fashion well becomming and complying with those tymes' bought it from the committee at Drury House. He then 'usurped the possession of that Tenement and received the rents issues and profitts' for a season and Spigurnell was viewed by Bragg as 'riding Tryumphantly on the Inheritance' of his father. Subsequently, about July 1656, Bragg entered into a treaty with Spigurnell for 'Retakeing the sayd estate' and agreed that for £50 Spigurnell would convey the property to Bragg. Spigurnell allegedly took the money and refused to give Bragg his conveyance and also threatened to sue him. Bragg thought Spigurnell was a man without a conscience and asked the Court of Chancery, in June 1662, to make a full account of the affair.[188] As Spigurnell lived about 100 miles from Bragg's father, he claimed he had never met him, or received any rent from him. He also claimed that Henry Bragg held the estate until it was purchased by Robert Coleby, gentleman in the name of William Tucker, at a time when Bragg expressed his 'affection and Engagement unto the then Parliament or pretended powers being then their volunteere souldier under Colonel John Gorge[s]'. Henry Bragg asked Spigurnell to help him purchase the estate from Tucker, Henry's neighbour, which he then did. Spigurnell, presumably in his capacity as an attorney, advised Henry Bragg about the back rents and if 'by the happye and hopefull restoration if his majesty' how the estate would return to the complainant's father, or to the complainant if his father was dead. Spigurnell pleaded to the High Court of Chancery to take his side in this case and not make him pay the £47 that was owed to Bragg.[189]

Another sequestered estate came into Spigurnell's possession on 17 June 1656. He acquired a short lease of all the 'tenths and tythes of Corne and Grayne ... to the said parsonage of Wyvelscombe and Fitzhead';[190] at that time Fitzhead was a chapelry of Wiveliscombe.[191] He agreed with a small group of individuals to hold this valuable asset from the 25 March 1656 for two years at the yearly rent of £150. However, like most of Spigurnell's activities with sequestered estates something went wrong. Hence in Easter terme 1657 he entered a bill in the Court of Exchequer against the Attorney General, William Hill, Lawrence Saunders and Henry Whipple.[192] The problem was that Spigurnell thought he was leasing the tithes from one group of owners, whereas the tithes were owned by a different group altogether!

Spigurnell claimed the right honourable William Steele Lord Chancellor of Ireland late Lord Cheif Baron of the Exchequer, Sir John Thorowgood knight, George Cooper, Richard Younge, John Pocock, Ralph Hall, Richard Sydenham, Edward Hopkyns, John Humfry and Edward Cressett esquires were seized in fee since 17 June 1656 of 'all tenths and tythes of Corne and Grayne yearely groweing ariseing encreaseing and renewing within the parish of Wyvelscombe and Fitzhead'. This was his two year lease at a rent of £150 per year. On the other side of the case were the Hills, Saunders and Whipple 'pretending tytle unto the said Tythes' who prevented Spigurnell collecting what was due to him and in the last year they collected the tithes for themselves. They claimed they did not know the other group were seized in fee of and in the said tithes, or that they had been demised unto Spigurnell.[193]

With two different claims on the table the facts had to be established. The rectory or prebend of Wiveliscombe and rectory of Fitzhead had been sequestered from Sir John Stawell knight.[194] John Gorges esquire demised the same on 12 July 1655 to Whipple and Saunders for one yeare from the 24th of June at the yearly rent of £55. About April 1656, Saunders, as Comissioner for Sequestrations for Somerset, demised the rectory of Wivelscombe to Jane Hill for one year from the 24th of June 1656 with a yearly rent of £100. Jane 'received and took all the tenths and tythes of Corne and Grayne within the said Rectory of Wyvelscombe' and she also had a grant from Saunders for the following year. Edmund Prideaux esquire, Attorney General, did not know the trustees were 'seized in Fee of the said Tythes or made any Lease thereof unto the said plaintiffs'. Prideaux knew the 'Impropriate Rectory of Wyvelscombe and Fitzhead' was part of the estate of Sir John Stawell and had been settled on William Skynner and others. Subsequently the rents should have been received by the Receiver General of Somerset. It materialised the defendants did receive the profits of the rectory by vertue of a demise or contract until 25 March 1657. However, they also denied that the Lord Protector in April 1656 'or any tyme before was intitled to the severall Rectories of Wyvelscombe and Fitzhead'. So the defendant was 'served with Proces appeared and joyned in Comission', the depositions were taken on both sides, then published and the cause was heard.

The court was of the opinion that a trial was needed 'att the Common Lawe concerning the tytle of the said Tythes' before it could 'receive a determinacion in Equitie'. All that was needed was to prove the plaintifs William Steele *et al* were, on 17 June 1656, seized in fee by the vertue of several 'Acts of Parliament and Ordinances of his Hignes the then Lord Protector' of all the 'tenths and tythes of Corne and Grayne' within the parishes of Wivelscombe and Fitzhead. If they were then they could have lawfully demised them to Spigurnell. The matter was ordered to be tried at the next assizes for Somerset.[195] Once again all did not go to plan. The Exchequer officers were informed on 18 June 1660 that the trial at assizes did not happen. To make matters worse on 14 November 1660 the 'cause being continued in the paper of causes' and as the late attorney general had died, it was ordered by the Court that the cause 'should bee continued in the paper' until an attorney general was appointed. They did not have to wait long as it was then ordered by the court, on 30 January 1660/1, that the plaintiff should declare and the said defendant should plead, and a trial should be held at the next assizes for Somerset. After consulting with the plaintiff and finding that the defendants failed to appear after 'a Declaracion in the Office of pleas of this Court' was served on them, the court gave them seven nights to plead. If they failed again the court would then hear the case.[196] A week later on the 6th of February the Exchequer Court ordered after 'long debate of the matter' and despite the defendant's counsel taking some 'excepcions to the yssue directed to bee tryed' it was ordered that both counsells:

shall agree upon the yssue to bee tryed or if they cannot agree concerning the same then counsell on both sides are to bee heard on Saturday next Unlesse the said Defendants shall appeare and plead soe as a tryall may bee had concerning the matter in question this next Assizes then an Attachment shalbe awarded against them.[197]

If a trial at Assizes was held then it did not generate an entry in the order book.

Exactly how many money making activities Spigurnell took advantage of during the Interregnum is not known but Bragg's description of him as 'A creature then in fashion well becomming and complying with those tymes'[198] appears to be wholey correct. How much money he actually made, or lost, is not known but his work for Parliament keeping courts of survey meant that by 1660 he was owed 'Great Sumes of Money ... from this Commonwealth' for that service.[199] He was involved in one case after the Restoration that brought him into conflict with his wife's family. It was a case that involved a very lucrative prize and Spigurnell used all of his legal knowledge to the full. It centred on his marriage portion with Elizabeth and the profits to be made out of the office of clerk of Taunton Castle.

The Taunton Castle clerkship controversy and Elizabeth Browne's marriage settlement

The period during which the Browne family and their kinsmen held the patent for the office of clerk of Taunton Castle was one of great controversy. Robert I had lived in the castle with his wife and three children until 1643 when his son Robert III died. It is possible the family moved to Wilton about that time to avoid the problems of living in a garrison town that was often under siege. The castle was also used as a gaol and housed many unsuitable prisoners that needed to be kept well away from young children. After Robert I's own death in 1648, his wife acquired the patent of clerk along with the existing holder John Browne III of Frampton (her husband's nephew). Matters could have changed dramatically when the bishop's manor was sold in 1647/8 as[200] the Brownes were facing the potential loss of their patent, but fortunately for them they held on to it. Such an action on the face of it suggests the Brownes were not openly supporting the Royalist cause at that time otherwise they would have been described as delinquents. However, whether this was correct, or not, their right to hold the patent for this office was brought to light in a Chancery Court case in 1654.

The new owners of the manor, Roger Hill of Poundsford esquire, Brampton Gurdon of Letton, Norfolk, esquire and John Hill of Taunton, gentleman, purchased the manor with a view to making money from it. Their purchase consisted of the castle and 'all manner of houses Buildings Barnes Stables Edifices Gardens Orchards Greenes' including the porter's lodge, gatehouse and a 'house adjoyninge to the Gate of the said Castle, the Gardings and Curtelages'.

Also included was a stable lately converted into a barn and 'Pounds Mootes or diches beinge neere or about the walles of the sayd Castle'. Some of these lands and buildings were also included in the grant of the patent of clerk, and as the Brownes held that patent it needed to be determined who held the rights to the lands, buildings and associated incomes that went with them. Thus the new owners brought a case against the widow Elizabeth, her nephew John Browne III (c.1608-1670/1) and her son George Browne III.[201] The outcome of the case is not recorded in the decree rolls,[202] so it is likely that the parties resolved the issue out of court as the Brownes held the office until Elizabeth's death. The establishment of the Brownes' rights and their defence of an action in the High Court of Chancery were beneficial for events that unfolded a few years later.

Although the Brownes survived the ravages of the civil wars and the Chancery case aginst the new lords, unfortunately for Elizabeth she became very ill in the late 1650s from the palsie. With no husband to look after her financial interests and her son being absent, her son-in-law Thomas Spigurnell appears to have made much of that situation. He brought to her sick bed, at her home at Sherford, a 'writinge touchinge the profitts of the office of Taunton', *i.e.* the office of clerk and porter valued at £100 (or £120) per annum. Spigurnell wanted his mother-in-law to sign over control of the office to him. But as she was too weak to sign anything and her voice too quiet to be heard, so Spigurnell put her seal on the document and then took her hand and put it on the seal. Did this action make the transaction legally binding? Spigurnell must have thought so. But after he left her chamber Mrs Browne, weak with the palsie, wept and complained he would keep the profits of the office and say he had used them for her benefit. She was lucid enough to discuss how she might live long enough to see the return of the king. Mrs Browne clearly had very little faith in her son-in-law's honesty.

Spigurnell appears to have acquired the offices in 1658 from his elderly and sick mother-in-law as he signed the 'booke of Fees in the exchequer court' in 1658. He also signed as recipient of the profits in 1659 and 1660, or at least Mrs Browne's share of it. But there were those who alleged he was an 'unjust man', mostly due to his support of the Parliamentary cause during the civil war, which may also reflect the politics of the time. During which time he not only purchased lands sequestered from Sir John Stawell but also, allegedly, endeavoured to have his house pulled down at Cothelstone, he 'meddled' with sequestered parsonages and tithes being 'much complayned of', was involved in an Exchequer Court case concerning the tithes of Burnham, procured 'Augmentacions for unworthy Ministres', involved in a case at the Court of Common Pleas, and was closely associated with two leading Civil War Parliamentarians in Somerset, Colonel John Pyne and Colonel Richard Bovett [10].[203] None of which would have endeared him to his brother-in-law George Browne III (whose precise activities in the 1650s are unclear), or to his mother-in-law who was one of the Fowkes family of Dorset. She was also related to the Gollops of North Bowood, one of whom, Thomas, was colonel of Portland Castle for the Royalist party.[204] But she managed to retain the patent of clerk during the 1650s,[205] possibly due to the Brownes service to parliament; for the relevant relationships between the Fowkes and Gollop families see pedigrees 4 and 5.

The matter of this falsely acquired office and the income from it, as well as further allegations of him appropriating personal effects belonging to his mother-in-law (who died in May 1661),[206] came to a head after her death. But what drove Spigurnell to allegedly take such actions? As a member of a younger branch of a landed family it was an accepted practice for daughters, such as Spigurnell's second wife Elizabeth, to bring to their marriage a 'portion'. This was a financial sum, or property, that was normally provided by the bride's parents to give her an income during her married life. So the Brownes allegedly promised to provide a settlement with Spigurnell for Elizabeth to have £2,000 on their marriage [10]. However, following her marriage she did not receive the money she was due for her settlement. Was this what motivated Spigurnell to seek some sort of redress from his mother-in-law? The redress being the profits of the office of clerk and his mother-in-law's household valuables.

Subsequently in May 1661 George Browne III's kinsman, Mr John Browne III of Frampton (the other patent holder) made an award to try and settle the dispute between his cousin George III and Spigurnell, with whoever defaulted having to pay £2,000. Therefore, on the 24 June 1661, the stage was set for settling the dispute, the location being the exchequer of Taunton Castle. Present were George Gollop of North Bowood, Dorset, his brother-in-law George III, Mr Prockter a merchant of Taunton St Mary, William Lane a gentleman of Totnes, Devon, John Rowland a whitebaker of Taunton, John Porter the ever reliable deputy steward and clerk of the castle, Thomas Harvey the deputy clerk, and an un-named minister in the company of Spigurnell. The award required George III to pay Spigurnell £300 for deeds and writings held by the latter, which amount he duly presented to him in bags, which were partially counted before Spigurnell handed it over to the minister. Browne then demanded Spigurnell hand over the deeds and writings which were subject to the award, at the same time presenting Spigurnell a document for him to sign. This second transaction would release to George III all Spigurnell's 'clayme and interest in the office and estates of Robert Browne esquire deceased and Mrs Elizabeth Browne'. The document was then read out and when the reading was complete Spigurnell stood at the door, looked into the room and said nothing of 'dislike or take any exceptions to the same'. But for some unfathomable reason Spigurnell did not seal or execute the document. To make matters worse he did not deliver the papers subject to the award, only stating to his brother-in-law 'if he pleased' to sue him for not performing the award. He then threatened to carry away the money and dispose of it how he pleased. The situation then became even worse as Spigurnell had not handed over the bond for the £300, so Gollop and Prockter tried to persuade him for 'quitnesse sake' to accept the money and perform his part of the award. Not surprisingly he refused. The £300 was then left in the exchequer at around 7p.m. with George III ready to perform the award but Spigurnell was nowhere to be seen. Why did Spigurnell undertake such a disagreeable action before so many worthy men? Spigurnell's most unusual action set in motion a train of events that did nothing to foster good relationships between the Browne and Spigurnell families for years to come.

Any differences which then remained between the two were brought into the wider public gaze in the High Court of Chancery in the following year, when George III's case appeared to be much stronger than Spigurnells [10]. In the mean time, on 7 February 1661/2, George III of Wilton and John Gollop of North Bowood had taken out a new patent of office, by which date the manor had reverted back to the Bishopric of Winchester from Messrs Gourdon and Hill. Thus by obtaining such a grant there was absolutely no doubt that Spigurnell had no more right to the offices of clerk and porter and the fees it attracted. The fact this took over eight months after old Mrs Browne passed away at Wilton appears to have gone without notice.

The 31st of March in the year 1663 must have been an interesting day in the ongoing dispute between the Spigurnells (Thomas and Elizabeth) and George III. This was the day the deponents had to assemble before the commissioners in order to give their verbal evidence. Exactly where in the town the depositions were taken is not recorded on the roll but the whole proceedings were likely held at one of the larger inns situated in the borough, or at the castle. Overseeing proceedings were Thomas Dyke, William Doble and Henry Plucknett.[207] It was the principal job of these commissioners, all of them legal men, to examine the witnesses and make sure the depositions were recorded correctly and without ambiguity. Without a doubt the fact that 'the defendant Thomas Spigurnell was against the Kinge, and Complainant for the Kinge' meant the witnesses called by each party reflected those interests.

The nature of the interrogatories (or questions) put to the deponents reveals the strategy of the parties. The complainant, George III, tabled 32 interrogatories, followed by 22 from the Spigurnells; many interrogatories were made up of multiple questions. George III started by building a picture of his father, mother and the legitimacy of the documents presented on that day in Taunton. Next came George's efforts to discredit his brother-in-law. The nature of the fifth and sixth interrogatories dragged up many of the painful results of the wars, particularly sequestrations and the money Parliamentarians made from them. Interrogatory number seven tried to show Thomas was not a person of quality, and, reading between the lines, was in George's opinion a thoroughly unsuitable match for his sister. Number eight established the value of Robert and his wife's estate and what, if anything, was lost during the wars. Next, number nine, was an attempt to establish the character of his mother Elizabeth; was she weak, discreet, foolish, prudent, provident or improvident, and what was her spending ability? The question of money was also raised in interrogatory number ten, especially that held in the 'Exchequer of the Castle of Taunton'. If there was any held there it had been facilitatied by John Porter who was clerk of Taunton Castle, but at the time of the depositions he had also passed away and could not give any evidence apart from the writings he left behind in the castle. This led to the next interrogatory that concerned all the details that could be brought to light regarding the highly contentious issue of Thomas and Elizabeth's marriage portion. But questions over old Mrs Browne's health and her ability to manage any aspect of her estate were the substance of the next interrogatory and one of the longest series of questions that followed. It was not just her daughter's marriage portion that was of interest, but also her own jointure, the terms of her inheritance, how the Spigurnell newly weds interacted with her, including her ability to sign and seal documents. The final sub-question was one of the Spigurnells' loyalties to the 'Kinge and the Royall interest' or whether they were elsewhere.

Other interrogatories concerned matters such as documentation, the disposal of Mrs Browne's lands, where the Spigurnells lived after they were married and the relationships between them. Perhaps the most telling were interrogatories 28 to 31 that dealt with the award of 1661 that was drawn up between the parties. In reply the Spigurnells tabled their questions that overall helped fill in some of the gaps in the story. They also show how George III may have deliberately avoided asking some questions in order to strengthen his own case. Questions were asked about goods that were lost in the war, what George III did during his minority and how he was financially supported, the validity of the evidence given by James King, Dr Palmer's role at All Souls, the Stoke Hill property and the profits Thomas received when he married into the Browne family. In all well over 150 sub-questions were tabled but not all were answered [10].

Just before the depositions were taken, Spigurnell brought an action to recover a debt of £31 from George Browne III. Spigurnell's complaint, dated 14 February 1662/3 [9] was answered by George III on 25 May 1663 [11]. Two years after Elizabeth had remarried, with her new husband Edward Chard of Long Sutton gentleman, she rejuvenated their claim against George Browne III, sometime after June 1665 [12-13]; George's answer is dated 18 April 1666 [14]. The Chards were not done with the High Court of Chancery as they also brought a case against the new joint patent holder of the office of clerk of Taunton Castle before 13 May 1667 [15] when John Gollop gave his answer [16]. Eventually the matters under dispute had to be resolved. Thus on 11 April 1668 a decree was issued in the High Court of Chancery. It recited George III's bill of complaint of 1660 against Thomas Spigurnell gentleman, Elizabeth his wife and Elizabeth Browne II his mother. It established the lands, goods and profits of the clerkship of Taunton Castle left to George III's mother 'worth three thousand pounds and upwards' were in trust for George and his sister. Also how Thomas Spigurnell attempted to gain the whole estate from his mother-in-law in her time of weakness. How Thomas and his wife brought their own complaint in 1661 against George Browne, John Gollop gentleman and John Browne in which Spigurnell claimed he had a marriage 'treaty' with Elizabeth his wife worth £200. But with George's agreement this was actually established at £1,000 and it materialised that his mother Elizabeth had agreed to this in 1659. All of which eventually led to the infamous event whereby George was ready to pay Spigurnell £300 in the exchequer of Taunton Castle but it all fell through.

The decree also established how despite Spigurnell's death, the Chards subsequently exhibited their bill of reviver in 1665 opening up the unresolved dispute. But George III exhibited his own bill of reviver in 1666 against the Spigurnell children and their father's executors. As the children were under age their guardian and mother, Elizabeth Chard, did not put in an answer to their uncle George's bill. But the right honourable Sir Orlando Bridgeman knight and baronet, Lord Keeper of the Great Seal of England (by authority of the High and Honourable Court of Chancery), ordered George III to:

> pay the said Three hundred pounds and seaventy pounds for the damages thereof into the hands of such person or persons and att such time and place as Sir Moundeford Gamston Knight one of the masters of this Court shall nominate and appointe in Trust for the Complainant Elizabeth.

But Elizabeth was not happy with this, claiming that she had other debts caused by her brother's actions. The court finally ordered Elizabeth Chard's estate and debts be examined and a person appointed to 'give good security to pay the interest of the residue' of the debts. They also ordered what appears to be a further £370 to be 'left to the hands of the said Elizabeth for her livelyhood and meyntenance dureing her life', after which it was to be left to her children. On George's handing over the money the Chards had to hand over all the documents concerning Robert I and his wife Elizabeth II, at the same time introducing an order to protect Thomas's executors. When the Spigurnell children came of age they were to be added to the 'Conveyance and Assignment', similarly George's children were to 'hold and enjoy all the reall and personall estate of his said ffather and mother and likewise the said Offices' of clerk of Taunton Castle. If any problems occurred the matter was to be referred back to the master in Chancery [17].

All these disputes were costly to those involved. George Browne claimed in

1666 that he had already spent £200 on such cases and 'vexatious suites' [14]. But despite their problems during the civil wars, including having their house at Sherford plundered by soldiers and losing around £1,000, the Browne's remained a reasonably wealthy family of some standing, with George III appearing in Blome's *Britannia* in 1673, described as being 'esquire' and a resident of Wilton.[208] He died in 1679 and Gollop continued to hold the patent for another year before it was taken up by Thomas Gerrard esquire,[209] who held on to it until 1697 when it fell into the hands of the Morleys.[210] The Morley family held it for a further twenty years and today the Taunton Court Leet continues to observe many of the ancient traditions witnessed during the years of the Browne versus Spigurnell controversy.[211]

But this was not the end of the affair. In 1684, over two decades after Spigurnell's death, Elizabeth Chard, described as the 'sole daughter and onely childe and issue liveing of Robert Browne deceased late whilst he lived of Taunton Castle' once again was involved in a dispute in Chancery. She recited all the lands owned by her father in Bridport and Huish Champflower, along with his marriage settlement drawn up in 1631 which settled all of his estate on his wife after his death. After her death it was Robert I's intention for the lands to pass to their children, if they had any, and 'to the survivor and the heires of such survivor'. As her brother Robert III died when he was eleven, followed by their mother, so Elizabeth and George were the heirs of the estate. At some stage John Beresford of Taunton, a gentleman and lawyer, was given responsibility for this estate and asked to raise some money for the Brownes by mortgaging Middleton (in Huish Champflower). However, like so many other cases there was a problem. It was alleged that after the parents (Robert I and Elizabeth II) died, Elizabeth III's brother George III took possession of the estate and concealed all the deeds and writings from his sister. He also took out a mortgage on a farm for £800 from Thomas Strode, serjeant at law, but then died in 1679 leaving a wife Ann, a son Robert and five daughters [19].[212] To make matters worse Ann 'under pretence' of borrowing a further £400 from Strode caused the five daughters to levy a fine on the estate to Strode. At the time it was claimed that Elizabeth Chard was barred by the statue of non claim from any part of the estate, something that was not helped by the fact that any 'evidences' regarding title to the estate were allegedly either hidden or destroyed.

Beresford, who was now living in Taunton Castle, once home to the Browne family [19], had a different view of events. In his defence Beresford recited how he entered a judgement in His Majesty's Court of Record at Westminster against Ann Browne for the recovery of the £800 (mortgage) and two writs of *fieri facias* (a writ to a sheriff for executing a judgement) for the sheriff of Somerset to levy the goods of George Browne that were in the hands of his widow (Ann) to be administered. But only £200 was raised out of the £800 that was supposed to have been recovered. Beresford, a man of the law, recited the previous suits between the Brownes, Spigurnells, Dryer and Pyne and how the High Court of Chancery ordered £370, Middleton and other lands to be set over to George Browne on 1 April 1669. Beresford also somehow knew that Robert I did not want any of his lands to pass to his daughter from his son. The reason he gave was that she had inherited the greater part of her father's personal estate but by making such a claim Beresford had more to gain from George inheriting the lion's share rather than his sister. He also knew there were other lands involved that had not previously been mentioned in the Chancery cases he recited. Several grants and assignments for land at Benvill in Corscombe, Dorset by George Browne, as well as old writings and leases relating to Middleton, some of them made by Ann Browne were eventually brought to light. The most important document was one by George Horner, late sheriff of Somerset, for £800 for a grant and sale of Middleton to Beresford for 1,000 years, including the clause for the tenant to pay the high rent and perform any services due to the lord of the manor.[213]

Conclusion

Thomas Spigurnell was not a man who came out of nothing, which as a servant working on his master's horses might suggest. His father was a mercer, his grandfather a man of the Church and his teenage years were spent under the tuition of Sir Henry Sambourne a relative by marriage on his mother's side. This connection brought young Thomas under the wing of Dr Thomas Palmer and a potential career in medicine. However, possibly due to the tumults of the 1640s, after time at All Souls he trained in the law and entered Clement's Inn as an attorney. After which he spent more time in Taunton, married twice and had three children by his second wife. The failure to receive an alleged marriage portion for his second marriage led to a dispute he brought in the High Court of Chancery. Subsequently a rift between the Brownes of Wilton and the Spigurnells (and later Chards) lasted almost two decades. It cost the parties hundreds of pounds in legal fees and may have changed their fortunes for the generations that followed.

In between all this activity Thomas Spigurnell became embroiled in a number of investments and disputes. He was a 'creature' of Parliament and took advantage of sequestrations, in the process he became closely involved with the Taunton cabal of John Pyne, Samuel Whetcombe, George Searle and Richard Bovett senior. His involvement with such men saw him branded as a confederate. But the pendulum of fate swung back in favour of the Royalists. The Interregnum offered many Royalists the chance for retribution, much to Thomas Spigurnell's dislike. Despite his efforts to prove his loyalty to Parliament in the 1650s, then prove his loyalty to the Crown in the 1660s, there was nothing he could do to prevent his early demise aged 33, or thereabouts. Sadly his financial management caused immediate problems for his widow and three young children. One of his legacies can be seen today at Long Sutton Court where his initials mark the renovations he oversaw in the late 1650s when it was a farm. His professional activities can be seen in numerous records in the High Court of Chancery, the Court of Common Pleas and Court of Exchequer. The publication of a handful of these documents in this volume reveals something of the world of a mid-seventeenth century lawyer who practised in Somerset, married above his station (twice), fell out with his Royalist relatives, often did not pay his debts, but built many friendships in the local Parliamentary elite and with numerous figures in the legal profession. His life was unique and the documents he generated are of value to local, social and legal historians over three and a half centuries after he died in Taunton at an inn.

It is ironic that old Sir Henry Sambourne outlived Thomas.[214] As for his other associates, only his old friend Richard Bovett senior went on to leave a significant mark on history, playing a major role in the Monmouth Rebellion, whereas others slipped into obscurity. It is a possibility that Spigurnell has been painted in a bad light due to the type of records that reveal the main events of his life. Most of these records are legal disputes and by their nature reveal two different conflicting sides of some sort of disagreement. There is also a possibility that some of the Chancery documents associated with these disputes have not survived the ravages of time. Nevertheless there is no smoke without fire and it is up to the reader to decide whether Spigurnell was the type of character some of the documents claim he was. It is my opinion that he can be classed as both a confederate and pettyfogger who appears to have taken full advantage of any opportunity to make money at other people's expense.

Sometimes documents hint at events and circumstances that are not proven facts. Those printed in this volume leave little doubt of Thomas Spigurnell's sharp practice. But were the tailors who supported his case men who made his clothes? Was the inn where he died in Taunton also his business premises where he gave legal advice to the Taunton confederates? Did his penny-pinching activities when instructing his tithe collector an underlying theme, especially when it came to mourners enjoying the food and drink at his wake? Was Thomas simply a man who would rather take his chances with going to court rather than pay his debts? Many more questions can be asked about his life, especially his activities as a surveyor that appear to have been overlooked by historians.

Pedigree 1 : Browne family of Frampton and Taunton

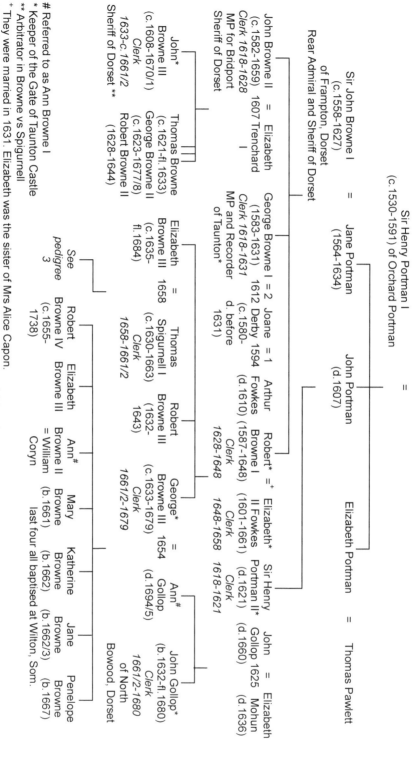

+ They were married in 1631. Elizabeth was the sister of Mrs Alice Capon.

Note: Other siblings are not shown, only those people referred to in the text of this volume.

Principle sources: G. D. Squibb, *The visitation of Somerset and the City of Bristol 1672*, Harl. Soc. New Series 11 (1992), 136–7. Somerset and Dorset parish registers.

* Arbitrator in Browne vs Spigurnell
** Keeper of the Gate of Taunton Castle
* Referred to as Ann Browne I
# Referred to as Ann Browne I

Pedigree 2: Spigurnell family of Maidenhead and Sambourne of Moulsford, Berkshire

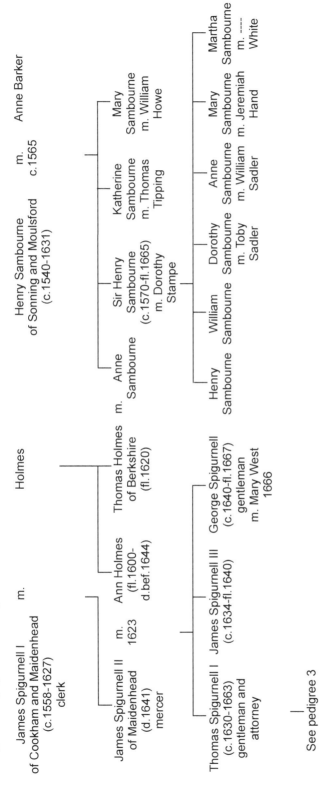

Sources: Berkshire Record Office, D/A1/16/598 will and D/A1/213/146 probate inventory; S.H.C., D/D/OI 36 29 November 1662: D/P/l.sut/2/1/1 Long Sutton registers; T.N.A., C 6/167/18 joint answer of Thomas and Elizabeth Spigurnell, c. 1661; C 78/639 no.17 decree, 1658/9; CP 40/2498 case, 1642; C. Kerry, *The history and antiquities of the Hundred of Bray, in the county of Berkshire* (London, 1861), 8; V.C. Sanborn, *Genealogy of the family of Samborne or Sanborn in England and America 1194-1898* (Privately printed, 1899), 17-18.

Pedigree 3 : Spigurnell family of Long Sutton and Godwin of Wells

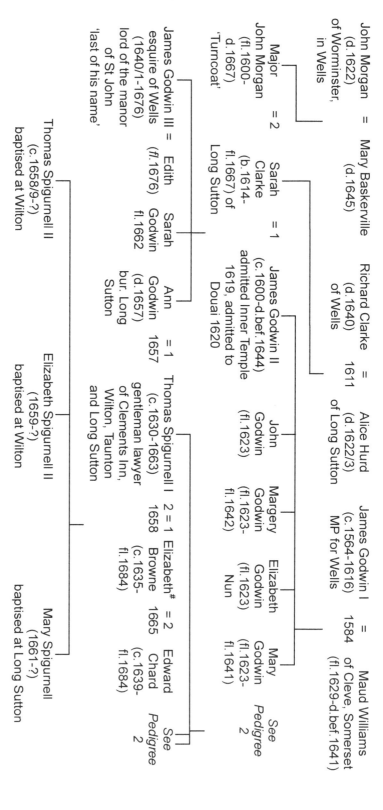

John Morgan
(d.1622)
of Worminster,
in Wells

= Mary Baskerville
(d.1645)

Richard Clarke
(d.1640)
of Wells

= 1611

Alice Hurd
(d.1622/3)
of Long Sutton

James Godwin I
(c.1564-1616)
MP for Wells

= 1584

Maud Williams
of Cleve., Somerset
(fl.1629-d.bef.1641)

Major
John Morgan
(fl.1600-
d.1667)
'Turncoat'

= 2

Sarah
Clarke
(b.1614-
fl.1667) of
Long Sutton

= 1

James Godwin II
(c.1600-d.bef.1644)
admitted Inner Temple
1619, admitted to
Douai 1620

John
Godwin
(fl.1623)

Margery
Godwin
(fl.1623-
fl.1642)

Elizabeth
Godwin
(fl.1623)
Nun

Mary
Godwin
(fl.1623-
fl.1641)

See
Pedigree
2

James Godwin III
esquire of Wells
(1640/1-1676)
lord of the manor
of St John
'last of his name'

= Edith
Godwin
fl.1662

Sarah
Godwin
bur. Long
Sutton

Ann
Godwin
(d.1657)

= 1 1657

Thomas Spigurnell I
(c.1630-1663)
gentleman lawyer
of Clements Inn,
Wilton, Taunton
and Long Sutton

2 = 1 1658

Elizabeth#
Browne
(c.1635-
fl.1684)

= 2 1665

Edward
Chard
(c.1639-
fl.1684)

See
Pedigree
2

Thomas Spigurnell II
(c.1658/9-?)
baptised at Wilton

Elizabeth Spigurnell II
(1659-?)
baptised at Wilton

Mary Spigurnell
(1661-?)
baptised at Long Sutton

Referred to in this volume as Elizabeth Spigurnell I
Sources: S.H.C., DD/FS/48/5/1-2 lease, 1662; DD/WY/2/53/3 assignment, 1644; D/P/l.sut/2/1/1 Long Sutton registers; T.N.A., C 78/639 no.17
decree, 1658/9; CP 40/2498 case, 1642; PROB 11/184/551 will of Richard Clarke of Long Sutton, 1640; PROB 11/355/213 will of James Godwin
of Wells, 1676; Stoate and Howard, Somerset Protestation returns and lay subsidy, 1641-2; Visitation of Somerset, 3 volumes.

Pedigree 4: Fowkes family of Symondsbury, Dorset and Harringworth, Northamptonshire

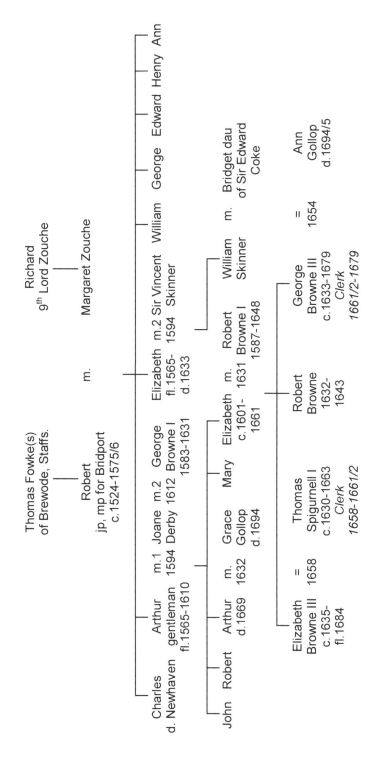

Selected people only included.

George Browne I and Robert Browne I were brothers.

Principal sources: W.C. Metcalfe ed., *The visitation of Dorsetshire, A.D. 1565* (Exeter, 1887), 15; J.P. Rylands ed., *The visitation of the county of Dorset, taken in the year 1623*, Harl. Soc. XX (London, 1885); G.D. Squibb, *The visitation of Dorset, 1677*, Harl. Soc. 117 (1977), 31-2.

Pedigree 5: Gollop family of North Bowood, Dorset

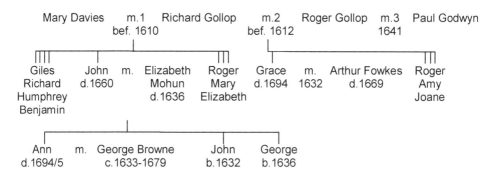

Selected individuals only included.
Principal sources: W.C. Metcalfe ed., *The visitation of Dorsetshire, A.D. 1565* (Exeter, 1887), 15;
J.P. Rylands ed., *The visitation of the county of Dorset, taken in the year 1623*, Harl. Soc. XX
(London, 1885); G.D. Squibb, *The visitation of Dorset, 1677*, Harl. Soc. 117 (1977), 31-2.

Select chronology of the main events

** Documents transcribed in this volume

1618	Sir Henry Portman II of Orchard Portman and John Browne II of Frampton, Dorset obtain the patent of office of Clerk of Taunton Castle
1628	George Browne I and Robert Browne I of Frampton, Dorset purchase the patent of office of Clerk of Taunton Castle
1630	Thomas Spigurnell is born around this date
1633	14 May – Robert Browne I and John Browne III the younger purchase the patent of office of Clerk of Taunton Castle
1640s	Thomas Spigurnell is in Taunton with Dr John Palmer
1644-1645	Taunton under siege
1645	Dr John Palmer elected one of the members of parliament for Taunton
1647/8	The Bishop of Winchester's Taunton manors, including Taunton Castle, are sequestered and sold
1649	King Charles the First is beheaded
1651	Thomas Spigurnell was at All Souls College, Oxford and becomes involved with sequestered estates
1656	Thomas Spigurnell was at Clement's Inn
1657	Thomas Spigurnell married Ann Godwin of Wells and she died shortly afterwards
1658	Thomas Spigurnell married Elizabeth Browne III of Wilton
1660	May – Restoration of King Charles the Second
	29 September – George Browne III of Wilton exhibits his bill of complaint against Thomas Spigurnell in Chancery
	14 November – George Browne III of Wilton enters his bill of complaint versus Elizabeth Browne II widow (of Robert), Thomas Spigurnell gentleman and Elizabeth his wife **
1660/1	1 February – Answer of Elizabeth Browne II widow of Wilton, Somerset **
1661	24 April – Answer of George Browne III **
	15 May – Elizabeth Browne II widow buried at Wilton
	24 June – Arbitration meeting at Taunton Castle
	16 July – Answer of Thomas and Elizabeth Spigurnell to George Browne's III bill of 14 November 1660
	29 September – Thomas Spigurnell entered his bill against George Browne III for his marriage portion
1661/2	7 February – John Gollopp armiger and George Browne III purchase the patent of office of Clerk of Taunton Castle
1662	14 June – Examination and reply of John Browne III to the bill brought by Thomas Spigurnell
1662/3	14 February – Complaint of Thomas Spigurnell of Long Sutton gentleman against George Browne III
1663	31 March – Witnesses examined at Taunton in the case of Browne versus

Spigurnell

25 May – Answer of George Browne III esquire in reply to Thomas Spigurnell's compaint (of 14 February 1662/3)

30 August – Thomas Spigurnell is buried at Long Sutton

1666   26 May – Bill of complaint of George Browne III esquire of Wilton

1667   13 May – Edward Chard and Elizabeth Chard versus George Browne III, John Gollopp and John Browne III regarding Thomas Spigurnell's bill for his marriage portion against George Browne III

1668   11 April – Final decree in Chancery in Chard versus Browne in favour of Browne

1669   1 April – Decree in Chancery for the assignment of a debt to George Browne III

1679   George Browne III esquire of Wilton died

1680   24 September – Lease of Middleton from Ann Browne of Sherford (widow of George Browne deceased) to John Beresford of Taunton Castle

1684   19 November – Edward and Elizabeth Chard (only daughter of Robert Browne I of Taunton Castle) bring an action against John Beresford gentleman and Anne Browne widow

1694/5 Ann Browne died

Glossary

attorney – a person, typically a lawyer, appointed to act for another in business or legal matters

clerk of Taunton Castle – a manorial office responsible for administration

confederate – a person in an alliance, or local group

demurrer – an objection to a point in an opponent's evidence

esquire – a man who bore a coat of arms and of independent means

fieri facias – a writ to a sheriff for executing a judgement

fifths - 20% of the value of an estate

interregatory – a written question which is formally put to one party in a case by another party and which must be answered

marriage portion – financial settlement usually agreed before the marriage by the bride's family

marriage settlement – as above

particular - a type of account

patent – a legal grant to hold a manorial office

pettyfogger – a lawyer whose methods are petty, underhanded, or disreputable

porter – a manorial office similar to a gatekeeper

rayment – clothing

reader - a post in an inn of court

Sequestration Committee – set up for conficating Royalist estates

Abbreviations

B.L.	British Library
B.R.O.	Berkshire Record Office
B.R.S.	British Record Society
C.	High Court of Chancery series of records at T.N.A.
C.P.	Court of Common Please series of records at T.N.A.
C.C.C.	M.A.E. Green ed., *Calendar, Committee for Compounding*, 5 volumes (London, 1889-1892)
C.C.E.D.	Clergy of the Church of England Database
E.	Court of Exchequer series of records at T.N.A.
H.A.	Hampshire Archives
H.S.	Harliean Society
H.T.	R. Holworthy ed., *Hearth Tax for Somerset 1664-1665* (Herne Bay, 1916)
H.T.E.	T.L. Stoate ed., *Dwelly's Index to the Somerset Hearth Tax Exemption Certificates of 1670 and 1674 ; with a Completion of Part 5 of Dwelly's National Records, volume 2* (Almondsbury, 1976)
L.M.A.	London Metropolitan Archives
n.d.	no date
P.A.	Parliamentary Archives
P.S.A.N.H.S.	*Proceedings of the Somersetshire Archaeological and Natural History Society*
S.D.N.Q.	*Somerset and Dorset Notes and Queries*
S.H.C.	Somerset Heritage Centre
S.P.	State Papers series of records at T.N.A.
S.P.R.	T.L. Stoate and A.J. Howard eds, *Somerset protestation return and lay subsidy rolls, 1640-1641* (Almondsbury, 1975).
S.R.S.	Somerset Record Society
T.Cal.	E.A. Fry ed., *Calendar of wills and administrations in the court of the Archdeacon of Taunton : parts I and II, wills only, 1537-1799*, B.R.S. (1912)
T.N.A.	The National Archives [of England and Wales]
U.N.S.C.	University of Nottingham Special Collections
W.Ca.A.	Wells Cathedral Archive
W.Cy.A.	Wells City Archive
W.S.R.O.	Wiltshire and Swindon Record Office

Select Bibliography

Sir J. Baker, *Legal education in London 1250-1850* (London, 2007).

Sir J. Baker, *Reports from the note books of Edward Coke volume I 1572-1579* (London, 2022).

E.A. Bates ed., *Graves' memoirs of the Civil War* (Edinburgh, 1927).

J. Batten, 'Somerset Sequestrations during the Civil War' in *P.S.A.N.H.S.* IV (1853), 60-77.

J. Batten, 'Somerset Sequestrations', *P.S.A.N.H.S.* XVI (1870), 13-34.

J.A. Bennett, *The manuscripts of the late Reverend W. Pyne, of Charlton Mackerel, and of Pitney, Somerset, and of the Reverend A.J. Woodforde, of Ansford, Somerset*, Historical Manuscripts Commission 9th report appendix 2 (London, 1883).

A. Bevan, *Tracing your ancestors in the National Archives* (London, 2006).

B. Brooks and M. Herber, *My ancestor was a lawyer* (London, 2015).

C.W. Brooks, *The admissions registers of Barnard's Inn, 1620-1869*, Selden Society (1995).

C.W. Brooks, *Pettyfoggers and vipers of the Commonwealth. The 'Lower Branch' of the Legal Profession in Early Modern England* (Cambridge, 2004).

H. Cary, *Memorials of the Great Civil War in England*, 3 volumes (London, 1842).

C. Churches, "The most unconvincing testimony': the genesis and historical usefulness of the country depositions in Chancery' in *The Seventeenth Century*, 11 (1996), 209-27.

W.H. Coates ed., *The journal of Sir Simonds D'ewes* (Yale, 1923).

M. Dowling 'Public Record Office Research: The Equity Side of Chancery, 1558-1714' in *The Review of English Studies* 8:30, pp. 185-200.

A. Fletcher, *The outbreak of the English Civil War* (London, 1985).

E.A. Fry ed., *Index of Chancery proceedings (Reynardson's Division)*, 2 volumes, British Record Society (1903-1904).

R.S. Gardiner, *History of the great Civil War, 1642-1649*, 4 volumes (1886-1905).

I. Gentles, *The New Model Army* (Blackwell, 1992); contains numerous references to individuals.

D. Gerhold, *Courts of equity, a guide to Chancery and other legal records* (Pinhorn, 994).

M.A.E. Green ed., *Calendar of the proceedings of the Committee for Compounding etc 1643-1660*, 5 vols (London, 1889-1892).

W. Gibson, *Religion and the enlightenment, 1600-1800: conflict and the rise of civic humanism in Taunton* (Oxford, 2007).

T. Hearing and S. Bridges ed., *Dorset Quarter Sessions order book, 1625-1638*, Dorset Record Society 14 (2006).

C. Hill, *The world turned upside down* (London, 1972).

H. Horwitz, *Chancery Equity Records and Proceedings 1600–1800*, P.R.O. Handbook No. 27, 2nd edn. (London, 1998).

H. Horwitz, 'Chancery's "Younger Sister": the Court of Exchequer and its Equity Jurisdiction, 1649–1841' in *Historical Research* 72 (1999).

E. Hyde, Earl of Clarendon, *The history of the Rebellion and Civil Wars in England*, six volumes (Oxford, 1888).

M. Jansson, *Proceedings in the opening session of the Long Parliament, 1640-1641*, 7 volumes (Rochester, 2000-2007).

S.C. Lomas ed., T. Carlyle, *The letters and speeches of Oliver Cromwell*, 3 volumes (London,

1904).

N.L. Matthews, *William Sheppard, Cromwell's law reformer* (Cambridge, 1984).

C.H. Mayo, *The minute books of the Dorset Standing Committee, 23rd Sept. 1646 to 8th May 1650* (Exeter, 1902).

S. Moore, *Family feuds: an introduction to Chancery proceedings* (London, 2003).

J.S. Morrill, *Revolution in the provinces, 1630-1648* (London, 1998).

P. Newman, *Royalist officers in England and Wales, 1642-1660* (London, 1981).

S. Peachey and A. Turton, *War in the West Part 1. The fall of the West volume 5. The military units Dorset Wiltshire and Somerset* (Backwell, 1994).

W. Phillimore, *Index nominum to the Royalist composition papers first and second series* (London, 1901).

S. Porter, *Destruction in the English Civil Wars* (Stroud, 1994).

E. Razzell ed., *The English Civil War: a contemporary account, 1625-1675*, 5 volumes (London, 1997).

R. Robson, *The attorney in eighteenth-century England* (Cambridge, 1995).

C. Scott, *The maligned militia: the west country militia of the Monmouth Rebellion, 1685* (Abingdon, 2015)

V.F. Snow and A.S. Young, *The private journals of the Long Parliament* (Yale, 1987).

G.D. Stawell, *A Quantock Family. The Stawells of Cothelstone and their descendants, the Barons Stawell of Somerton, and the Stawells of Devonshire and the County Cork* (Taunton, 1910).

D. Underdown, *Somerset in the Civil War and Interregnum* (Newton Abbot, 1975).

J. Waylen, *Chronicles of the Devizes, being a history of the castle, parks and borough of that name; with notices statistical, parliamentary, ecclesiastic, and biographical* (London, 1839).

J. Wroughton, *The Civil War in Bath and North Somerset* (Bath, 1973).

J. Wroughton, *An unhappy Civil War: the experiences of ordinary people in Gloucestershire, Somerset and Wiltshire, 1642-1646* (Bath, 1999).

Series

Volumes in the following series of publications have been consulted:

Notes and Queries for Somerset and Dorset
List and Index Society
Proceedings of the Somersetshire Archaeological and Natural History Society
Somerset Record Society
Victoria County History of Somerset.

BRIEF BIOGRAPHIES

The information below concerning the deponents and selected characters involved in Thomas Spigurnell's life is not definitive. It has been presented to give some background information about the main characters in this story, as well as their relationship to others involved in Spigurnell's life. References to baptisms, marriages and burials are taken from parish registers held in the relevant county record office.

John Bartlett of Frampton, Dorset, gentleman, aged 33 was a witness for Browne at Taunton on 31 March 1663 [10]. A man of this name was buried at Frampton on 25 May 1688.

John Beresford (*c.* 1640-1699)

A gentleman lawyer who appears late in the Spigurnell story, over two decades after he died, when Edward and Elizabeth Chard (only daughter of late Robert Browne of Taunton Castle) brought an action against John Beresford gentleman and Anne Browne widow, 19 November 1684.[215] He married Barbara daughter of Walter Cliffe of Taunton Castle and they had four children.[216] Both men were appointed on 19 February 1660/1 as bailiff of the Bailiwick and Liberty of Taunton and Taunton Deane, with control of weights and measures for £4 per annum.[217] He acquired Middleton as his will of 11 September 1699 includes a bequest to his son John of his tenements 'Barton or Farme called Middleton ... And all that the Mannor and Royalty of Huish Champflower'.[218]

Richard Bovett (1611-1685)

Of all those involved in the dispute Richard Bovett was the most outwardly Parliamentarian supporter and anti-Catholic character that possibly ever set foot in Taunton in the 17th century. Baptised in Winsham, he lived in Chard for a time before moving to Wellington. After failing to hold Wellington House for Parliament his active involvement in the First Civil War is unclear. Although he is only mentioned in passing in the depositions, the fact that he was well enough known to be thought of as some sort of local figurehead during the wars makes him stand out as a leading character.

Bovett and his brother both married daughters of Dr John Palmer who as Spigurnell's patron became a close associate. These three men, who appear only briefly in the existing literature concerning Taunton were part of the Parliamentarian cabal based in the borough in the 1650s. After the wars were over Bovett took a leading role in the administration, both military and civil, in the district, including serving as mayor of Taunton. Spigurnell acted as Bovett's solicitor[219] and in return Bovett witnessed Spigurnell's will in August 1663, along with his son Richard.[220] Following the Restoration his fortunes dramatically changed and he was ostracised by the new Stuart Government. His anti-Catholic feelings saw him serve as one of the Duke of Monmouth's generals. After fleeing the battlefield, he was captured, tried and hung at Cothelstone in 1685. He is regarded as a Protestant martyr.[221]

Citing Bovett in the depositions is a clear statement that a politcal aggenda played an important part of this case, in addition to the financial implications.

John Bridle of the parish of Burton, Dorset, yeoman aged 'Threescore yeares or there abouts' was a witness for Browne and Spigurnell at Taunton on 31 March 1663 [**10**]. A man of this name married Jone Vennis at Burton Bradstock on 13 July 1629. 13 July 1686 a man of this name of Motcombe, Dorset wrote his will.[222]

Ann Browne (1626-1694/5)

George Browne III's wife was Ann (baptised 20 July 1626 at Netherbury) daughter of John Gollop gentleman. She married George Browne in 1654 at Bridport. In 1679 when George Browne died the office of steward was filled by John Gollop esquire; John and George had received the bishop's patents for the office of clerk and also of keeper of the castle gate in 1661/2. Also during her widowhood Ann entered into a financial agreement with another official of Taunton Castle, John Beresford the bailiff. She died in 1694/5.

Elizabeth Browne (*c.* 1601-1661)

Elizabeth was one of two daughter's (and three sons) of Arthur Fowkes and Joane Derby of Symondsbury, Dorset; she is referred to in this book as Elizabeth II to avoid ambiguity. Her mother's family were of farming stock from Askerswell but her father was a gentleman who bore a coat of arms.[223] However, her grandfather, Robert Fowkes (*c.* 1524-1575/6) married Margaret daughter of Richard 9th Lord Zouch of Haryngworth.[224] Elizabeth also held other illustrious connections thanks to her aunt of the same name. Aunt Elizabeth (d.1633) married Sir Vincent Skinner (1543-1616) who was a career m.p., constable of Bolingbroke Castle and Lincoln Castle in 1583. He was secretary to William Cecil, 1st Baron Burghley from about 1575 to 1593, after which he was appointed to the Exchequer as an auditor of the receipt. Thornton Abbey was one of his residences where he lived with Elizabeth Browne's aunt. Elizabeth and Vincent had a son, William, who married Bridget a daughter of Sir Edward Coke who is considered the greatest juror and barrister of the Elizabethan and Jacobean eras.

Elizabeth II married Robert Browne esquire (1608-1648) in 1631.[225] She inherited the office of clerk and porter from her husband after his death in 1648[226] but signed the audit book in 1645 and 1646; she also signed for the period 1648 to 1655.[227] In the will of her husband, dated 1637 and proved in 1648, when he was described as resident of Taunton Castle, he left the 'Office of Clerke and Porter' of the Castle of Taunton to Elizabeth for her use and that of his children. He also instructed John Porter to continue the office of clerk and deputy clerk, as well as overseer of his will,[228] which explains why whe signed the audit book until 1655.[229] At the time of the sale of the manor of Taunton in 1648 she was in possession of the lands leased in 1633 from the bishop of Winchester for the lives of three sons of John Browne of Frampton, Dorset, esquire, called Knowlwood and Smokeham with 2 cottages thereon, garden and orchard of 1 rood, meadow of 1 acre, Quarry Close of 3 acres, 2 enclosed pastures of 11 acres, 3 pieces of arable of 13 acres, the Coppice of 10 acres, Smokeham Coppices of 4 acres, all in the hundred of Holway and parish of Stoke St Mary, abutting west on the land of Thomas

Boone Esq., east on the land of John Bellringer, south on the land of John Slape, north on Henley Woodes, as well as the great barn, now converted into a stable, within the Greene or Yard of the Castle of Taunton near the Pound, with all ponds, moats and ditches about the walls of the Castle, and banks and parcels of land on each side of the Pound, late of John Browne (leased to him in 1633 by the bishop for rent of two quarters of oats, hay and litter for the horses of the steward and his servants, valued at 30s).[230]

Elizabeth Browne of Sherford, widow in 1653 by an enrolment, according to the custom of the manor, was granted a 32 feet by 2 feet of the lords waste 'lying before the garden of the said Elizabeth in Sherford greene and xxii foote in length and six foote in bredth of the lords wast lying before parte of the house of the said Elizabeth in Sherford Greene aforesaid in the tithing of Galmington'.[231] So despite the sale of the manor in 1648 she retained a financial interest. She made her will on 7 May 1661 and was buried at Wilton eight days later, presumably having moved out of the castle some years before. She was 'sick of the sicknesse whereof she died', according to her nuncupative will. She made a clear declaration that she did not want her son-in-law Thomas Spigurnell to be her executor, preferring her only son George instead, something that was repeated to Mary Phillips.[232] It was alleged that because of the 'unnaturall deportment of her said sonne shee the said Elizabeth [Browne senior, widow] was reduced to poverty and was constreyned to borrow and take up money' from Thomas Spigurnell [9]. This was the only time such an allegation was made.

Elizabeth Browne III (*c.* 1635-fl. 1684) – *later Elizabeth Spigurnell, then Elizabeth Chard*

The daughter of Robert and Elizabeth (née Fowkes) was probably born in the mid 1630s. She married Thomas Spigurnell in 1658, then after he died in 1663 she married Edward Chard in 1665. She is one of the main characters in this long running saga. Along with her young children she suffered after Spigurnell's death. Her marriage to Edward Chard lasted over 20 years and saved her from poverty. Her first husband's legacy haunted her during her widowhood and her subsequent marriage. An example of this can be seen when Francis Naylor, an associate of her first husband Thomas Spigurnell, brought a case against her in 1681 in Chancery for money owed to him.[233]

George Browne I (1583-1631)[234]

Born in 1583 he was the eldest son of Sir John Browne of Frampton. Through his mother's family he became involved in parliamentary matters in Taunton. Elected as m.p. for Taunton in 1625 with Sir Robert Gorges, then again in 1628 with his cousin Hugh Portman (d. 1632). His wife was the widow of Arthur Fowkes. George's brother Robert married Elizabeth Fowkes in 1631.

George Browne II (*c.* 1623-1677/8)

Born around 1623 to Sir John Browne. He was first cousin to Elizabeth, Robert and George Browne of Taunton Castle and Sherford. He was a Royalist.

George Browne III (*c.* 1632-1679)

Born around 1632 to Robert and Elizabeth (née Fowkes). Although only a young man during the civil wars he was part of a group that were jeered 'for being Cavaleers' [10]. He married Ann Gollop in 1654 at Bridport and he claimed to have 'married into a family of quality and with a Gentle woeman against whom noe excepcions could bee taken' [4]. The couple are two of the main characters in this story. George Browne III and his wife Ann were living at Wilton in 1661 when their daughter Mary was baptised at the parish church, followed by Katherine on 25 March 1661/2, Jane on 4 March 1662/3 and Penelope on 1 August 1667. In the mid 1660s he lived at Wilton in a house with seven hearths.[235] On 28 February 1662/3 he took out a lease from the Bishop of Winchester of land and woodland at Stoke St Mary.[236] He served as parish overseer in 1674.[237] His sister married Thomas Spigurnell. George was one of the principal harrangers of his brother-in-law Spigurnell. His bill of complaint, dated 26 May 1666, describes him as a resident of Wilton.[238] He died in 1679. His daughter Ann married William Coryn of Treworden, Cornwall and they retained an interest in the family lands in Bridport, Sherford and Stoke Hill in 1682;[239] Mrs Anne Corin was buried at Kenwyn on 18 March 1734/35.[240]

Robert Browne I (1587-1648)
Grandson of Sir Henry Portman, and son of Sir John Browne. After his brother John II gave up the patent of clerk Robert took it up in 1628. He married Elizabeth Fowkes in 1631 and they had three children Elizabeth III, Robert III and George III.

Robert Browne III (1632-1643)
Son of Robert I and Elizabeth. He was buried at Taunton St Mary Magdalene on 24 August 1643 described as an esquire. Five years later his father died and subsequently Robert III's brother George III became the only surviving male in this branch of the family.

Robert Browne IV (c. 1655-1738)
Born in 1655 at Netherbury and was the only son of George III and Ann. At the time of his father's death he became 'much in debt' in 1679. He moved to Graston, Dorset and 'lost' the manor in 1696. He married at Bridport in 1701. He died at Heddon Street, St James Westminster on 12 June 1738.[241]

Alice Capon of Wilton, widow aged 55 and 'upwards' was a witness for Browne and Spigurnell at Taunton on 31 March 1663. She was a sister of Elizabeth Browne II [10].

Richard Carpenter of Taunton, upholsterer, aged 32 was a witness for Spigurnell at Taunton on 31 March 1663 [10]. He lived in a house with 12 hearths in Fore street, one of which was 'beaten up'.[242] He was involved in a Chancery case in 1662 and 1663.[243] A man of this name was buried at Taunton St Mary on 31 July 1666.

Edward Chard (c. 1639-fl. 1684)
Described as a gentleman of Long Sutton he married Thomas Spigurnell's widow, Elizabeth (née Browne). On 29 June 1665 when he took out a marriage allegation he was described as a bachelor of St Martin in the Fields, Middlesex, aged about 26. They

were allowed to be married in the parish church of St Peter and Pauls Wharf or Bridewell Precinct, London.[244] Chard became step father to Spigurnell's children and was involved in their financial interests. Subsequently he was involved in numerous Chancery cases and property transactions with his wife's attempts to protect the interests of her children.[245]

Elizabeth Chard *see Elizabeth Browne III*

William Doble (1628-1663) was one of the commissioners when the depositions were taken at Taunton in 1663 [**10**]. He was the son of William Doble (1599-1628) and Margaret Every of Cothay. William senior was also a lawyer. William junior entered the Inner Temple in 1644 and was called to the Bar in 1652. He held the advowson of Ashbrittle and West Monkton. He was living in a house in Fore Street in 1660 in the centre of Taunton.[246] He was buried at Kittisford 'in the newly erected vault of my friend William Every of Cothay'.[247]

John Dryer was one of several generations of this family which contained a John Dryer. The family farmed at Long Sutton in the 1620s[248] and he lived near the Spigurnells. John Dryer the elder was buried at Long Sutton on 27 August 1638, thus John son of John Dryer the elder of Long Sutton, husbandman left a will that was proved in 1657.[249] John Dryer (father of John deceased) was one of the executor's of Spigurnell's will.[250] After Spigurnell's death Dryer (with John Pyne, Henry Cotton, John Barker and George Spigurnell) was involved from 1665 in a Chancery suit versus the Spigurnell children.[251] He was also involved with Browne v Pyne and Dryer v Cotton, all of which meant he was party to four cases in three years.[252] Then, in 1667, Dryer was involved in another Chancery case, this time with Roger Hurley of Taunton Magdalene, husbandman against Charity Grigg.[253] This family had connections with Taunton and Monmouth.[254]

Thomas Dyke was one of the commissioners when the depositions were taken at Taunton in 1663 [**10**]. Not of the Inner Temple, Middle Temple, Lincoln's Inn or Barnard's Inn. He may have been the son and heir of William Dyke esquire of Frant, Sussex addmitted to Gray's Inn on 7 August 1623. A man of this name who claimed to be an esquire held numerous Taunton Deane lands.[255]

Mary Fry was the wife of Thomas Fry of Bishops Hull, tailor, aged 27 who was a witness for Spigurnell at Taunton on 31 March 1663 [**10**]. Two children of this couple were baptised at Bishops Hull in the mid 1650s but neither parent appears in the Hearth Tax returns or the exemption certificates for Taunton or Bishops Hull.

George Gollop of 'Northboard' (North Bowood), Dorset, gentleman, aged 27 was brought as a witness for Browne at Taunton on 31 March 1663 [**10**]. George was Ann Browne's brother and George Browne's brother in law. The Gollop family were landed gentry[256] and their pedigree appears in the published *Visitation of Dorset in 1677*.[257] Their relationship with the Fowkes and Browne families is through Mary Davies (or Davis) who married three times, as outlined in the pedigree 5 on page lii.

John Gollop of North Bowood, gentleman, aged 30 was a witness for Browne at Taunton on 31 March 1663 [**10**]. John was Ann Browne's brother and George Browne's brother in law. The Gollop family were landed gentry[258] and their pedigree appears in the published *Visitation of Dorset in 1677*. Elizabeth Browne of Wilton's brother Arthur married Grace Gollop a step sister once removed to John and Ann.[259]

Thomas Harvey of Taunton, gentleman, aged 36 was a witness for Browne and Spigurnell at Taunton on 31 March 1663 [**10**]. Described as living at Taunton Castle when he was appointed deputy steward of the manor of Taunton Deane on 12 January 1656/7 by John Porter, steward of Taunton Deane.[260] He was involved in the case of Jeane v Spigurnell in 1660.[261] As a potential resident of the castle he does not appear in the Hearth Tax of 1665. He held Taunton Deane land in Poundsford from 1666.[262] He was involved in Chancery disputes in 1668, 1669 and 1670.[263] A burial for Thomas Harvey at Taunton St Mary appears at the end of July 1672. A joint account book for Thomas and William survives and shows how after Thomas died William took over his relative's business.[264] An appointment of William Harvey to serve as deputy steward was made in 1674.[265]

John Herring of Taunton. One of the confederates in 1654 when he was described as a shoemaker.[266] About this time he became known to Spigurnell when he was described as an innholder.[267] In 1660 he was living with his wife in Fore Street.[268] At the time of Spigurnell's death he was described as Mr John Herring,[269] a Taunton innholder,[270] who lived in Fore Street.[271] Herring claimed he arranged the transportation of Spigurnell's body from Taunton to Long Sutton and paid for the funeral.[272] Spigurnell's will and codicil were both witnessed by Herring.[273]

John Hewes of Bishops Hull, 'Wostard Comber', aged 42, was a witness for Spigurnell at Taunton on 31 March 1663 [**10**]. He does not appear in the either the Hearth Tax returns or the exemption certificates. A burial for a man of this name occurred on 7 November 1682 at Taunton St Mary.

Alexander Hill of Taunton, gentleman, aged about 50 was a witness for Spigurnell at Taunton on 31 March 1663 [**10**]. There were several men of this name in the Taunton area. A man of this name was ordered to 'settle £20 per annum for ever upon the church of Mary Magdalen in Taunton ... for which his whole fine of £192 8s is remitted'.[274] The Hill family were staunch Parliamentarians and he was called by the Parliamentarian Spigurnell to give evidence [**10**]. In 1635, Alexander son of Robert was executor to his father and in 1703 Alexander's will was proved by Alexander his son and executor;[275] the latter are mentioned in a will of 1687.[276] He was involved in three cases in Chancery.[277]

Robert Hucker of Bishops Hull, woolstapler, aged about 56 was a witness for Browne at Taunton on 31 March 1663 [**10**]. A man of this name was baptised at Taunton St Mary Magdalene 14 October 1613 son of John Hooker (buried 21 September 1642 at Taunton St Mary Magdalene). Was this Robert a sequestrator in Trull[278] or the man of the same name who married Mary Herring there in 1634; if it was it could not have been him as a man of this name was buried at Pitminster on 22 May 1657. There were two men of this name who appear in the Protestation return in Taunton.[279] And in 1640 Robert son of Robert Hucker was buried at St Mary's on the 19th of August. In September 1656 he gave his age as 52 and his ocupation as a yeoman; he served as a rent collector or bailiff for the Taunton cabal but refused to collect any rents for them.[280] In 1658 he served as constable of the borough[281] and the year later as one of the portreeves.[282] In 1653, or 1654, he petitioned Quarter Sessions to have an alehouse near the castle in Taunton to be suppressed.[283]

Described as a gentleman of Taunton who with William Chaplyn leased Lower Poundsford and two pastures called Peircies lawne-close all in parish of Pitminster, the castle and manor of Taunton and Taunton Deane with the appurtenances, messuages and lands called Smokeham in Knowle Wood in the parish of Stoke St Mary (in the tenure of Elizabeth Browne), the great barne or stable at Castle Green, Taunton with several parcels of ground used therewith (also in the occupation of Elizabeth Browne) in 1659.[284] He lived in a house with three hearths in Bishops Hull in 1665.[285] He was buried on 19 November 1679 at Taunton St Mary Magdalene. His will, with a codicil dated 1679, describes him as a yeoman. He left bequests to Mr George Newton minister of the Gospel of 40s and seven other ministers of 20s each, plus money to the poor.[286] Hucker was also part of the cabal.

Roger Hurley of Taunton appeared in two cases involving Spigurnell's land transactions with Richard Grigg in 1660 and in 1667.[287] Hurley benefitted from the sale of Royalist estates. He witnessed the will of Christopher Hurley on 12 April 1658[288] of which there was a senior and junior in 1656; Christopher junior gave his ocupation as a clothier.[289] Roger was buried at Taunton St Mary on 12 July 1677.

Richard Jeane of Middlezoy, Somerset, gentleman and attorney, aged 33 was a witness for Browne at Taunton on 31 March 1663 [10] and was no friend of Spigurnell.[290] John Jean of Greylake (in Middlezoy) who as an attorney during the Civil Wars claimed he 'could not satisfy his conscience to take up arms for Parliament' and 'never bore arms for the King',[291] suggesting he was sympathetic to the Royalist cause. In 1659, Richard Jeane of West Monkton took Spigurnell to Chancery.[292] In 1667 Richard took John Jeane *et al* to Chancery over lands at Bradford and Middlezoy.[293] A will for John Jeane, gentleman of West Monkton survives for 1663[294] and one for Richard Jeane of Taunton, gentleman, was proved in 1680.[295]

James Kinge of Taunton Magdalene, carpenter aged 60 was a witness for Browne at Taunton on 31 March 1663 [10]. He married Elizabeth Ford on 7 July 1634 and was in Taunton in 1640/1.[296] Buried 24 December 1678 at Taunton St Mary. He lived with the widow Kinge in 1671 when he was exempt from paying the Hearth Tax in Holway.[297]

Tristrum Lane of Taunton, husbandman, aged 35 was a witness for Spigurnell at Taunton on 31 March 1663 [10]. He was a local man baptised at Bishops Hull on 26 January 1622/3 and buried at Taunton St Mary on 23 September 1673. In September

1656 he gave his age as 30 and his occupation as a groom.[298] He does not appear in the Hearth Tax in the 1660s.

William Lane of Totnes, Devon, gentleman, aged 19 was a witness for Spigurnell at Taunton on 31 March 1663 [**10**].

Robert Leigh of Milverton, Somerset, gentleman aged 25 was a witness for Browne at Taunton on 31 March 1663 [**10**]. There were several men of this name.[299] It is possible that he was one of the commissioners in 1662/3 [**9**].

Philip Lissant. Although not one of the deponents, his name appears in two of the documents. He was at Mr Christopher's house in Taunton on 11 May 1661 and witnessed the answers given by Elizabeth Browne and Thomas Spigurnell [**3**]. There were several men of this name in Taunton during the 17th century who were involved in numerous Chancery cases, including two who appear in the Protestation returns.[300] He held numerous Taunton Deane lands.[301] In 1624 and 1625 a man of this name served as churchwarden of St Mary's and as a borough court juror in the 1630s.[302] Philip junior served as constable of the borough in 1642.[303] This man lived in Fore Street in a house with five hearths and one had 'fallen downe' in 1665.[304] He is likely to have been the Philip whose will mentions a son of the same name.[305] The father's probate inventory (appraised by George Lissant and Robert Prouse), dated 12 February 1667/8, totalled £1,232 12s 6d and included a lease of property at Bradford.[306] There was also a Philip who worked as a haberdasher who lived in London.[307]

William Mantle of Bishops Hull, tailor, aged 64 was a witness for Spigurnell at Taunton on 31 March 1663 [**10**]. Mantle was the second witness for Spigurnell who was a tailor by trade. There were more than one men of this name in Taunton, one of whom lived at Shuttern in 1637,[308] one appears in Taunton in the Protestation returns.[309] He does not appear in the Hearth Tax returns or the exemption certificates. A man of this name was buried in 1666, 1677/8 and 1679 at Taunton St Mary. Perhaps, coincidentally, Mary Mantle, widow aged 69 of Taunton gave evidence in Spigurnell v Dryer in 1668.[310]

John Mare of Nettlecombe, Somerset, yeoman, age 42, was a witness for Browne at Taunton on 31 March 1663 [**10**]. John was a son of Sibble Mare (d. before 1663); Sibble was involved with a lease of Middleton with Joane Mare the elder, Joane Mare the younger and Thomas Mare [**10**]. A man of this name served as churchwarden for Nettlecombe in 1640/1.[311] He married Joane Hooper on 20 April 1657 at Nettlecombe. A son William was baptised in 1667 and died the following year; a daughter Sibil was baptised at Nettlecombe in 1669/70 and died in 1679.

Doctor John Palmer (*c.* 1609-1659/60)
Described as a son of an apothecary from Taunton of the same name.[312] Whilst at Queen's College he claimed to be a gentleman, where he matriculated 21 November 1628 aged 19, followed by a B.A. 3 December 1628, B.Med. 2 December 1630 and returned many years later to achieve a D.Med. on 12 April 1648. In 1647 he married a

granddaughter of the First Earl of Marlborough. John Palmer alias Vaux was put in as warden of All Souls College by the same authority that ejected his predecessor on 30 March 1648, a position he held until his death, which partly explains why Spigurnell was there in 1651.[313] He served as M.P. for Taunton from *c.* November 1645 until 1653, and described as a "great Rumper" in 1659.[314] He was one of a group of 'confederates' who prior to October 1654 included Walter Cliffe of Exeter, gentleman, Edward Theare of Taunton, yeoman, John Herring of Taunton, shoemaker and Thomas Spigurnell of Taunton, yeoman.[315] It is possible he was back in Taunton in 1656 when he was involved in a Chancery suit.[316] His nuncupative will, made about the last day of February 1659/60 and he died 4 days later. He was buried at upper end of the College chapel.[317] Although he was not a deponent he was subject of one of the interrogatories and Spigurnell's patron. He remained a close associate of Spigurnell, hence his appearance in the records.

Henry Plucknett was one of the commissioners when the depositions were taken at Taunton in 1663 [**10**]. He does not appear in the entry books for the Inner Temple, Middle Temple, Grays Inn, Lincoln's Inn or Barnard's Inn. He acted as Spigurnell's attorney in 1657 in the High Court of Chancery during Hillary Term 1657.[318]

John Porter (*c.* 1591[319]-*c.* 31 March 1663) [10]

He was the reliable gentleman clerk of Taunton Castle who served clerical and lay masters, both Parliamentarian and Royalist. He appears to therefore have been of neutral leanings. He ensured the continued operation and smooth running of the "bank" of Taunton in the form of the manorial system in the Hundred of Taunton and Taunton Deane. Porter was known to hundreds of people who undertook transactions recorded in the exchequer of Taunton Castle.

Sir William Portman (*c.* 1610-1649)

Sir William Portman (Fifth Baronet) initially supported Parliament in 1642 but changed his allegiance to the Royalists. In June 1643 Orchard House wass used briefly as the Royalist headquarters during the king's campaign to establish control in Somerset. His house was used as a staging post by both forces during the ensuing sieges of Taunton Castle. In February 1645 the Parliamentarians imprisoned Sir William in Taunton Castle. There was a bitterly fought battle at Orchard Portman between both forces in May and the end of Royalist siege of Taunton. On the 14th of June at the Battle of Naseby Sir William escaped and fought for the king. He was taken by Cromwell's men to the Tower of London where he died in 1649. The Portman estates were sequestered by Parliament and the funds raised from their sale was used to compensate the people of Taunton.[320]

Robert Prockter, merchant of Taunton St Mary Magdalene aged 45 was a witness for Browne and for Spigurnell at Taunton on 31 March 1663 [**10**]. He was baptised at Taunton St Mary's on 14 September 1617 the son of Robert and Anne (née Prestcott). There was another Robert who lived at Wilton who appears in the Protestation returns.[321] A man of this name was described as a merchant of Henlade in 1651.[322] He held numerous Taunton Deane lands.[323] The Hearth Tax for East Street records 'Mr Procter of Heydon' as a house owner.[324] Robert Procter of Taunton, merchant, was a witness in

1648 to the will of Robert Browne esquire of Taunton Castle, who postumously became Spigurnell's father-in-law [**9**]. His will, proved 13 March 1682/3, describes him as being of Taunton and mentions his manor or lordship of Angersleigh alias Knightsleigh.[325]

John Pyne the elder of Curry Mallett esquire (1600-1678)

Of all the characters involved in this case John Pyne was by far the most high profile of them all. He was a leading figure in Somerset during the Parliamentary cause during the civil wars and Interregnum. Pyne was one of Spigurnell's executors and entrusted with his estate.[326] The son of Thomas Pyne (d. 1629) and Amy Hanham (d. 1640) he had two surviving sons (John and Charles) by his first wife, Eleanor Hanham (1609-1662). The Pyne's manor house at Curry Mallet was a very substantial buiding that contained 16 hearths.[327] Pyne's second wife, Amy White (see under her name) was also one of the deponents in 1663.[328] His own will, dated 1676, makes no mention of the Spigurnell family or any of their mutual cronies.

John Rowland of Taunton, whitebaker, aged 52 was a witness for Browne at Taunton on 31 March 1663 [**10**]. He married Mary Dimond at on 25 November 1631 and he was in Taunton in 1640/1.[329] He held Taunton Deane land in Holway from 1651.[330] He was buried on 5 April 1687 at Taunton St Mary's. He served as tithingman for North Street in 1665 where he lived in a house with ten hearths.[331] He was involved in the Lottisham v Bovett case.[332]

John Spencer of Netherbury, Dorset, husbandman, aged 74 was a witness for both Browne and Spigurnell at Taunton on 31 March 1663 [**10**]. He was baptised at Netherbury on 18 December 1585 and married Margaret Whiffin in 1624/5. He was buried on 27 April 1664 at Netherbury.

Elizabeth Spigurnell *see Elizabeth Browne III.*

Elizabeth Spigurnell daughter of Thomas I senior (below) and Elizabeth was baptised at Wilton on 8 November 1659.

Mary Spigurnell was the third child of Thomas I senior (below) and Elizabeth. She was baptised at Long Sutton in 1661.

Thomas Spigurnell I *see the Introduction.*

Thomas Spigurnell II son of Thomas Spigurnell I (above) and Elizabeth was baptised at Wilton on 14 January 1659/60. His fate is unknown. A man of this name married Mary Meales at Westminster St Marylebone in August 1688.

Osmond Spreate

A butcher of Taunton, aged about 50 when he was a witness for Browne and for Spigurnell at Taunton on 31 March 1663 [**10**]. He was the son of Anthony, a grocer of Taunton, and married Bridget Nation on 22 October 1632 at Taunton St Mary. He lived in a substantial house with seven hearths in Fore Street in 1665.[333] As a man of business and property interests he was involved in six Chancery cases from 1648 to 1669. In 1655, with Grace Spreat and Sarah Crocker they were presented to the manorial court for stopping up 'the ancient Rhine or Watercourse flowing from Pool Wall Mills to the River Tone' much to the annoyance of their neighbours.[334] His will was proved in 1671.[335]

Sir John Stawell (1600-1662)
Although not subject of the depositions, Stawell certainly played a part in Spigurnell's life on more than one occasion. He was a leading figure for the Royalist party in Somerset during the First Civil War and served as governor of Taunton. He used his lordship of multiple manors to raise funds and troops for the King.[336] Stawell found himself besieged in Exeter on 14 April 1646 and on 15 July 1646 was in London to compound. He refused to acknowledge the new order, remaining fiercely loyal to the King and on the 13th of August was committed as a prisoner to Ely House. Five days later he was sent as a delinquent before the House of Commons and thence committed to Newgate for high treason, kept there for 4 years then sent to the Tower (by July 1650). An act for his trial was published in 1650. Another of 16 July 1651 declared his estate forfeit for treason and was sold. He appealed against this and went to great lengths to retain as much of his wealth as he could, claiming how he ought to have had the benefit of the Exeter Articles. Stawell's manors of Cothelstone, Cushuish and Priestly were bought by Dr John Palmer by 14 May 1652 and two others for Taunton was in part of 7,000li granted to the town by Parliament to repair their great losses and sufferings. Later in the year Merridge manor (part of the Stawell estate) was bought by Richard Bovett by 24 December 1652. The compensation was dealt with by a local committee of men that included Dr John Palmer.[337] It was his confiscated estates on the great hill of Quantock that attracted Spigurnell and his cohorts. The Grigg case directly involved Spigurnell.

John Stocker gentleman was one of the commissioners when the depositions were taken at Taunton in 1663 [10]. A man of this name lived in Somerton in the 1660s and 1670s.[338]

Nicholas Strode of the Inner Temple, a lawyer, whose will dated 10 September 30 Chas II describes him as a knight late of Chapsted, Kent.[339] Not to be confused with Thomas Strode (below) who lent money for mortgage.[340] He examined documents in a later Chancery case involving Elizabeth Chard and John Beresford [18].

Thomas Strode of Parnham in Netherbury, a lawyer, who loaned money to George Browne III by way of a mortgage[341] that was inherited by his son Robert.[342]

Jane Tower aged 45 was the wife of William Tower late of Wilton, carpenter, was a witness for Spigurnell at Taunton on 31 March 1663 [10]. Neither appears in the Hearth Tax returns or the exemption certificates.

George Treagle
George Treagle was not a deponent but had two significant interactions with Spigurnell. As the first recorded seller of printed books in Taunton he was from a business family.

His father, or possibly grandfather, was a wollen draper who had business connections with a Taunton apothecary in 1573 and 1585, a London grocer in 1573, Hugh Preston of Cricket St Thomas in 1584 and an Exeter man in 1585.[343] George married Annes Deane on 20 January 1593/4 at Taunton St Mary Magdalene and a child called George was baptised on 15 October 1596; this George became the bookseller involved with Spigurnell. Only one George appears in the Protestation return for Taunton and he was assessed for 5s in 1642 in the borough and for a property in Holway.[344] He served as bailiff in the borough in 1642.[345] In October 1656, he gave his age as 59 and his occupation as mercer[346] rather than a bookseller, perhaps revealing his dual occupations. In 1660, he appears in the poll tax list with his wife as a resident of Fore Street.[347] On 10 May 1664 Anstice Treagle married John Capon at St Mary's but is not known if he was related to Alice Capon who gave evidence in the Browne v Spigurnell case [10].

In 1660, Spigurnell took Treagle to Chancery over money matters. There was no political aggenda in this case as it involved Roger Hill esquire of Taunton and the trustees of Sir John Stawell's sequestrated lands. It appears Treagle had borrowed various sums of money claiming that he was possessed of certain land on Quantock Hill. Spigurnell was acting as steward or surveyor for the trustees and Bovett owed Treagle £10.[348] George the bookseller was buried at Taunton St Mary Magdalene on 8 March 1666/7, as was his widow Frances on 8 November 1667. A lasting memorial to the couple can be seen in the trade token they issued which bears George's name and a symbol of his trade, with both their initials on the reverse.

Henry Tymewell of Taunton Magdalen, vintner, aged 45, was a witness for Browne at Taunton on 31 March 1663 [10]. A man of this name was a juror for the borough court in 1631.[349] He married Elizabeth Ridler 6 June 1639 at Taunton St Mary. Two sons were baptised there; Henry in 1640 and Hugh in 1649. Described as gentleman when he was a witness for Spigurnell at Taunton on 31 March 1663 [10]. He held Taunton Deane land in Holway from 1664.[350] He lived in North Street in a house with ten hearths and 'he hath pulled down 2'.[351] He was involved in a Chancery case in 1683.[352] He was buried 4 April 1698 at Taunton St Mary.

Samuel Whetcombe
A Samuel married Grace Cooper on 4 February 1639/40 at Taunton St Mary. In 1647 Elizabeth Whetcombe, aged 27, daughter of Samuel, gentleman of Taunton, married Thomas Earle of Litton, Devon, clerk.[353] He served as constable of the borough in 1645 and 1650,[354] as well as mayor of Taunton.[355] On 20 July 1648 the borough of Taunton was sold to Whetcombe and George Searle (one of its Members of Parliament) for £868 14s 4d who supported Parliament throughout the civil war.[356] He was a close associate of Bovett during the Interregnum,[357] served as a sequestrator for the Committee for Compounding[358] and was involved in numerous Chancery cases. He held Taunton Deane land in Holway from 1652.[359] A burgess of the borough of Taunton in 1656 alongside men like Bovett, Christopher Hurley and Roger Hill of Poundsford[360] he was one of the cabal. Alice wife of Samuel Whetcombe, gentleman died 20 March 1654 and her memorial was in St Mary's church.[361] The banns of his proposed marriage to Alathia Barnes of St Clement Danes, spinster, in March and April 1656 describe him as a

gentleman of Taunton.[362] He was still alive in 1660 when he was involved in case of Jeane v Spigurnell[363] and in 1662 with Spigurnell v Grigg.[364] He died before 1664 and Athalia was possibly still in Taunton in 1664 during her widowhood.[365] No entry appears in burial registers for Somerset for her unless she remarried.

Amy White (1635-1692)

Amy White of Chedon Fitzpaine, single woman, gave her age as 30 years and upwards. She was a witness for both Browne and Spigurnell at Taunton on 31 March 1663 [**10**]. She was described as Mrs Browne's woman. She claimed that she lived at Wilton and was related to Elizabeth Browne. She was a daughter of Martin White a lawyer of Fiddleford in Sturminster Newton, Dorset and Mary daughter of Francis Moore of Taunton; she was baptised 27 September 1635 at Melcombe Regis. Martin's first wife was Penelope or Anne daughter of Serjeant Thomas Hanham of Wimborne, Dorset.[366] A marriage license for John Pyne widower of Curry Mallet esquire and Amy White aged about 50 issued on 30 December 1667 suggests Amy did not know exactly when she was born, or if she did she was keeping it close to her chest.[367] Thus Amy married one of the leading Parliamentary leaders in Somerset and has a double connection to the Taunton controversy. Amy was his second wife and John conveyed all of his manors to her on 11 August 1671. His will, dated 12 August 1676, was proved by Amy on 14 June 1678. Pyne was well connected and left bequests to Mr Amos Poulett, his kinsman Sir Edmund Wyndham Knight Marshall to His Majesty's Household and £10 to Sir William Wyndham knight and baronet, and the same to Sir Edward Phillips.[368] Her will, proved 14 February 1692/3, proves she was the daughter of Martin of Fiddleford.[369] Mrs Amy Pyne was buried at Curry Mallet on 11 August 1692.

---

1   T.N.A., C 8/197/125 bill of complaint, 12 February 1668/9. I am grateful to Susan Moore for this information.

2   T.N.A., E 134/9AND10CHASI/HIL29 deposition of John Porter gentleman, 1634-1635; C 22/767/33 depositions in Browne v Spigurnell, 31 March 1663.

3   www.nationalarchives.gov.uk/currency-converter/#currency-result, accessed 8 August 2021.

4   H.R.O., 11M59/E2/155655 appointment of Portman and Browne, 4 June 1618.

5   H.R.O., 11M59/E2/155655 appointment of Browne and Browne, 14 May 1633.

6   See the History of Parliament website.

7   H.R.O., 21M65/A1/32 appointment of Browne and Gollopp, 7 February 1661/2.

8   T.N.A., C 8/334/64 Bragg v Spigurnell, the complaint of Henry Bragg of Crewkerne, 24 June 1662; T.N.A., C 10/92/9 Spigurnell's answer, 9 December 1662.

9   *C.C.C.* vol. 3, 1984.

10 Anon, A *view of the proceedings of the Western-counties for the pacification of their present troubles: as also of the plots and purpose to disturbe the same* (London, 1642), 3.

11 A.R. Brayley, *The great Civil War in Dorset 1642-1660* (Taunton, 1910), 25.

12 S.H.C., D/D/Ol 36 29 November 1662 George Spigurnell was a bondsman for the marriage license between Richard Jeanes of Long Sutton, widower, husbandman and Ann Salmon a 30 year old spinster from Pitney; 11 June 1664 George Spigurnell was a bondsman for the administration of John Jeanes of Long Sutton who died intestate; D/D/Ol 37 he was bondsman on 19 May 1664. All documents describe him as a gentleman of Wells.

[13] I am grateful to Dr Julia Wood of Wells for checking her records for any evidence of George and his wife in the city records. A George Spigurnell was in Nevis in 1670 which, if he is the same man that was in Wells, may explain why he disappears from records in Somerset (V.L. Oliver, *The history of the island of Antigua, one of the Leeward Caribbees in the West Indies, from the first settlement in 1635 to the present time* (London, 1894), 90.

[14] V.C. Sanborn, *Genealogy of the family of Samborne or Sanborn in England and America 1194-1898* (Privately printed, 1899), 17-18.

[15] Buckinghamshire Archives, PR31/1/1 Burnham marriage register.

[16] Berkshire Record Office, D/A1/16/598 will and D/A1/213/146 probate inventory.

[17] J.H. Lea ed., *Abstracts of wills in the Prerogative Court of Canterbury at Somerset House, London, England* (London, 1904), 324, will number 986.

[18] C. Kerry, *The history and antiquities of the Hundred of Bray, in the county of Berkshire* (London, 1861), 8.

[19] B.R.O., D/EX 506/1 deed mentioning Nicholas Spygernel and his wife Alice, 1324.

[20] G.C. Gorham, *An account of the chapelry, chauntry and guild of Maidenhead, Berkshire* (1838), 37.

[21] British History Online and the Clergy of the Church of England Database have been thoroughly searched.

[22] Gorham, *An account*, 37.

[23] B.R.O., D/A1/213/146 probate inventory of James Spigurnell, clerk, 1627.

[24] B.R.O., D/A1/16/598 will of James Spigurnell, mercer, 1640.

[25] T.N.A., C 6/12/160 Spigurnell v Andrews, 1644. The Quart Pot Inn was still in Maidenhead in 1852 (*Slater's, late Pigot & co., royal national and commercial directory* (London, 1852), 21.

[26] T.N.A., C 6/12/160 Spigurnell v Andrews, 1644.

[27] Kerry, *The history and antiquities*, 17.

[28] T.N.A., C 21/C14/29 Cotton v Chafey: depositions taken in the country, 7 April 1654.

[29] Anon, *Parnassus biceps. Or Severall choice pieces of poetry, composed by the best wits that were in both the universities before their dissolution. With an epistle in the behalfe of those now doubly secluded and sequestred Members, by one who himselfe is none* (London, 1656).

[30] By the King, *A proclamation of His Majesties grace, favour, and pardon to the inhabitants of his county of his citty of Exeter* (Oxford, 1642).

[31] Sanborn, *Genealogy*, 17-18.

[32] J. Lenthall, *A list of all the prisoners in the Upper Bench prison, remaining in custody the third of May, 1653. Delivered in by Sir John Lenthall to the committee appointed by the Councell of State, for examining of the state of the said prison, with the times of their first commitment, and the causes of their detention. And also the substance of the propositions made by the committee to the prisoners, with their answer thereunto. Published for information of all such as are concerned herein. By the appointment of the committee, Coll: Thomas Pride. Coll: Tomlinson. Coll: Cooper. Mr. John Fountaine. Mr. Richard Wollaston. Mr. Margets Judg Advocate* (London, 1653), 3.

[33] *Friends of Lydiard Tregoz report* number 14 (Lydiard Tregoz, 1981), 30-2.

[34] W. Dugdale, *The antiquities of Warwickshire illustrated from records, leiger-books, manuscripts, charters, evidences, tombes, and armes : beautified with maps, prospects and portraictures* (London, 1656), 157, 186, 605.

[35] R. Thoroton, *The antiquities of Nottinghamshire extracted out of records, original evidences, leiger books, other manuscripts, and authentick authorities : beautified with maps, prospects, and portraictures* (Londn, 1678), 267-8.

[36] W. Dugdale, *The history of imbanking and drayning of divers fenns and marshes, both in forein parts and in this kingdom, and of the improvements thereby extracted from records, manuscripts, and other authentick testimonies* (London, 1662), 44.

37 Hertfordshire Archives and Local Studies, AH 925 endowment, 1323.

38 C. Kerry, *The history and antiquities of the Hundred of Bray, in the county of Berkshire* (London, 1861), 8.

39 T.N.A., C 22/619/5 Dryer v Spigurnell, 1668. The deposition of John Herringe of Taunton, innholder, mentions he knew Spigurnell for seven years prior to his death in 1663.

40 T.N.A., C 22/222/4 Attorney General v Pyne and others: depositions taken in the country, 1656.

41 T.N.A., C 6/12/160 Spigurnell v Andrews, 1644.

42 T.N.A., PRO 30/26/74/1 Clement's Inn addmission book, 1656-1790.

43 J. Diprose, *Some account of the parish of Saint Clement Danes (Westminster) past and present* (Westminster, 1868).

44 Memorial slab in Long Sutton church.

45 T.N.A., SP 16/10 f.89 list of Recusants in Somerset, 28 Nov. 1625. Mawdi Godwyn of Wells is recorded as having 'one corslett, one halberd delivered into the custodie of the constable of Wells'.

46 J. Hasler and A. Nott eds, *Wells Convocation* Act Books, 1589-1665,Part 2: 1662-1665, S.R.S. 91 (2004), 971.

47 S.H.C., DD/WY/2/53/3 lease, 18 Jan. 1643/4.

48 T.N.A., C 6/180/47 Spigurnell v Pyne, 1665.

49 J.R. Guy, "Under the Dean's nose' recusancy in early seventeenth-century Wells' in *South Western Catholic History* 1 (1983), 10-18; A. Nott, *Under God's visitation* (Wells, 2010), 25-6.

50 *Report of the commissioners for inquiring concerning charities, 1818-1837* (London, 1895), 388-9.

51 A. Hamilton, *The chronicle of the English Augustinian Canonesses Regular* (London, 1904), 217-218, 247; Guy, 'Under the Dean's nose', 16.

52 E.H. Burton and T.L. Willians eds, *The Douai College Diaries*, vol. 1, Catholic Records Soceity vol. 10 (1911), 180.

53 T.N.A., E 179/172/406 subsidy for the Hundred of Wells Forum, 1641.

54 S.H.C., D/D/Ca/412 index to excommunications, 1625-1641.

55 S.H.C., D/P/w.st.c/2/1/1 Wells St Cuthbert parish register.

56 T.N.A., PROB 11/355/213 will of James Godwynn, gentleman of Wells, Somerset.

57 J. Britton, *Memoir of John Aubrey, F.R.S., embracing his autobiographical sketches, a brief review of his personal and literary merits, and an account of his works : with extracts from his correspondence, anecdotes of some of his contemporaries, and of the times in which he lived* (London, 1845), 54.

58 https://wiki.bcw-project.org/royalist/foot-regiments/robert-phelips (accessed 20 July 2021).

59 T.N.A., SP 23/185/1 received 30 April 1646.

60 In 2022 Ann Spigurnell's memorial slab in the church at Long Sutton was covered by the organ.

61 T.N.A., PROB 11/355/213 will of James Godwyn, gentleman of Wells, Somerset.

62 I am very grateful to John Spiers for showing me around the house and giving permission to photograph it.

63 S.H.C., DD/SP/1679/48 inventory of George Browne, 1679.

64 T.N.A., C 6/180/47 Spigurnell v Pyne, 1665.

65 T.N.A., C 8/159/55 Dryer v Chard *et al*, 1667.

66 T.N.A., C 6/180/47 Spigurnell v Pyne, 1665.

67 T.N.A., C 8/159/55 Dryer v Chard *et al*, 1667.

68 T.N.A., C 6/180/47 Spigurnell v Pyne, 1665.

69 T.N.A., C 22/619/5 Dryer v Spigurnell, 1668. The woods were assigned to Edward Parsons of Langport Eastover, innholder, in 1665.

70 T.N.A., C 22/619/5 Dryer v Spigurnell, 1668.

71 T.N.A., C 6/180/47 Spigurnell v Pyne, 1665.

72 T.N.A., C 6/180/47 Spigurnell v Pyne, 1665. Francis Naylor, an associate of her first husband Thomas Spigurnell, brought a case against her in 1681 in Chancery for money owed to him (T.N.A., C 7/242/63 Naylor v Chard, 1681).

73 T.N.A., C 22/619/5 Dryer v Spigurnell, 1668.

74 T.N.A., C 6/180/47 Spigurnell v Pyne, 1665.

75 T.N.A., C 22/619/5 Dryer v Spigurnell, 1668.

76 T.N.A., C 6/180/47 Spigurnell v Pyne, 1665.

77 T.N.A., C 22/619/5 Dryer v Spigurnell, 1668.

78 T.N.A., C 22/619/5 Dryer v Spigurnell, 1668. Christopher Chapple had his estate sequestered at Barton St David by Edward Curle (*C.C.C.* vol.1 p.141).

79 T.N.A., C 10/67/41 Chapple v Ewtey, 1662. Ewtey was presented by the earl of Cleveland (T.F.T. Baker ed, 'Stepney: Churches', in *A history of the county of Middlesex: volume 11, Stepney, Bethnal Green* (London, 1998), 70-81).

80 T.N.A., C 22/619/5 Dryer v Spigurnell, 1668.

81 T.N.A., C 10/67/41 Chapple v Ewtey, 1662.

82 S.H.C., D/D/Pg8 survey of Barton St David, n.d..

83 T.N.A., C 10/67/41 Chapple v Ewtey, 1662.

84 T.N.A., C 22/619/5 Dryer v Spigurnell, 1668.

85 T.N.A., PROB 11/313/117 will of Thomas Spigurnell of Long Sutton, 1664.

86 T.N.A., C 22/222/4 Attorney General v Pyne and others: depositions taken in the country, 1656.

87 T.N.A., C 22/619/5 Dryer v Spigurnell, 1668. The deposition of John Herringe of Taunton, innholder, mentions he knew Spigurnell for seven years prior to his death in 1663.

88 T.N.A., C 22/619/5 Dryer v Spigurnell, 1668.

89 T.N.A., E 179/172/418 poll tax for the Hundred of Taunton Deane, 1660.

90 T.N.A., C 22/619/5 Dryer v Spigurnell, 1668.

91 T.N.A., SP 28/242 payments, 1650-1651.

92 S.H.C., D/P/tau.m/2/1/1 Taunton St Mary baptism register, 1558-1696.

93 *H.T.*, 8.

94 S.H.C., DD/SP/1665/3 inventory.

95 T.N.A., C 22/619/5 Dryer v Spigurnell, 1668.

96 T.N.A., C 22/170/33 Spigurnell v Dryer, 1668.

97 T.N.A., C 22/619/5 Dryer v Spigurnell, 1668.

98 *H.T.*, 3.

99 T.N.A., C 22/170/33 Spigurnell v Dryer, 1668.

100 T.N.A., C 22/619/5 Dryer v Spigurnell, 1668.

101 T.N.A., C 22/170/33 Spigurnell v Dryer, 1668.

102 T.N.A., C 22/619/5 Dryer v Spigurnell, 1668.

103 S.H.C., D/P/l.sut 2/1/1.

104 T.N.A., C 22/170/33 Spigurnell v Dryer, 1668.

105 T.N.A., C 6/180/47 Spigurnell v Pyne, 1665.

106 T.N.A., C 22/619/5 Dryer v Spigurnell, 1668.

107 T.N.A., C 22/170/33 Spigurnell v Dryer, 1668.

108 T.N.A., PROB 11/313/117 will of Thomas Spigurnell of Long Sutton, 1664.

109 T.N.A., C 22/619/5 Dryer v Spigurnell, 1668.

110 T.N.A., C 22/170/33 Spigurnell v Dryer, 1668.

[111] T.N.A., C 8/159/55 Dryer v Chard et al, 1667.

[112] T.N.A., C 8/159/55 Dryer v Chard et al, 1667.

[113] T.N.A., C 22/170/33 Spigurnell v Dryer, 1668.

[114] T.N.A., C 22/619/5 Dryer v Spigurnell, 1668.

[115] T.N.A., C 22/170/33 Spigurnell v Dryer, 1668.

[116] T.N.A., C 22/619/5 Dryer v Spigurnell, 1668.

[117] T.N.A., C 6/180/47 Spigurnell v Pyne, 1665.

[118] T.N.A., C 22/170/33 Spigurnell v Dryer, 1668.

[119] T.N.A., C 22/619/5 Dryer v Spigurnell, 1668.

[120] T.N.A., C 22/170/33 Spigurnell v Dryer, 1668.

[121] T.N.A., C 22/619/5 Dryer v Spigurnell, 1668.

[122] L.M.A., MS 10091/26 London and Surrey, England, Marriage Bonds and Allegations, 1597-1921.

[123] Clement's Inn records do not cover the period Spigurnell was admitted (T.N.A., PRO 30/26).

[124] T.N.A., SP 28/80 f.802 letter, 22 Sep. 1651. A warrant by the trustees for the 'sale of lands and estates forfeited to the Common-wealth for Treason' released £60 to Henry Cotton in return for Spigurnell's work as a surveyor, dated 1 April 1653, is in T.N.A., SP 28/275 f.110.

[125] T.N.A., SP 23/118 f.1131 petition of Thomas Spigurnell, 14 January 1651/2.

[126] T.N.A., SP 23/167 list of contracts renewed by the Commissioners for sequestrations in Somerset since the last return of 22 May 1652, f.227 Thomas Hopkins delinquent.

[127] *S.D.N.Q.*, 13 part 100 (Dec. 1912), 158.

[128] T.N.A., C 10/59/149 Spigurnell v Treagle, 1660. Spigurnell gave his evidence on 11 July 1660 and Treagle on 18 October 1660.

[129] Sir J. Baker, *Reports from the note books of Edward Coke volume I 1572-1579* (London, 2022), lxxiii, lxxix, lxxxiv. I am particularly grateful to William Hancock for drawing my attention to this reference and for making available other law books.

[130] T.N.A., C 6/180/47 Spigurnell v Pyne, 1665; C 8/145/62 Jeane v Spigurnell, 1659-1660.

[131] Clement's Inn records do not cover the period Spigurnell was admitted (T.N.A., PRO 30/26).

[132] Sir J. Baker, *Legal education in London 1250-1850* (London, 2007), 13.

[133] https://en.wikipedia.org/wiki/Inns_of_Chancery#Inner_Temple_attachments, accessed 8 August 2021.

[134] Baker, *Legal education*, 13-14.

[135] F.A. Inderwick ed., *A calendar of the Inner Temple records, vol. II, 1603-1660* (London, 1898), 288-318.

[136] C.W. Brooks, *Pettyfoggers and vipers of the Commonwealth. The 'Lower Branch' of the Legal Profession in Early Modern England* (Cambridge, 2004), 151-72.

[137] T.N.A., E 179/172/418 poll tax for the Hundred of Taunton Deane, 1660.

[138] R. Robson, *The attorney in eighteenth-century England* (Cambridge, 1959), 4, 6.

[139] B. Brooks and M. Herber, *My ancestor was a lawyer* (London, 2015), 35-7.

[140] T.N.A., C 6/180/47 Spigurnell v Pyne, 1665.

[141] T.N.A., C 7/418/74 complaint of Roger Hill of Poundsford, Somerset and Brampton Gurdon of Letton Hall, Norfolk esq. and John Hill of Taunton, gent., 24 October 1654.

[142] S.H.C., DD/X/WA/2 Treasurer's certificate for the sale of the manor of Taunton Deane, 15 March 1647/8.

[143] S.H.C., DD/SAS/C112/20/3 grant to Walter Cliffe, 1631.

[144] T.N.A., C 7/418/74 complaint of Roger Hill of Poundsford, Somerset and Brampton Gurdon of Letton Hall, Norfolk esq. and John Hill of Taunton, gent., 24 October 1654.

[145] T.N.A., C 78 contains no ruling under Hill or Gurdon from 1655-1665.

[146] T.N.A., C 21/C14/29 Cotton v Chafey: depositions taken in the country, 7 April 1654.

[147] https://en.wikipedia.org/wiki/Robert_Hunt_(Parliamentarian), accessed 14 August 2021.

[148] T.N.A., C 21/C14/29 Cotton v Chafey: depositions taken in the country, 7 April 1654.

[149] T.N.A., SP 23/167 list of contracts renewed by the Commissioners for sequestrations in Somerset since the last return of 22 May 1652, f.227 Thomas Hopkins delinquent.

[150] T.N.A., C 6/180/47 Spigurnell v Pyne, 1665.

[151] T.N.A., C 21/C14/29 Cotton v Chafey: depositions taken in the country, 7 April 1654.

[152] T.N.A., C 78/544 no. 12.

[153] T.N.A., C 22/222/4 Attorney General v Pyne and others: depositions taken in the country, 1656.

[154] T.N.A., C 6/180/47 Spigurnell v Pyne, 1665. He also dealt with the lease of 7 acres on a former royal manor in Cornwall in April 1657 (T.N.A., SP 28/287 Spigurnell to the Trustees for the Sale of Fee Farm Rents, 22 April 1657; he is described as being of Clement's Inn).

[155] T.N.A., C 8/145/62 Jeane v Spigurnell, 1659-1660.

[156] T.N.A., C 6/180/47 Spigurnell v Pyne, 1665.

[157] T.N.A., E 179/252/32 part 28.

[158] T.N.A., PROB 11/446/154 will of Henry Cotton, gentleman of St Clement Danes, Middlesex, 1698.

[159] T.N.A., C 8/145/62 Jeane v Spigurnell, 1659-1660.

[160] B.L., AddMS 34012 list of royalists, 1655 for Cornwall, Devon, Dorset, Gloucestershire, Somerset and Wiltshire.

[161] T.N.A., C 8/145/62 Jeane v Spigurnell, 1659-1660.

[162] Berkshire Record Office, D/A1/16/598 will of James Spigurnell, mercer, 1640.

[163] T.N.A., C 8/145/62 Jeane v Spigurnell, 1659-1660.

[164] Rev. W. Phelps, *The history and antiquities of Somersetshire* (London, 1836), 66-7.

[165] T.N.A., C 8/145/62 Jeane v Spigurnell, 1659-1660.

[166] https://en.wikipedia.org/wiki/John_Desborough, accessed 14 August 2021.

[167] Rev. E.H. Bates Harbin, *Quarter Sessions records for the county of Somerset, Commonwealth*, vol. III, S.R.S. 28 (1912), 278.

[168] T.N.A., C 8/145/62 Jeane v Spigurnell, 1659-1660.

[169] T.N.A., C 10/55/150 Spigurnell v Wyndham, 1658.

[170] S.H.C., DD/WY 14/9 draft case papers for Spigurnell v Burrowe and Younge, 1657.

[171] T.N.A., C 6/180/47 Spigurnell v Pyne, 1665.

[172] T.N.A., C 10/55/150 Spigurnell v Wyndham, 1658.

[173] S.H.C., DD/WY 14/9 draft case papers for Spigurnell v Burrowe and Younge, 1657.

[174] T.N.A., C 10/464/177 Stibbens and Spigurnell v Wyndham, 4 June 1658.

[175] P.A., HL/PO/JO/10/2/7B Main Papers (Parchment Collection), Petition and remonstrances of inhabitants of County Somerset, 10 December 1641.

[176] T.N.A., C 10/464/177 Stibbens and Spigurnell v Wyndham, 4 June 1658. Jones petitioned parliament for his losses at the Restoration when he was still a clerk living in Bridgwater (*Calendar of the House of Lords manuscripts*, column 7 part 1 (London, 1879), 123).

[177] T.N.A., C 10/55/150 Spigurnell v Wyndham, 1658.

[178] S.H.C., DD/WY 6/1/6 Someone, many decades ago, correctly pencilled in the front of this volume that it belonged to Wadham Wyndham '9th son of Wyndham = Portman Baptized 29 Oct. 1609 died Xmas day 1668 at Law'.

[179] *C.C.C.2 1423-1466; An act for the tryal of Sir John Stowel Knight of the Bath, David Jenkins Esq; Walter Slingsby Esq; Brown Bushel, William Davenant, otherwise called Sir William Davenant, and Colonel Gerrard* (London, 1650); *An answer of the purchasers of the lands, late of Sir John Stawel, by Act of Parliament exposed to sale for his treason, to a pamphlet intituled 'The humble remonstrance of Sir*

John Stawel' ... (London, 1654). There are numerous cases in Chancery that mention the dispersal of his estate e.g. C 7/276/91.

[180] T.N.A., C 8/138/75 Grigg v Spigurnell, 1660. Complaint of Grigg 12 July 1660, Spigurnell's reply 9 ovember 1660.

[181] T.N.A., C 10/59/149 Spigurnell v Treagle, 1660. Spigurnell gave his evidence on 11 July 1660 and Treagle on 18 October 1660.

[182] T.N.A., C 8/138/75 Grigg v Spigurnell, 1660. Complaint of Grigg 12 July 1660, Spigurnell's reply 9 ovember 1660.

[183] T.N.A., C 8/196/17 complaint of Thomas Spigurnell, 25 November 1662.

[184] T.N.A., C 78/722 no.22 Grigg and Spigurnell, 18 May 1663.

[185] T.N.A., PROB 11/312/231 will of Richard Grigg, dated 25 August 1663. He left several bequests to children under six years of age and those people who lived on the common.

[186] T.N.A., C 6/180/47 Spigurnell v Pyne, 1665. The Western Circuit Assize order book contains no mention of Spigurnell or Browne during the period 1660-1663 (T.N.A., ASSI 24/22 Western Circuit Assize order book, 1652-1677). I am exceptionally grateful to Susan Moore for providing copies of the order book.

[187] T.N.A., C 8/323/239 Hurley and Dryer v Spigurnell, 1667.

[188] T.N.A., C 8/334/64 Bragg v Spigurnell, the complaint of Henry Bragg of Crewkerne, 24 June 1662; T.N.A., C 10/92/9 Spigurnell's answer, 9 December 1662.

[189] T.N.A., C 10/92/9 Bragg v Spigurnell, Spigurnell's answer, 9 December 1662.

[190] T.N.A., E 134/1657/58Hil3 Depositions by Commission dated 28 November 1657, with depositions taken at Taunton on 25 January 1657/8. John Porter, clerk of Taunton Castle was one of the commissioners.

[191] Gloucestershire Record Office, D678/2/T1/6/1-26 Prebendary and tithes of Wiveliscombe and Fitzhead and the manor of the Prebendary of Wiveliscombe, 1633-1772. See A.J. Monday, *History of the Yea family of Pyrland Hall*, Appendix N xliii-xliv and pp. 34-36 where there is a discussion about Fitzhead's tithes not being sufficient to support the maintenance of a minister.

[192] T.N.A., E 134/1657/58Hil3 Depositions by Commission dated 28 November 1657, with depositions taken at Taunton on 25 January 1657/8. John Porter, clerk of Taunton Castle was one of the commissioners. The commission was issued from the Exchequer on 28 November 1657 and the depositions were taken at Taunton on 25 January 1657/8.

[193] T.N.A., E 126 number 6 f.251r Entry Book decree, 28 June 1658.

[194] F. Hancock, *Wifela's Combe* (Taunton, 1911), 116-117.

[195] T.N.A., E 126 number 6 f.251r Entry Book decree, 28 June 1658.

[196] T.N.A., E 126 No. 7 f.135r an interlocutory order, 30 January 1660/1.

[197] T.N.A., E 126 no7 f.137v an interlocutory order, 6 February 1660/1. Further papers relating to the tithes can be found at Gloucestershire Record Office, D678/2/T1/6/1-26 Prebendary and tithes of Wiveliscombe and Fitzhead and the manor of the Prebendary of Wiveliscombe, 1633-1772. I am grateful to William Hancock for this reference. Many Assize records from this period have not survived and, to make matters worse, the result is not mentioned in the order book.

[198] T.N.A., C 8/334/64 Bragg v Spigurnell, the complaint of Henry Bragg of Crewkerne, 24 June 1662.

[199] T.N.A., C 8/145/62 Jeane v Spigurnell, 1659-1660.

[200] S.H.C., DD/X/VNL 1 copy of the Hill cartulary.

[201] T.N.A., C 8/132/67 Hill v Browne, 1654-1655.

[202] T.N.A., C 78 Chancery decree rolls.

203 In his will dated 1663 he mentions both the Bovett and Pyne families (T.N.A., PROB 11/313). His mother-in-law was buried at Wilton in 1661.

204 Brayley, *Dorset*, 479.

205 Sir Edward Waldegrave's Regiment of Horse (http://wiki.bcw-project.org/royalist/horse-regiments/sir-edward-waldegrave) and P.J. Norrey, The relationship between central and local government in Dorset, Somerset and Wiltshire, 1660-1688 (University of Bristol thesis, 1988) (https://research-information.bris.ac.uk/ws/portalfiles/portal/34496592/DX082795.pdf) accessed 4 October 2021).

206 Although Mrs Browne tried to 'hide, convey away, disperse' her goods she lost by plundering and the 'troubles of the tymes', a great deal of her household goods to the vale of £1000 'more especially while the Seiges were att Taunton'. She managed to keep some of her jewels and similar valuables from being plundered, as well as her lands at Benfield and Graston, Dorset, her house and lands at Sherford and an estate called Middletons at Huish Champflower, from being sequestered (T.N.A., C 22/767/33).

207 T.N.A., C 22/767/33 depositions in Browne v Spigurnell, 1663. John Stocker gentleman is also mentioned as one of the commissioners but he did not sign any of the membranes of depositions.

208 *Somerset and Dorset Notes and Queries* 4 pt xxxii (December 1895), 355.

209 S.H.C., DD/DP 43/4/13.

210 H.R.O., 11M59/E2/155656.

211 I am grateful to Dr Dunning for inviting me to a court leet held in Taunton in 2007 in order to witness proceedings.

212 Only four children are mentioned in a document of 1682 (Dorset History Centre, D/FRY/32 deed, 1682).

213 T.N.A., C 7/58/30 Chard v Beresford, 1684.

214 T.N.A., C 9/39/25 Sambourne v Hand, 1667.

215 T.N.A., C 7/58/30 Chard v Beresford and Browne, 1684.

216 G.D. Squibb, *The visitation of Somerset and the City of Bristol 1672*, H.S. New Series 11 (1992), 119.

217 H.R.O., 21M65/A1/32 appointment.

218 T.N.A., PROB 11/454 will of Thomas Beresford, 1699.

219 T.N.A., C 22/222/4 Attorney General v Pyne and others: depositions taken in the country, 1656.

220 T.N.A., PROB 11/313/117 will of Thomas Spigurnell of Long Sutton, 1663.

221 A biography of Bovett is being worked upon by the author.

222 T.N.A., PROB 11/385/293 will of John Brydle of Motcombe, Dorset, dated 1686.

223 W.C. Metcalfe ed., *The visitation of Dorsetshire, A.D. 1565* (Exeter, 1887), 15; J.P. Rylands ed., *The visitation of the county of Dorset, taken in the year 1623*, H.S. XX (London, 1885).

224 History of Parliament website, accessed 20 Jan. 2020; Metcalfe, *Dorsetshire*, 15.

225 T.N.A., PROB 11/204 will of Robert Browne, dated 1637 and proved 1648; Squibb, *The visitation of Somerset*, 136-7.

226 T.N.A., PROB 11/204 will of Robert Browne, dated 1637 and proved 1648.

227 S.H.C., DD/SP/329 audit books of fees, 1626-1734.

228 T.N.A., PROB 11/204 will of Robert Browne, dated 1637 and proved 1648.

229 S.H.C., DD/SP/329 audit books of fees, 1626-1734.

230 S.H.C., DD/X/VNL 1 copy of the Hill cartulary.

231 S.H.C., DD/SP/98 Turn of Hock court book, 1653.

232 T.N.A., PROB 11/310/585 sentence; PROB 11/312/51 will of Elizabeth Browne, widow,

1663; PROB 20/331 supplementary will of Elizabeth Browne, widow, 1663.

[233] T.N.A., C 7/242/63 Naylor v Chard, 1681.

[234] He is not to be confused with George II who in 1677 was described as of Foston in Charminster, Dorset, esquire aged 53 and was buried at Godmanstone on 1 January 1677/8. His will was proved on 2 July 1678 and he passed away before 1679 when George III was still in office.

[235] *H.T.*, 36.

[236] H.A., 11M59/D1/2 lease, 28 Feb. 1662/3.

[237] *H.T.E.*, 314.

[238] T.N.A., C 10/472/12 although badly damaged the details recited in this document are very similar to the deposition case.

[239] Dorset History Centre, D/FRY/32 deed, 1682. The Coren family were from the parish of Kenwyn (T.L. Stoate ed., *Cornwall Hearth and Poll Taxes, 1660-1664* (Almondsbury, 1981), 64).

[240] Kresen Kernow, Kenwyn parish registers.

[241] R. Browne, *The genealogy of the Browne family*, accessed 28 Nov. 2019 at https://my-tripartite.co.uk/Brownes.htm.

[242] *H.T.*, 2.

[243] T.N.A., C 5/419/6; C 10/67/36.

[244] London Metropolitan Archives, MS 10091/26 London and Surrey, England, Marriage Bonds and Allegations, 1597-1921.

[245] For example T.N.A., C 7/58/30 Chard v Beresford and Strode, 1683.

[246] T.N.A., E 179/172/418 poll tax for the Hundred of Taunton Deane, 1660.

[247] I am grateful to Charles Doble for the biographical information relating to William Doble.

[248] S.H.C., Q/SR/53108-109 and 113 examinations, 1625.

[249] T.N.A., PROB 11/265/283 will of John Drier of Long Sutton, 1655.

[250] T.N.A., PROB 11/313/117 will of Thomas Spigurnell of Long Sutton, 1663.

[251] T.N.A., C 6/180/47-48 Spigurnell v Pyne *et al.*; C 8/159/55 bill of complaint of John Dryer of Long Sutton, husbandman, 1667.

[252] T.N.A., C 6/180/48 and C 10/472/112.

[253] T.N.A., PROB 11/312/231 will of Richard Grigge, yeoman of Staple Fitzpaine, Somerset, 1663; T.N.A., C 8/323/239 Hurley etc v Grigg, 4 December 1667.

[254] J.F. Dryer, *Ancestry of Rufus K. Dryer with notes on William Dryer of Rehoboth and some of his descendants* (Rochester, N.Y., 1942), 1-3, 110-130.

[255] S.H.C., DD/SP/317 index of fines.

[256] J. Burke, *A genealogical and heraldic history of the commoners of Great Britain and Ireland, enjoying territorial possessions or high official rank; but univested with heritable honours*, vol. 1 (London, 1835), 95.

[257] G.D. Squibb, *The visitation of Dorset, 1677*, H.S. 117 (1977), 31-2.

[258] Burke, *A genealogical and heraldic history*, vol. 1, 95.

[259] Squibb, *Dorset*, 31-2.

[260] S.H.C., DD/SP/346 manor of Taunton Deane, 1621-1784.

[261] T.N.A., C 8/145/62 complaint of Richard Jeane of West Monkton gentleman and attorney, 14 June 1659; answer of Thomas Spigurnell, gentleman of Wilton, 21 April 1660.

[262] S.H.C., DD/SP/317 index of fines.

[263] T.N.A., C 8/169/2; C 8/185/149; C 8/197/125; C 10/473/1.

[264] S.H.C., DD/SP/363 account book of Thomas and William Harvey, 1663-1707.

[265] S.H.C., DD/SP/18/42 Lawday court file, 1684.

[266] T.N.A., C 7/418/74 complaint of Roger Hill of Pounsford, Somerset and Brampton Gurdon

of Letton Hall, Norfolk esq. and John Hill of Taunton, gent., 24 October 1654.

267 T.N.A., C 22/619/5 Dryer v Spigurnell, 1668.
268 T.N.A., E 179/172/418 poll tax for the Hundred of Taunton Deane, 1660.
269 T.N.A., C 22/170/33 Spigurnell v Dryer, 1668.
270 T.N.A., C 22/619/5 Dryer v Spigurnell, 1668.
271 *H.T.*, 3.
272 T.N.A., C 22/619/5 Dryer v Spigurnell, 1668.
273 T.N.A., PROB 11/313/117 will of Thomas Spigurnell of Long Sutton, 1664.
274 W. Scott, *A collection of scarce and valuable tracts*, vol. 5 (London, 1811), 142.
275 A.J. Webb ed., *Somerset wills extracted by Miss Olive Moger*, S.R.S. 94 (2008), 172-3, 177.
276 M. Siraut ed., *Somerset wills extracted by A.J. Monday*, S.R.S. 89 (2003), 157.
277 T.N.A., C 8/128/74; C 8/148/72; C 10/29/59; C 10/64/38.
278 S.H.C., D/P/tru/24/52 account of Rogert Mattock, *c.* 1650.
279 *S.P.R.*, 116.
280 T.N.A., C 22/222/4 Attorney General v Pyne and others: depositions taken in the country, 1656.
281 H.B. Sheppard, *Courts Leet and the Court Leet of the Borough of Taunton* (Taunton, 1909), 59.
282 S.H.C., DD/SP/54 Taunton Borough court book, 1652-1665.
283 S.H.C., Q/SPET/1/123.
284 S.H.C., DD/X/WA/7 lease for a year, 1659.
285 *H.T.*, 32.
286 T.N.A., PROB 11/362/533 will of Robert Hucker of Taunton, yeoman and codicil, 1679.
287 T.N.A., C 8/138/75 Grigg v Spigurnell, 1660.
288 T.N.A., PROB 11/286/65 will of Christpher Hurley of Taunton dated 1658. A petition to the manorial court by Christofer Hurley mentions two males named Roger Hurley. One was Christopher's nephew and the other was his brother (H.R.O., 11M59/E1/144/7/22 petition of Christofer Hurlye, 1595X1605).
289 T.N.A., C 22/222/4 Country Depositions series II, Attorney General v Pyne and others: depositions taken in the country, 1656, abstracted in British Archivist pages 115-116.
290 T.N.A., C 8/145/62 Jeane v Spigurnell, 1659-1660.
291 *C.C.C.*, vol. 2, 1412.
292 T.N.A., C 8/145/62 Jeane v Spigurnell, 1659-1660.
293 T.N.A., C 7/191/59 Jeane v Jeane, 1667.
294 T.N.A., PROB 20/1422 will of John Jeane of West Monkton, 1663.
295 T.N.A., PROB 11/363/418 will of Richard Jeane, Gentleman of Taunton, 1680.
296 *S.P.R.*, 116.
297 *H.T.E.*, 163.
298 T.N.A., C 22/222/4 Country Depositions series II, Attorney General v Pyne and others: depositions taken in the country, 1656, abstracted in British Archivist pages 115-116.
299 S.H.C, DD/SF/2/39/68 Milverton deeds, 1652-1662.
300 *S.P.R.*, 116.
301 S.H.C., DD/SP/317 index of fines.
302 S.H.C., DD/SP/52 Taunton borough court book, 1630-1639.
303 S.H.C., DD/SP/53 Taunton borough court book, 1639-1652.
304 *H.T.*, 2.
305 T.N.A., PROB 11/326/249 will of Phillip Lissant of Taunton, 1668.
306 T.N.A., PROB 4/4454 inventory of Philip Lissant the elder, mercer, 12 February 1667/8.
307 T.N.A., PROB 11/409/396 will of Phillip Lissant, haberdasher of London, 1692.
308 S.H.C., Q/SR/76/106-108 examinations, 1637.

309 *S.P.R.*, 116.

310 T.N.A., C 22/619/5 Dryer v Spigurnell, 1668.

311 *S.P.R.*, 164.

312 S.H.C., DD/SP/317 contains two mentions of a John Palmer in 1629 and 1645.

313 T.N.A. SP 28/80 f.802 letter, 22 Sep. 1651.

314 T. Hearne, *The lives of ... John Leland, Thomas Hearne, and Anthony à Wood* ..., volume 2 (Oxford, 1772), 193; T.N.A., PROB 11/303/295 will of Dr John Palmer, 11 February 1660/1.

315 T.N.A., C 7/418/74 complaint of Roger Hill of Pounsford, Somerset and Brampton Gurdon of Letton Hall, Norfolk esq. and John Hill of Taunton, gent., 24 Oct. 1654.

316 T.N.A., C 7/276/91 Palmer v Musgrave, 1656.

317 Hearne, *The lives*, volume 2, 193; T.N.A., PROB 11/303/295 will of Dr John Palmer, 11 February 1660/1.

318 S.H.C., DD/WY 14/9 draft case papers for Spigurnell v Burrowe and Younge, 1657.

319 T.N.A., E 134/9AND10CHASI/HIL29 deposition of John Porter gentleman, 1634-1635.

320 T.W. Mayberry, *From Somerset to Portman Square* (Taunton, 2016).

321 *S.P.R.* 120.

322 S.H.C., DD/SP/98 Turn of St Martin court book, 1651.

323 S.H.C., DD/SP/317 index of fines.

324 *H.T.*, 8.

325 T.N.A., PROB 11/377/197 will of Robert Prockter, merchant of Taunton St Mary Magdalene, 1684.

326 T.N.A., PROB 11/313/117 will of Thomas Spigurnell of Long Sutton, 1664.

327 *H.T.*, 179.

328 T.N.A., PROB 11/357 will of John Pyne the elder of Curry Mallett esquire, 1676.

329 *S.P.R.* 117.

330 S.H.C., DD/SP/317 index of fines.

331 *H.T.*, 6.

332 S.H.C., DD/SF/12/10/14-16 and DD/SF/12/14/28.

333 *H.T.*, 2.

334 Sheppard, *Courts Leet*, 37.

335 *T.Cal.*, 369.

336 *O.D.N.B.* entry for Sir John Stawell.

337 *C.C.C.2* 1423-1466; *An act for the tryal of Sir John Stowel Knight of the Bath, David Jenkins Esq; Walter Slingsby Esq; Brown Bushel, William Davenant, otherwise called Sir William Davenant, and Colonel Gerrard* (London, 1650); *An answer of the purchasers of the lands, late of Sir John Stawel, by Act of Parliament exposed to sale for his treason, to a pamphlet intituled 'The humble remonstrance of Sir John Stawel'* ... (London, 1654). There are numerous cases in Chancery that mention the dispersal of his estate e.g. C 7/276/91.

338 See for example S.H.C., DD/S/BT/28/8/1, DD/WEL/32, DD/CH/126/3, DD/CH/112/5, DD/DN/2/16/1.

339 T.N.A., PROB 11/373/522 will of Sir Nicholas Strode of the Inner Temple, 1683.

340 T.N.A., C 7/58/30 Chard v Beresford, 1684.

341 T.N.A., C 7/58/30 Chard v Beresford, 1684.

342 R. Browne, *The genealogy of the Browne family* at https://my-tripartite.co.uk/Brownes.htm, accessed 28 Nov. 2019.

343 T.N.A., CP 40/1317-1318 Trinity 1573; CP 40/1423 Hilary 1584; CP 40/1436 Hilary 1585.

344 *S.P.R.*, 118, 258, 263.

345 S.H.C., DD/SP/53 Taunton borough court book, 1639-1652.

346 T.N.A., C 22/222/4 Country Depositions series II, Attorney General v Pyne and others:

depositions taken in the country, 1656, abstracted in *British Archivist* pages 115-116.

[347] T.N.A., E 179/172/418 poll tax for the Hundred of Taunton Deane, 1660.

[348] T.N.A., C 10/59/149 Spigurnell v Treagle, 1660. Spigurnell gave his evidence on 11 July 1660 and Treagle on 18 October 1660.

[349] S.H.C., DD/SP/52 Taunton borough court book, 1630-1639.

[350] S.H.C., DD/SP/317 index of fines.

[351] *H.T.*, 6.

[352] T.N.A., C 2/212/6.

[353] J. Foster *et al*, *London marriage licences, 1521-1869* (London, 1887), 436.

[354] *P.S.A.N.H.S.* 55 (1909), 8, 58.

[355] T.N.A., C 22/222/4 Attorney General v Pyne and others: depositions taken in the country, 1656.

[356] S.H. Cassan, *The Lives of the Bishops of Winchester* (London, 1827), 30; www.wikipedia.org/wiki/Taunton_(UK_Parliament_constituency)#MPs_1640, accessed 14 August 2021.

[357] T.N.A., SP 18/156 f.103.

[358] T.N.A., SP 20/13/2.

[359] S.H.C., DD/SP/317 index of fines.

[360] S.H.C., DD/X/WA/5 agreement with covenants, 1656.

[361] J. Savage, *History of Taunton* (Taunton, 1822), 158.

[362] L.M.A., St Clement Danes marriages, 1653-1675.

[363] T.N.A., C 8/145/62 Jeane v Spigurnell, 1659-1660.

[364] T.N.A., C 8/196/179 Spigurnell v Grigg, 1662.

[365] S.H.C., DD/SP/317 index to fines.

[366] Squibb, *Dorset*, 75.

[367] J. Foster *et al*, *London marriage licences, 1521-1869* (London, 1887), 1104.

[368] T.N.A., PROB 11/357/85.

[369] T.N.A., PROB 11/413/317 will of Amy Pyne, widow of Curry Mallet, Somerset includes a bequest to Elizabeth daughter of my nephew Ignatious White of Angers, Dorset deceased; Squibb, *Dorset*, 75.

THE TRANSCRIPTS RELATING TO THE DISPUTES

Description:

1. The complaint of George Browne, 14 November 1660 [T.N.A., C 6/167/18]

2. The complaint of Thomas and Elizabeth Spigurnell, 30 November 1660 [T.N.A., C 10/85/85]

3. Answer of Elizabeth Browne widow to George Browne's complaint, 1 February 1660/1 [T.N.A., C 6/167/18]

4. Reply of George Browne to the complaint of Thomas and Elizabeth Spigurnell, 27 March 1661 [T.N.A., C 10/85/85]

5. The joint answer of Thomas and Elizabeth Spigurnell to George Browne's complaint, after 11 April 1661 [T.N.A., C 6/167/18]

6. The answer of John Browne to George Browne's complaint, 24 April 1661 [T.N.A., C 8/191/30]

7. Further answer of Thomas Spigurnell gentleman to George Browne's complaint, 11 May 1661 [T.N.A., C 6/167/18]

8. The answer of John Browne to George Browne's complaint, 14 June 1662 with amendments 14 February 1662/3 [T.N.A., C 8/192/102]

9. The complaint of Thomas Spigurnell in Thomas Spigurnell v George Browne, 14 February 1662/3 [T.N.A., C 10/78/62]

10. The depositions taken at Taunton in the case of Browne v Spigurnell, 31 March 1663 [T.N.A., C 22/767/33]

11. The answer of George Browne esquire to Thomas Spigurnell's complaint, 25 May 1663 [T.N.A., C 10/78/62]

12. Complaint of Edward Chard of Long Sutton gentleman and Elizabeth his wife versus George Browne, after June 1665 [T.N.A., C 6/176/18]

13. Complaint of Edward Chard of Long Sutton gentleman and Elizabeth his wife versus George Browne, after June 1665 [T.N.A., C 6/176/18]

1.

Description: The complaint of George Browne, 14 November 1660 in the case
of George Browne v Elizabeth Browne widow, Thomas Spigurnell gentleman
and Elizabeth his wife
Reference: T.N.A., C 6/167/18
Editorial note: Another similar version of George Browne's complaint dated 13
November 1660 is in T.N.A., C 8/191/30, and the answer of John Browne esquire
(T.N.A., C 8/191/30) is printed as number **4** in this volume.

[*Headed*] 14 November 1660
[*Marginated*] Trinity 1664
[*Annotated*] Longeville

To the right honourable Edward Lord Hide Lord Chancellor of England
Humbly complayning your Orator George Browne of Wilton in the County of
Somersett Esquire only sonne and heyre of Robert Browne late of the Castle of
Taunton in the saide County Esquire deceased sheweth to your Lordshipp That your
Orators said late father having in his life tyme long before his death lawfully setled and
conveyed his lands of inheritance which are of the yearely value of two hundred
pounds per Annum and upwards uppon and unto Elizabeth his wife your Orators
mother (who is yet living and enioyeth the same) for her life for her Joynture, and
being soe seized to him and his heyres according to the Custome of the Mannor of
Taunton Deane of and in a certaine Messuage and Tenement at Marystoake parcell of
the said Mannor of the yearely value of five pounds or therabouts and alsoe interested
and possessed for the residue of a terme of one Thousand yeares or some other long
terme of yeares yet enduring of and in a certaine Messuage or Tenement or lands
called Middleton lying in the parish of Huish Champflower in the said County of the
yearely value of ffourescore pounds and upwards and being alsoe interested and
possessed of se much ready money Creditts plate bedding linning and other goods
Chattles and household stuffe as well as Three Thousand pounds and upwards or
some other greate somme of money and having yssue only your Orator and Elizabeth
his daughter who were very young and tender not of discretion sufficient to manage
an estate or in truth to governe themselves and your Orators said father being in or
about the nineteenth day of August in the yeare of our lord One Thousand six
hundred Thirty and seaven sicke and weake and having a very greate confidence in
your Orators said Mother and intending to make provision for a reasonable
maintenance for your Orator and his said sister during theyr minority out of his reall
and personall estate not in Joynture to your Orators said mother and to have a
convenient porcion raysed out of the same after his death for your Orators said sister
and intending that the residue therof should come unto your Orator and yet however

3

to leave a seeming overaweing power in your Orators said mother touching the same your said Orators father uppon or about the second day of August in the said yeare of our Lord One Thousand six hundred thirty and seaven made his last <will> and Testament in writing and therein amongst divers other things did express and declare that as touching his personall estate both reall as his lease at Stokehill his Coppyhold of Taunton Deane and his lease for a Thousand yeares of the land called Middleton in the said parish of Huish Champflower and his personall Chattles all his plate lynnen bedding and all his household stuffe and other goods whatsoever he therby gave the same to your Orators said mother in trust for your Orator and his said sister and therby did declare his meaning to bee that your Orators said mother should have the use of his said goods for her widdowhood and dispose of the them for the proferrment of your Orator and his said sister as should bee meete and they should meete And your Orators sayd father did further by his said will declare that though hee were very confident of the intire affeccion which your Orators sayd mother bore unto his Children and that she would doe them all the good she could yet it was his will and pleasure that if she should marry after his death she should then relinquish all her right to his said reall <and> personall estate content herselfe with her Joynture and such goods only as belonged to her person according to the ranke and make over the residue <of his estate> to your Orators said fathers Overseer nominated in his said will for the use of his Children to bee distributed as hee should thinke fitt And your Orator further sheweth that his said late father and one John Browne now of Frampton in the County of Dorsett Esquire your Orators said fathers brothers sonne whose name was used only by your Orators said father in trust for the benefitt of your orators said father and such to whome hee should assigne the advantage thereof were in the life tyme of your Orators said father lawfully seised for the termes of theyr naturall lives and the life of the survivor of them in trust for your Orators said late father as aforesaid of and in the office of clerk of the Castle ville and lordshipp of Taunton in the County of Somersett with all and singuler the hundreds and members and of all the Annuall fees Annuityes emoluments and profitts of the same with the rights members and appurtenances to the said office belonginge or appertaining which was and is of the yearely value of one hundred and eighty pounds beyond all repryzes and being therof soe seised in trust for your Orators said later father as aforesaid, your Orators said father in and by his said last will and Testament did alsoe give the same Office to your Orators said mother during her widowhood to the use of his Children to maintayne them and proferr them and to rayse porcions for them and did thereby further direct that imediately after his death the said office should bee bought for another life to bee added to the sayd John Browne in trust for his said wife and children as aforesaid and this his said will made your Orators said mother Executrix and one John Porter then his Overseer and shortly after dyed after whose death your Orators said mother in due forme of law proved the said will and tooke uppon her not only the burthen of the execucion of the same but alsoe the execucion of the severall trusts in the said will mencioned and by your Orators sayd father in her reposed as aforesaid which your Orator doth believe his said mother would have faithfully performed had she continued in such a measue of health and strength of body and minde as she was in and did enioy at the tyme of the death of your Orators

4

said father But doe it is may it please your Lordshipp that after the death of your
Orators said late father your Orators said mother growing weake and sickly and for
many yeares last past having bene by a dead palsey depirved of the use and exercise of
her limbs and by her age and weakness she lost those abilityes which she had at the
death of your Orators sayd late father, and your Orators said sister being growne
marriageable and noe fitt match provided for her or tendered to her whereof one
Thomas Spigurnell a person of <noe> value and a servant to one Doctor Palmer
whoe some tymes lived in the towne of Taunton aforesaid and was a neighbour to
your Orators said mother taking notice and having yett some interest in the men of
power in the late distracted tymes by his false and insinuating waye, and Courses and
sometymes by threat wrought soe much uppon the weaknesses of your Orators said
mother and gott soe farr unto the good opinion of your Orators sayd sister that
without the privity or knowledge of your Orator he in short tyme after to witt about
five yeares since married your Orators said sister and therby getting the oportunity to
looke into your Orators said late fathers will and to discover the nature of his estate
and how hee had disposed of it and living with your Orators said mother in the same
house and designing to gayne the whole estate both reall and personall of your
Orators said late father and alsoe the said office to himselfe and wholly to deprive your
Orator of the benefitt and advantage intended to your Orator by his said late grant of
the same by unworthy false and indirect Courses and suggestions laboured to bring
your Orators said mother into an ill opinion of your Orator suggesting to her that
your Orator was an enimy to the then Government and an undutifull sonne and by
other his unworthy insinuations and false aspercions cause your Orator said mother
without any just cause at all to withdraw much of her affeccion from your Orator and
the better to accomplish his uniust end of gayning all your Orators said late fathers
estate to himselfe and into hir owne hands the said Thomas Spigurnell prepared or
brought prepared to your Orators said mother in her greate weaknes when she did not
not nor could understand the tenor or designe of a conveyance one or more writing or
writings to bee sealed by your Orators said mother to the said Thomas Spigurnell and
his wife or one of them of some other person or persons to the use of them or one
of them or in trust for them or one of them who in such her weaknesse was by the
said Thomas Spigurnell and Elizabeth his wife or one of them prevayled to seale and
deliver the same the contents whereof she did not then know nor was or were the
same reade unto her nor doth she know what they doe concerne but your Orator is
confident that when the same shall bee seene and discovered it will appeare that hee
hath drawne your Orators said mother by reason of her said weakness and infirmity to
violate the trust in the reposed by your Orators said father as aforesaid and as much as
in her lay wholly to deprive your Orator of the benefitt and advantage intended to
your Orator by his said late father out of his estate in and by his said last will and
testament which your Orator hath the greater reason to believe for that the said
Thomas Spigurnell under Colour and pretence of the same hath possessed and
disposed of all or the greatest parte of the personall and testamentary estate of your
Orators said late father made severall entryes on his reall estate and lands not in
ioynture and ever since received not only the profitts of the same but alsoe the profitts
of the said office and your Orator as wholly deprived of the same <out of which

there hath bene little or no porcions or maintenance allowed unto your Orator contrary to the intent and will of his said father> and the said Thomas Spigurnell the better to furnish his designs and wholly to destroye and <ruyne> your said Orator hee hath confederated with the said John Browne whose name was used only in trust in the patent or grant of the said office for the benefitt of your Orators late father and by a Combynacion betweene them they have or one of them hath made severall grants and assignments of the same office to persons unknowne to your Orator without any due consideracion who were notwithstanding will acquainted with the said trust and the said John Browne contrary to all truth equity and good Conscience and in apparent breach of the trust in him reposed by your Orators said late father as aforesaid doth sometymes deney the said trust and claime to have a peculier right and interest to himselfe in the same office and without any trust whatsoever and at other tymes gives out that hee hath or will grant and assigne the same to the said Thomas Spigurnell which is contrary to the trust reposed in him the truth being and the said John Browne well knowing that his name was used in the grant of the said office only in trust for your Orators said father and that the whole profitts of the said office was in the life tyme of your Orators said late father received by him alone and have since his death bene received by your Orators said mother without any Accompt soe rendred or demanded by him for the same and although the said John Browne doth well know or hath bene at least informed that the trust of the said office doth not atall apppertaine unto the said Thomas Spigurnell and that noe further estate can bee bought therin according to the direccion of your Orators said late fathers will unlesse the said John Browne doth surrender his estate therin the same being in the grant of the Bishopp of Wynton yet the said John Browne although hee hath in all friendly manner <in order to the taking of such further estate therein as by the will is directed> be requested to surrender the same accordingly yet hee doth refuse to surrender his estate the said office for the taking of a further estate therin according to the direcion and desire <of> your Orators said late father in his said will contrary to the trust reposed in him and to the greate disadvantage and hazard of your Orator In tender Consideracion wherof and to the end the uniust practizes of the said Thomas Spigurnell in working on the weaknessed and infirmitye of your Orators said mother and in obtayning the deeds and writings to <be> sealed and delivered by her <as aforesaide> may bee fully discovered and made knowne and receive the examinacion judgment and decree of this honourable Court and that your Orator may have a convenient porcion and maintenance raysed and allowed unto him, out of his sayd fathers estate and to the end the said Thomas Spigurnell and Elizabeth his wife may uppon theyr severall corporall oathes discover or sett forth the same the severall dates tenor effect and substance of the same when and uppon what condicion made and who were wittnesses to the same and what right title interest or clayme the said Thomas Spigurnell and Elizabeth his wife or either of them have or make to all or any and what parte of the reall or personall estate late of your Orators said late father and to the said office and by and under what right title interest or authority hee hath disposed of the same or received all or any of the profitts thereof. And forasmuch as your Orator is without all remidy to inforce the die execucion and performance of the before mencioned trusts or of any or either of them or to examine discover and bee

6

releived touching the breach of the same but in a Course of Equity before your Lordshipp in this honourable Court to the end therfore that the miscarriage and mistake of your Orators said money in the execucion and performance of the severall trusts in her reposed as aforesayd which have bene cheifly occasioned by her age weaknes and infirmities and by the undue practices of the sayd Thomas Spigurnell taking advantage of and working on the same may by the order and decree if this honourable Court bee all certifyed and sett right <and> the sayd severall trusts performed according to the true intent and meaning of your Orators said father the said Thomas Spigurnell bee compelled to accompt aswell for all the reall and personall estate of your Orators said late father which hath since the death of your Orators said father bene in his hands or bene disposed by him as alsoe for the profitts of the said office which hee hath received and to the end all the said deeds and writinge which have bene yett by surprize from your Orators said mother as aforesaid may bee by the like order and decree of this honourable Court vacuated nulled and prove voyd and that the said John Browne may pursueant to the will of your Orators said late father bee by the order and decree of this honourable Court compelled to surrender his estate and interest in the said office for the taking of a further estate therin by your said Orator and to the end your Orator may been otherwise releived by by the order and decree of this honourable Court in all and singuler the premisses according to equity and good conscience May it please your Lordshipp to grant unto your Orator his Majestys most gratious writt of subpana to bee directed to the said Elizabeth Browne your Orators mother John Browne Thomas Spigurnell and Elizabeth his wife therby commanding them and every and either of them at a certaine day and under a certaine payne therin to bee limited personally to bee and appeare before your Lordship in the high Court of Chancery then and there to answere all and singuler the premisses uppon theyr severall Corporall oathes and further to stand to abide such further order and direcion in the said premisses as to your Lordships shall seeme meete and most agreeable to equity and good conscience And your Orator as his duty is shall every pray &c.

[*signed*] John Ryves

[END OF DOCUMENT]

2.

Description: The complaint of Thomas and Elizabeth Spigurnell, 30 November 1660
Reference: T.N.A., C 10/85/85
Note: This complaint was drawn up only two weeks after the complaint of George Browne [1].

[*annotated*] 30 November

The the Right Honourable Edward Earle of Clarendon Lord High Chancelor of England

Complayneing sheweth unto your Lordship your Dayly Orators Thomas Spigurnell of the parish of Long Sutton in the County of Somersett Gentleman and Elizabeth his wife Daughter of Elizabeth Browne late of Taunton deceased That Robert Browne late of Taunton aforesayd ~~esquire~~ in the County of Sommersett Esquire and father to your oratrix Did in or about the yeare of our Lord God one thousand six Hundred thirty and three purchase of Walter the lord Bishop of Winton the Office of Clerke of the Castle and Burrough and Lordship of Taunton aforesayd unto himselfe and unto John Browne (then the sonne of John Browne Esquire of Frampton in the County of Dorsett ~~esquire~~ since deceased) for the Terme of their lives and the life of the longestt Liver of them which was an office antiently granted by the Bishops of Winton who had power in right of his Bishopprick to grant the same and as by the Instrument itselfe under the Bishops seale if it might bee produced would more playnly appeare, which sayd purchase was contracted for and made by the sayde Robert Browne alone and the fyne or Consideration therfore given was payd by the sayd Robert Browne and with his proper moneyes and the name of the sayd John Browne the younger incerted in the pattent or Instrument of grant of the sayd offices by the directions and appoyntement of the sayd Robert in trust for him his executors Administrators and Assignes and accordingly he the sayd Robert Browne entred into the sayd Office alone and had tooke and Converted to his owne use all the rents and yearly profitts of the sayd Office and premissed dureing the then future Terme of his life which was for sixe yeares and upwards Dureing all which time the sayd John Browne did not Intermeddle in the said offices or receave any rents or profitts thereof though the same was worth one hundred and forrty pounds a yeare, And the sayd Robert being thereof soe seized and haveing Issue by Elizabeth his then wife Two Children viz George her onely sonne and your Oratrix Elizabeth the onely daughter made his last Will and Testament in writeing bearing date the second day of August which was in the yeare of our Lord God one thousand six hundred thirty seaven And Contendeing as the truth was and is that hee might Limitt and appoynt thereby the Bennefitt of the

Trust which after his death by the sayd Pattent and grant would rest in the sayd John Browne and Intending to settle and appoynt have the Trust should bee disposed of and employed Did by his sayd last will amongst other things give and appoynt the said office and premisses which hee held under the Bishop of Winton for his owne Life and the life of the sayd John Browne to his sayd wife dureing her widdowhood to the use of his Children to maynteyne and prefer them and to rayse portions for them as in her discretion shall bee thought fitt and with the advice of his overseer And thereby further appoynted that Instantly after his death the sayd office[1] should bee bought of the Bishop for another life in trust for his wife and Children and of his said will made his sayd wife whole and sole executrix and one John Porter Gentleman his overseere thereof or by the sayd will relation being thereunto had if produced would alsoe more fully appeare, And shortly thereafter the sayd Robert Browne dyed and <the sayde> John Browne ... him survived and because solely e..... in the sayd Office but upon the Trust aforesayd And your Orator further sheweth unto your Lordship[2] That your Orator haveing an estate of Lands in the said County worth neare two hundred pounds a yeare to the knowledge of the sayd Elizabeth Browne <the widdowe> executrix of the sayd Robert Browne; after some Treaty betweene your orator and the sayd Elizabeth Browne touching a marriage to bee had betweene your Orator and Oratrix and uppon your Orators and Oratrixe Consent it was about foure yeares since agreed on betweene your orator and the said Elizabeth Browne the executrix <By and with the Consent[3] of the sayd George Browne that a marriage should bee had between your Orator and Oratrixe> And that ~~a portion~~ your sayd orator should have as a ~~portion~~ marriage portion with his sayd wife one thousand pounds to bee raysed out of the profitts of the sayd Office by vertue of the said Trust over and above besides the Porters office and some other Lands worth about ~~threehun~~ two hundred pounds, And the sayd Elizabeth Browne the mother and Executrix as well in persuance of the said marriage agreement as alsoe of the Trust and power granted her by the said will of her husband with the Consent and knowledge of the sayd George Browne Did by Deed under her hand and seale Charge the sayd Office with the rayseing of one thousand pounds part of the portion of your Oratrix, And the said Elizabeth the mother to further ~~to further~~ the Raysing of the sayd portion Did give directions unto John Porter who Executed the sayd Office and had knowledge of the sayd appoyntment made by the said Elizabeth Browne the mother to passe and accompt with and pay the profitts unto of the said office ~~unto~~ your Orator as the same should bee raysed which accordingly was done by the said John Porter without any Contradicion of the sayd John Browne who had perfect notice of the sayd ~~Agreement~~ appoyntment And your Orator further sayeth that shortly after the sayd marriage to witt in or about the yeare ......[4] 1659 the said George Browne did exhibitt a bill in the Court of Exchequer against his sayd mother to Compell her to sett forth what estates shee had setled on your Orator as a porcion with which his sister to which bill the sayd Elizabeth gave answeare that shee had Charged the sayd Office with the payment of the sayd thousand pounds which answeare being receaved by the sayd George Browne hee waved that Court and dismissing that his bill exhibited a bill in this Honourable Court of Chancery (against his mother and the sayd John Browne the party trusted) to the same effect to which shee gave the like answeare The shee had for your Orators portion in marriage with the said Elizabeth the daughter Charged the sayd Office with the payment of the said thousand pounds All which the sayd Georg Browne will knew as the sayd John Browne the party trusted being a party to the said suites and had Coppyes of theise bills and answeares and gave his owne answeare thereunto <and agreed to performe the said trust and> Likewise the sayd John Browne and George Browne very well knew that there was noe other portion or mayntenance for the said Elizabeth your Oratrice <butt> ~~but~~ out of the profitts of the said Office, besides those those small things given your Orator as aforesayd) yet notwithstanding soe it is may it please your Lordship that the sayd George Browne although hee well knew that it was the directions of ~~this~~ the said Robert Browne his father by his sayd will That the life of the sayd John Browne should still bee Continued and that at the first opportunity ~~another~~ annother life should bee purchased and added to the sayd John Browne for the Bennefit of the Children of the said Robert Browne as is aforesaid and the sayd George Browne was privy and Consenting to the mariage <Agreement> aforesaid Hee the sayd George <and one John Gollopp> by combination had with the sayd John Browne and to the end to defraud and the said Trust and estate under pretence of pursuing of the directions of the sayd Will of the sayd Robert Browne <his father ......[5] promise that the life of the said John Browne should still be continued and stand in a new pattent or graunt to bee obteyned of the said office to the use of the said last will of the said Robert Browne> and that hee would onely add his owne life and by other sinister meanes hee the sayd George Browne <and John Gollopp> soe farr fore raysed with the said John Browne as that the sayd John Browne did deliver unto him the said George Browne <and John Gollopp or one of them> the sayd first <pattent> obteyned by the sayd Robert Browne with Letter of Attorney or other power to surrender the same which hee noe sooner had obteyned but contrary to his promise and the trust and directions of the said Last will of his said father in the name of the said John Browne did surrender up the pattent and ~~of~~ in stead of Inserting the name agayne of the said John Browne according to the Trust and directions of the said ..... tooke and obteyned from the present Lord Bishop of Winton (within whose Grant the sayd Office is a new pattent or grant thereof to himselfe for two other Lives or names <vizt him the said George Browne and John Gollopp> intending therby to defraud and defeate your Orator~~s~~ of his Trust and Interest in the profitts of the sayd Office and of the sayd Thousand pounds and damages for the same whereas the sayd new pattent ought in equitye to bee subject to the trust appoynted by the will of the sayd Robert Browne and consequently chargeable with the <sayd> Thousand pounds to your Orator and the sayd trust for your Oratrice, And your Orators sheweth that they haveing notice of this greate fraud tending to the utter Ruine of them did peticion the sayd Lord Bishop seking forth his right and title, and the fraud comitted by the sayd George Browne which the sayd Lord Bishop being ..sible off was pleased to grant uppon your Orators sayd peticion a letter of prohibicion unto the then Deane and Chapter of Winton Intimateing his being surprized by the sayd George Browne and to desire the sayd Deane and Chapter to forbeare the Confirmation of the sayd pattent Butt the sayd George Browne made such hast unto the sayd Deane and Chapter that hee obteyned a Confirmation of the sayd Pattent by the sayd Deane and Chapter some few houres before your Orator could gett thither which the sayd Letters of Prohibicion, And now the sayd George Browne <and John Gollopp> haveing thus surruptitiously obteyned the new Pattent and Confirmation thereof hee hath made some secrett estate or estates thereof to some person or persons unknowne to your Orator in trust for himselfe or uppon some other trust and will not permitt or suffer your Orator to receave his sayd of our porcion of One thousand pounds and damages out of the sayd Office or the profitts thereof although the sayd George Browne hath an estate left him by his sayd father and mother worth about six thousand pounds beside the sayd office there being noe other Children left by the sayd Robert but the sayd George Browne and your Oratrix Elizabeth who hath receaved nothing as yett of what was left or Intended for her by her sayd fathers will and the appoyntment of Elizabeth her mother to whom whee was ever obedient ser..viceable and pleaseing, And the sayd George Browne <and John Gollopp or one of them> hath gott into his Custody or the Custody of some other by his Consent delivery or privity the sayd last will of the sayd Robert Browne and Denyeth to Lett your Orator to have the same or the sight or perusall thereof In tender Consideracion whereof sayd that your Orators have noe Remedy by the strict Rules of Common Law of this Realme neither can your Orators by any Course of that Law Compell the sayd George Browne <and John Gollopp> to suffer your Orator by predptions of the profitts of the sayd Office to receave satisfaction of the sayd thousand pounds porcion and damages your Orator not as yett haveing receaved above thirty pounds out of the profitts of the said Office towards the sayd thousand pounds and dammages But your Orator hath his proper and endeed onely remedy before your Lordship in the high Court of Equity where Breach of trust frauds and Circumventions are properly exxamminable and remmediable, neither can your Orator for want of the sayd And pattent and last Will manifest and make out the trust and directions thereof or other the Transactions aforesayd elswhere or otherwise then in this Honourable Court uppon the Oathes of the sayd Confederates, many of the persons that Can or Could prove the same being since dead or gone beyond the seas or remote and unknowne unto your Orators But your Orators doe know that the Confederates Can and doe hope that they or one of them will uppon his or their Corporall Oath discover the particuler truth of the premisses which that they may doe and may make a perfect and particuler answeare to all and singuler the premisses And that your Orators may bee relived touching the same according to equity and good Conscience may it please your Lordship to grant Unto your Orators his majestyes most gratious writt of subpena to bee to them the sayd George Browne <John Gollopp> and John Browne directed thereby Commanding them and either of them at a certayne by and under a certayne payne therein to be Lymitted personally to bee and appeare before your Lordshipp in the high Court of Chancery then and there to Answear all and every promisses And to stand to and abide such further order and direction therein as to your Lordshipp shall seeme meeke And your Orators shall pray &c.

[signed] Jo: Fountayne

[END OF DOCUMENT]

3.

Description: Answer of Elizabeth Browne widow in the case of George Browne v Elizabeth Browne widow, Thomas Spigurnell gentleman and Elizabeth his wife, 1 February 1660/1
Reference: T.N.A., C 6/167/18
Note: Elizabeth was the widow of Robert Browne esquire of Taunton Castle.

The severall Answeare of Elizabeth Browne widdow one of the defendants to the Bill of Complaint of George Browne Esquire Complainante

[*endorsed*] Penrodoc

The said defendant now and att al times hereafter saveinge to herselfe the benefitt and advantage of Exception to the incertainties insufficiences and imperfeccions of the said bill of Complaint and the matters therein contained for answere thereunto saith That it is true that Robert Browne Esquire in the Complainants bill named this defendants late husband did in his life time settle and convey his lands of inheritance which are of the yearly value of Sixscore Pounds a yeare uppon this defendant for her life for her Jointure in which right shee ever since his death hath enioyed and doth still enioy the same, And this defendant doth beleeve it to bee true that her said late husband was in his life time and died seised of a Messuage and tenement lyinge att Mary Stoake parcell of the Mannor of Taunton Deane of the yearely value of ffive pounds of thereavouts and that hee was in his life time and att his death interested and possessed for the residue of a long terme of yeares the certainty of which this defendant is not well able to expresse of and in a messuage and tenement called Middleton lyinge in the parish of Huish Champflower of the yearely value of Fiftie Pounds or thereabouts and that hee was in his life time and att his death alsoe interested and possessed of a personall Estate in ready money debts, plate Jewells, Utensills of househol and household stuffe to the value of ffive hundred pounds or thereabouts and that hee had issue att the time of his death only the said Complainant and Elizabeth the now wife of Thomas Spigurnell who were then very young (that is to say) the said Complainant of the age of tenn yeare or thereabouts and the said Elizabeth of the age of seaven yeares or thereabouts, And this defendant doth alsoe confesse it to bee true that this defendants said late husband had a great confidence in this defendant of her this defendants care and tendernesse of her said children and in that confidence did on or about the time in the said bill of Complaint in that behalfe mencioned hee beeinge then in good health and memory make his last will and testament in writeinge wherein hee did give all his reall and personall estate to this defendant in trust for the said Complainant and his said Sister and did declare his meaneinge to bee that this defendant should have the use of the same duringe this defendants widdowhood and should dispose thereof for the proferment of his said children. And this defendants said late husband did further by his said will declare that if this defendant shoulld after his death marry againe that this defendant should then relinquish all her right to his said reall and personall estate and content herselfe with this defendants Joynture and such Goods as belonged to this defendants person accordinge to this defendants ranke and make over the residue of his estate to John Porter gentleman Overseer nominated in the said will for the use of his said children; and this defendant saith that shee doth not nor never did conceive that shee had or hath any other right or title to the said reall or personall estate of her said late husband but in trust for her children And this defendant doth alsoe confesse that her said late husband and John Browne in the said bill of Complaint named were seised for their naturall lives and the life of the Survivor of them of and in the office of Clerke of the Castle ville and Lordshipp of Taunton and of the annuall fees emoluments and proffitts of the same which this defendant doth believe is of the yearely value of Sicscore pounds beyond all reprizes in the purchase of which this defendant knoweth that the name of the said John Browne was used only in trust for the benefitt of this defendants said late husband which office this defendant doth confesse that her said late husband by his said last will and testament did give to this defendant dureinge <her> widdowhood for the use of her said children to maintaine them and proferre them and to raise porcions for them, and by his said will did direct that imeadiately after the death of this defendants said late husband another life should bee bought into the said office, and added to the life of the said John Browne in trust for this defendant and her said children as aforesaid and in his said will made this defendant his Executrix and the said John Porter his Overseer as in and by the said will it selfe whereunto this defendant for the greater certainty doth in all thinges referr herselfe it doth and may appeare; shortly after which time this defendants said late husband dyed, and afterwards this defendant did make probate of his said will and tooke uppon her the execicion of the severall trusts therein contained with a full intent accordinge to the trust in her reposed faithfully to discharge the same, which dureinge all the time it pleased God to continue her health and strength unto her shee hopeth shee accordingly did. But this defendant doth confesse that of late yeares shee hath laboured under very great weaknesses by reason of a Palsey which hath seised uppon her and longe confined her to her chamber and bedd, by meanes whereof shee hath not beene able soe well as formerly to discharge the same nor in truth to undertake the management of her owne estate, And the defendant doth alsoe confesse it to bee true That the said Thomas Spigurnell hath married this defendants said daughter, to the now great alliccion of her, aswell as of this defendant, to whome this defendant did give a porcion of one thousand pounds in marriage with her to bee raised out of the office of this defendants said late husband which was much beyond his merritt. And the defendant doth alsoe confesse it to bee true that the saide Thomas Spigurnell did by his insinuacions and an overawing greatnesse which hee assumed to himselfe having been an active person in the late unhappy revolutions, against the King, labour to sett differences betweene this defendant and the said Complainant and to bringe him into the disesteeme and disaffeccion of this defendant and whiles this defendant did retaine her parts and strength of reason did often labour to gaine from this defendant all the said reall and personal estate of this defendants said late husband, And the said office,

13

whereto this defendant did ever refuse to assent; though the said Thomas Spigurnell had prepared instruments and writeinges in in order to it; And this defendant saith that shee doth <not know> that shee did ever grant, assure, convey or make over to the said Thomas Spigurnell, or to any other person or persons, all or any parte of the said reall or personall estate, of this defendants said late husband other then the said . one thousand pounds, or the said office of Clerke of the Castle of Taunton, of the rents, issues, or yearely income thereof, or of any part thereof, but doth hope and believe that and disposicion of this defendant and that shee hath not at all by any Act deprived the said Complainant of the same, to whome this defendant doth confesse the same <will> intended, after a competent porcion, raised out of the same for this defendants said daughter. And this defendant saith, that if the said Thomas Spigurnell, hath obtained or conveyance of the said reall or personall estate of this defendants said late husband, or any parte thereof, other then the said summe of one thousand pounds office of Clerke of the Castle; the same was obtruded uppon this defendant in some time or times of her very great weaknesse, and gained by surprise, when this or understand therof, or was able to take notice of the same; And therefore as shee hopeth not of force to conclude this defendant or to deprive the said Complainant of by his said late father. And this defendant saith that shee hath beene of late informed, that the said Thomas Spigurnell and his wife, have stolne the greatest part of the goods and household stuffe left to this defendant as aforesaid, for which this defendant hath sent unto him, who most unjustly doth refuse to deliver the same to this defendant, And this defendant the said Thomas Spigurnell and his said wife, have alsoe gott into their hands many deeds and writeings concerneing the said reall estate of this defendants said alsoe unjustly detaine, And this defendant saith, that shee is very desirous that the intencions of her said late husband, by this defendant herein formerly expressed without that, that any other matter or thinge in the said Bill of Complaynt contained material or effectuall in the Lawe for this defendant to make herein before sufficiently answered unto confessed and avoyded, traversed or denyed is true in such manner and <forme> as in the said Bill is all prayeth to bee dismissed out of this Honourable Courte with her reasonable Costs and charge in this behalfe most wrongfully sustayned

Capta fuit haec responsio primo die Februarii Anno Regni dominio Caroli secundi Regis decimo tertio apud Wilton in Commitatus Somerset super sacramentum supra nominate defendentis Coram nobis[6]

John Slape   John Sowthey
[*endorsed*] 9 February 1660
Before Aldred Seaman W Glascock
Executio istius patet in quadans scedula huic brevi annexa
[*a note on a seperate piece of vellum*] The Execcution of this Commission appears by the answeare heerunto anexed taken by us the xi[th] day of May Anno Domini 1661 [*signed*] Philip Lissante Sam: Whetcombe

[END OF DOCUMENT]

4.

Description: The answer of George Browne esquire to the complaint of
Thomas and Elizabeth Spigurnell, 27 March 1661
Reference: T.N.A., C 10/85/85
Note: Unfortunately the far right side of this document is badly damaged, folded with
some loss and much of it is illegible. Therefore the text below is an accurate transcript
of what is readable.

[*annotated*] Longueville

The severall answere of George Browne Esquire one of the defendants to the bill of
Complaint of Thomas Spigurnell and Elizabeth his wife Complainants

The said defendant now at all times hereafter saving to himselfe the benefitt and
advantage of excepcion to the Incertaintyes insufficiencyes and imperfeccions of the
said bill of Complainte and the matters therin contayned for answere therunto sayeth
that hee doth beleive it to bee true that Robert Browne Esquire deceased late father of
Elizabeth did in his life tyme, but in or about what yeare this defendant doth not
knowe purchase of Walter then Bishopp of Winton the office of Clerke of the Castle
Burrough and Lordshipp of Taunton unto himselfe and John Browne of Frampton
Esquire in the saide bill of Complainte named for the terme of their lives and the life
of the longest liver of them and beleiveth that the said office is an office anciently
granted by the Bishopps of Winton who as this defendant doth allsoe beleive had
power in the right of the said Bishoppricke to grante the same when voyd by death or
surrender, and doth beleive that the said purchase was soe made by this defendants
said Father alone and that the fine and consideracion that was payd for the same was
payd by this defendants said late fathers owne <proper> moneyes and that the name
of the said John Browne the younger was used and incerted in the Patent or
instrument of grante of the said office by the direccions and appointment of this
defendants said late father in trust for this defendents said father his heyres and
assignes and that this defendants said late father entred into the said office alone and
had and received the rents yssues and profitts therof during the them residue of his
life to his owne proper use without redering any Account for the same or any parte .....
to the said John Browne during which tyme this defendant doth beleive that the said
John Browne did not intermeddle in the in the said office nor receive any of the rents
or profitts theroff but this defendant doth not beleive that the said office is of the
yearely value of one hundred .... pounds or worth more than one hundred pounds
<per Annum> Commibus Annis ultra repryses And this defendant doth beleive that
this defendants said father being therof soe seised had yssue by Elizabeth his then
wife this defendant his only sonne and the Complainante Elizabeth his only daughter
and that hee made his last will and Testament in writing dated uppon or about the

second day of August in the yeare of Lord one Thousand six hundred Thirty seaven and in respect this defendant and the Complainant Elezabeth were then infants and very younge and to thend the said Elizabeth his then wife might have a seeming .... power in this defendant his said sister in relacion to the estate which was their father, and this defendants father reposing Confidence in this defendants said late mother, that his said sister <the now Complainant Elizabeth> might have some Competent porcion out of the same and to thend that as well the said office as all other his reall and personall estate might after the said porcion raysed out of the same come free and cleare unto this defendant after the death of this defendants said mother this defendants said Father did in and by his said will give devise and dispose of the said office and of his estate reall and personall in manner and form ...ing that is to say hee willed that his house called the Bull in Bridporte – should after the death of this defendants said mother goe to his youngest sonne that should bee living at his death and as for his personall estate both reall as his lease for three lives at Stokehill with his Coppyhold of Taunton Deane and his lease for one Thousand years of the land called Middleton in the parish of Huish Champflower and his personall Chattles as his plate Linnen bedding and all household stuffe and other goods whatsoever hee gave to his said wife this defendants late mother in trust for his children and did declare his meaning to bee that she should .... use of them forever .... and should dispose of them for the behoofe and proferrment of her children was she should see fitt and they meritt and did declare his further will and meaning to bee that if she should marry againe then she should relinquesh all her right to his goods and Chattles aforesayd and content her with ... ... and such .... necessary for her person accordinge to her Ranke and that she should make them over to his Overseer to bee named or his assignes for the use of his Children to bee distributed to them as hee or they should thinke fitt And for the office of Clerke and Porter of the Castle of Taunton which this defendants father held of the Bishopp of Winton for his owne life and the life of the said John Browne hee gave the same in the same manner to this defendants said mother during her widdowhood to the use of his Children to maintayne them proferr them and rayse porcions for them as in her discretion with the advise of his Overseer should bee thought fitt And did declare his will to bee that instantly after his death the said office should bee bought of the Bishopp for another life to bee added to the said John Browne in trust for his said wife and Children and this defendants said father made his said wife executrix of his said will and one John Porter his Overseer as by the sayd will it .... remayning as this defendant doth beleive in the Registry of the Prerogative Court of Canterbury whereunto this defendant for the greater certainty doth referr himselfe it may appeare And this defendant doth beleive that afterwards to witt uppon or about the month of ~~day of~~ December in the yeare one Thousand six hundred Forty.... this defendants said late father dyed and that the said John Browne did him survive And that this defendants sayd late mother proved the said will and tooke uppon her the execucion therof but whether the Complainant Thomas Spigurnell hath or ever had any estate or lands worth neere Two hundred pounds a yeare or whether .... or what treaty or treatyes were had betweene the Complainant Thomas Spigurnell and this defendants said late mother touching a marryage to bee had betweene the said Complainants or what agreement or agreements were made betweene the Complainant Thomas Spigurnell and his said wife and this defendants said late mother touching the same marriage this defendant doth not knowe But for the full discovery of the truth this defendant sayeth that the said Thomas Spigurnell being at or about the begining of the late warrs betweene his late Majestie Kinge Charles the first of blessed memory and those in rebellion against his Majestie a servant in a meane Condicion attending ...on or a ...o..e unto one Mr John Palmer a Phisitian then a member of the long Parliament and a very active person against his said late sacred Majestie and the Complainant Thomas Spigurnell by the meanes of his said Master getting into the favour of the late usurpers and being clothed with Competent porcion of impudence to carry him to any undertaking hee was in the late unhappy troubles imployed by the saud Usurpers in surveying of the estates of severall loyall persons which the said Usurper thought fitt to seize on and put to sale wherin they finding him an active and a fitt agent for them did in severall other thinges imploy and intrust him by meanes wherof hee gotte a greate interest in severall persons then in greate power and usurped authority in and about the Towne of Taunton in the County of Somersett for which his said Master served as a Burgesse neere which Towne this defendants said Mother and sister then lived where the said Complainant then appeared as if hee had bene a person of some quality and as this defendant hathe been informed … as for justice as by those of the said rebellion represented to this defendants said late mother and moved for to bee admitted a suitor for marriage to the now wife this defendants sister wherunto whether this defendants said late mother did then or at any time consent, this defendant sayeth hee doth not knowe but believe that if she did she was de..w..d ....[7] it more out of feare then for any affeccion she bare unto the said Complainant Thomas Spigurnell she being of a contrary Judgment to him and very much abhorringe the accions hee was dayly guilty of in adhering to those in that Rebellion against his sacred Majestie however this defenant doth beleive that the said Elizabeth Spigurnell by her ....[8] and insinuating courses afterwards got the Consent of his now wife to marry her and beleiveth that they are married but this defendant is very sure it was without the consent of him this defendant and that with this defendant would have prevented had it bene in his power shortly after with M.... ....[9] said mother was taken with a dead palsy and by meanes therof grew soe very weake that she could not well bee without the help and assistance of her said daughter this defendant not being then married and tooke the said Complainants into her house, and provided for them and the said infirmity increasing on .... she in a short time .... soe very weake and infirm........[10] and soe decayed in her parts and understanding that she was not able to manage or dispose of her owne estate or performe the trust reposed in her by this defendants said father but by the practices and subtile insinuations of the said Complainant Thomas Spigurnell leste the sole management and disposing of the same to him ... ... may be and to her intended gayning of the whole estate of this defendants said father wherof hee dyed seized and possessed was not or could bee soe cleare and smoth as he desired soe long as this defendant did continue with his mother in her said house, the said Complainant Thomas Spigurnell laboured to sett differenceis Betweene this defendants ... ... said mother and to drawe her in to greate dislike of this defendant which by his false suggestions and infirmacions and the interest of those of the rebellion in those parts hee in a short time did effect, and though this defendant married into a family of quality and with a Gentle woeman against whom noe excepcions could bee taken and with whom this defendant hath had a very fayre fortune yet the said Complainant Thomas Spigurnell drew this defendants said mother into soe greate a dislike therof and distast therat against this defendant that this defendant and his sayd wife whiles the late usurpers had the government could not bee received into this defendants said mothers house nor without great .... be admitted to see her but were reproached for being Cavaleires had noe allowance from this defendants said mother out of this defendants sayd fathers estate <limited for maintenance as aforesaid> but the said Complainant Thomas Spigurnell wholly swallowed upp the same and received and had the rents yssues and profitts therof and of this defendants said mothers Joynture all which was of the yearely value of one hundred and twenty pounds and the said Thomas Spigurnell by reason of the weakness of this defendants said mother having thus farr wrought uppon her and this defendant knowing hee hath confidence to attempt any thinge this defendant doth beleive hee did indeavour by all meanes to gayne unto himself at least ..cosen to all the estate this defendants said father dyed <seized or> possessed <of> but what deeds or writinges hee hath gott this defendants said mother <in her weaknesse> in her life time to sett her hand and seale unto or to execute or how farr hee hath drawne her into the breach of the said trust reposed in her by this defendants said late father in his life tyme this defendant doth not knowe nor <that> hath hee never sealed or delivered or otherwise executed and deed or deeds unto him or if she did this is most confident that the said Thomas Spigurnell gott the same by surprize and this defendants said mother to seale and execute the same at such a tyme when she understood not what she did all which this defendant is .d... of the more to vile her for that this defendants said mother in an answere of hers in this honourable Court putt in by her in her lifetime to a bill here executed against her and the now Complainant Thomas Spigurnell by this defendant she hath sworne shee doth not know that she ever made any deed unto him or if she did she was surprised in it ...[11] answere it selfe remayning of record in this honourable Court wherunto this defendant for the greater certainty doth referr himselfe it may appeare And this defendant sayth that hee doth hope to make it appeare that if this defendants said late mother did in her life time make any such deeds to the said Complainant as in and by the said bill of Complainante are pretended by him it was an apparent breach of the trust reposed in her by this defendants said late father which this defendant hopes will not receive the least countenance or favour in this honourable Courte And this defendant denyeth that any such deed or deeds as in and by the said bill of Complainte is and are p[re]tended to be [used by][12] the said Complainant Thomas Spigurnell by this defendants said late mother were made or if any such were ever made that the same were soe made by or with the consent or knowledge of this defendant or with the consent of John Porter in the said bill of Complainte named to this defendants knowledge as in and by the said bill of Complainte is in that behalfe sett forth And this defendant confesseth that he did heretofore exhibite his bill of Complainte into the Court of Exchequer against this defendants said late mother and the said Complainant Thomas Spigurnell amongst other things to discover that esteate grante or grantes of this defendants said late fathers said estate the said Complainant Thomas Spigurnell had obtayned from this defendants said late mother to which bill an answere was made in the name of this defendants said late mother which was as this defendant doth beleive and hopes to prove contained and framed by the now Complainant Thomas Spigurnell but what the content thereof was this defendant hee doth not remember nor can sett forth and doth beleive that his said late mother never understood the contents of it And this defendant doth confess that hee being advised by his Councell that his said bill was in several things imperfect this defendant did cause his said bill to be dismissed with the usuall costs in such case awarded much to the same effect whereunto this defendants said late mother she then having freed herselfe from being surprized in her act as by the said Complainant Thomas Spigurnell made such answer as this defendant hath herein formerly sett forth and by the said answer itself remayning of record in this Honorable Court whereunto this defendant for the greater certainty does refer himselfe it will appeare upon which said bill soe exhibited by this defendant in this Honorable couurt this defendant did intend and would have proceeded with effect But it soe happened that before any further proceedings were had therein, this defendant and the said Complainant Thomas Spigurnell by the mediacion of John Browne esquire in the said bill of Complaint name cousin german to this defendant and the said Complainant Elizabeth referred ....[13] difference between them to the said John Browne and enterd into severall bonds to each other in severall greate penall somes of money to abide his award touching the same which bonds were deposited in his hands who after due Consideracion had of the premises and after much paynes taken by him therin and a discovery to his satisfaccion ....[14] what the estate of this defendants said late father was and what the Complainant Thomas Spigurnell had since his intermarriage with this defendants said late sister received out of the same thought it reasonable that this defendants said sister should have the same made up a Competent porcion and theruppon awarded that this defendant should pay him for the somme of Three hundred pounds at a day certaine now past and that the Complainant Thomas Spigurnell should deliver unto this defendant all the writinges in his hands concerning the estate and offices late of this defendants said father and mother and relinquish to this defendant all his right and title and interest in or to the same and that all suits betweene this defendant and the said Complainant Thomas Spigurnell should cease wherwith the said Complainant Thomas Spigurnell seemed to bee satisfied and theruppon in obedience to the said award this defendant at the day in and by the same award limited for payment of the same three Hundred pounds did tender the same unto the said Thomas Spigurnell and was ready to pay the said Three hundred pounds unto him soe as hee would have delivered upp unto this defendant the said writinges concerning the said estates of this defendants said late father and mother and have relinqueshed and assigned to this defendant his clayme right title and interest in and to the same according to the true intent and meaning of the said award and this defendant in further obedience to the said award did no further proceed on this defendants said bill exhibited as aforesaid in this honourable Court against the said Complainant and did alsoe forbeare to proceed at the Common law against the said Complainant in an accion wherin this defendant had a verdict for <twenty pounds> besides his Costs of suite but the said Complainant refusing to performe the said award on his parte to bee performed this defendant did not deliver the said Three hundred pounds unto him but allwayes hath bene and is ready to pay the same soe as the said Complainant Thomas Spigurnell will perform soe much of the said award as on his parte is to bee performed according to the true and meaning of the said John Browne And this defendant doth deny that there was noe other porcion or maintenance for the Complainant Elizabeth out of the profitts of the said office since the time of the pretended grant therof to the said Complainant Thomas Spigurnell by this defendants said late mother as in the said bill of Complaint is in that behalfe sett forth but on the contrary this defendant sayth that hee hopes to prove that a sufficient porcion for her suitable to her quallity and ....[15] the meritt of the other Complainant Thomas Spigurnell might have bene <and was> promysed out of the yearely yssues and profitts of this defendants said late fathers estate and offices lefte in trust by him to this defendants said late mother from the death of this defendants said late father untill the intermarriage of the said complainant and this defendant doth confesse that his said late father did by his said will declare it to bee his desire that instantly after his death the said office of Clerke of the Castle of Taunton should bee bought of the Bishopp of Winton for another life to be added to the said John Browne as this defendant hath herein falsely sett forth which not being accordingly done the same was held by the life of the said John Browne only from the death of this defendants said late father which happned uppon or about the time aforesaid untill about six moneths since when this defendant at his owne proper costs and Charges and ....[16] monyes did purchase of the now Lord Bishopp of Winton a second life therin and agreed for the exchange of the life of the said John Browne for another life to bee named in his steed And this defendant doth alsoe confess that the said John Browne did by letter of Atturney ....[17] authorise this defendant to surrender upp the saide patent or grante of the said office to the said Bishopp of Winton in order to do this defendants taking a further estate therin for two lives which this defendant doth confesse hee accordingly did and that the said Bishopp theruppon ....[18] this defendant and one John Gollop gentleman for the lives of this defendant and the said John Gollopp and the longest liver of them which grante hath bene since confirmed by the Deane and Chapter of Winton but this defendant doth deny that the said Bishopp did to this defendants knowledge give ....[19] hinder or obstruct the confirmacion of the same by the said deane and Chapter as in and by the said bill of Complaint is in that behalfe suggested or if hee did this defendant doth beleive the same was procured by the Complainant Thomas Spigurnell uppon some false suggestion and hopes that ....[20] if any such were done by the said Bishopp; as first to receive this defendants money and make a grante of the sayd office and afterwards to obstruct the execucion of his owne grante, will receive the least favor or Countenance in this honourable Court And this defendant doth deny that the said letter of Attorney ....[21] obtayned or the said surrender or new grante of the said office made uppon any such Consideracion promise or agreement or to any such end or purpose as in and by the said bill of Complainte is in that behalfe surmised and sett forth but this defendant saith that the said John Browne having aforesaid by his said awarde ended all the differenceis betwene this defendant and the said Complainant wherto all parties att least seemed to submitt and to acquiesce in, the said John Browne did in

20

pursueance of the said awarde and at the request of this defendant deliver the old patent or grant ....[22] to this defendant and gave this defendant the said lettre of Atturney to surrender the same which in all conscience as this defendant hopeth under favour of this honourable Court hee ought and was lawfull for him to doe and this defendant hopeth that the <saide> new patent or grante soe obtayned as aforesaid ....[23] defendants owne purchase and with his owne proper moneis is not nor wilbee by this honourable Court construed to bee at all subject to the pretended trust or interest which the Complainants clayme therin or at all lyable to the payment of the one Thousand pounds wherwith the said Complainant ....[24] bill of complainte indeavour to charge the same And this defendant denyeth that hee hath made any estate or estates of the sayd office to any person or persons whatsoever but confesseth that hee doth refuse to permitt or suffer the said Complainant or either of them to receive the said profits ....[25] or any parte therof out of [t]he said office or out of the profitts therof as this defendant hopeth made favour of this honourable Court is lawfull for him to doe And this defendant sayeth that if the grants and conveyances which the said Complainants have or hath <or are of therin> at least pretend to have ....[26] said late mother in her weakness, of this estate or offices wherof this defendants said late father and mother <or one of them> dyed seized and possessed be good in law or shall receive the favour of this honourable Court to support them this defendant is soe farr from having an estate lefte him by his said father ....[27] value of six Thousand pounds over and besides the said office that not one penny worth of the estate wherof this defendants said late father and mother dyed seized or possessed and was in the power of them or either of them to dispose of is or will ~~or can~~ come to this defendant ....[28] that the said Complainant Thomas Spigurnell doth not only indeavour to charge the said office of Clerke of the Castle of Taunton with the said somme of one Thousand pounds which is much more then the full value therof but hath already solde and disposed of a very greate and considerable part of the ....[29] said late father and mother and consisting in ready money plate clothes linnen wolling <bedding> pewter brasse and other Goods and household stuffe and by pretended grants and conveyances supposed to be p[ro]cured by him from the defendants said late mother in her weakness claymes all the rest and residue of the reall and personall estate of this defendants said late father and mother or either of them dyed seized or possessed and could dispose <of> and by his false and unworthy practices and courses doth endeavour to deprive and deceive this defendant of the same and of all the benefitt intended by this defendants said late father unto this defendant out of the same........[30] of th.. ... ... And this defendant doth deny that hee or any other by his consent delivery or privity have hath or ever had the originall last will and Testament of this defendants said late father in his or their Custody and denyeth all the practice and Combynacion in and by the sayd bill of Complaint ....[31] charged and sayeth that over and besides what the said Complainants have already solde and disposed of the estates of this defendants said late father and mother and the said somme of three hundred pounds awarded to bee payd by this defendant to the said Complainant Thomas Spigurnell as aforesaid this defendant [did][32] clayme to have all the reall and personall estate and offices of his said late father and mother and doth hope that hee shall not bee any way hindred <or impracticed> by this honourable Court in the enjoyment therof without that that any other matter or thing clause or sentance or allegacion in the said bill of Complaint contayned materiall or effectuall in the law for this defendant to answere unto and not herein or hereby sufficiently answered unto <confessed or avoyded> traversed or denyed is true all which this defendant is ready to <ever justify> prove as this honourable Court shall award and prayeth to bee hence [dismissed with his][33] reasonable Costs <and charges> in theis behalfe most wrongfully and without just cause sustained.

Taken at Milverton in the county of Somerset 27th of March in the 13th year of King Charles the Second
[*signed*] Aldred Seaman Rob Leigh

[END OF DOCUMENT]

5.

Description: The joint answer of Thomas and Elizabeth Spigurnell in the case of George Browne v Elizabeth Browne widow, Thomas Spigurnell gentleman and Elizabeth his wife, after 11 April 1661
Reference: T.N.A., C 6/167/18
Note: This sheet is very creased and contains many corrections. Every effort has been made to transcribe as much as possible.

Endorsed 16 July 1661.

The Joynte and Severall Answeres of Thomas Spigurnell Gentleman And Elizabeth his wife two of the defendants to the Bill of Complaynt of George Browne Complaynant

Penrodoc
All advantages or exceptions to the incertanties insuficiencies and other the imperfeccions of the said Bill of Complaynt to these defendants or either of them now and at all tymes hereafter saved and reserved to as much of the said Bill of Complaynt as anyway concerneth them These defendants or either of them to make answere unto these defendants each answere severally apart and for him and her selfe doe answere and say that they respectively believe it to bee true that the Complaynants father, and the father likewise of this defendant Elizabeth did in his life tyme settle certaine Lands of Inherit<ance> on Elizabeth his <then> wife one other of the defendants in the said Bill of Complaynt named being the Complaynants and this defendant Elizabeth her mother for Joynture who in her life tyme <en>Joyed the same as by the said bill is alleadged But whether hee did this settle on her all his lands of Inheritance or whether those lands were or are of the yearly value of Two hundred pounds or upwards as by the said Bill of Complaynt is pretended these defendants respectively knowe not but doe respectively believe it to be true that the Lands of Inheritance descened unto the Complaynant by his said father either in possecion or revercion or Remainder now upon the death of his said mother the defendant Elizabeth Browne are truly worth ffive thousand pounds But these defendants doe demise that to theire respective knowledge the said Robert Browne was at any tyme in his life tyme seised to him and his heires according to the custome of the mannor of Taunton Deane of any messuage Tenement or any other landes in Mary Stoake as by the said bill of Complaynt is pretended But these defendants doe respectively believe that the said Robert Browne was in his Life tyme seised to him and his Assignes dureing the lives of himselfe and Thomas Browne and George Browne sonnes of John Browne Esquire now deceased of a messuage or Tenement and certaine Lands thereunto belonging being in Mary Stoak aforesaid of the Value of Twenty pounds per annumb or there abouts of the demise of Walter late Bishopp of Winton by Indenture

dated on or about the thirteenth day of May which was in the yeare of our Lord God
one thousand six hundred thirty and three which messuage or tenement as these
defendants doe respectively conceave is the messuage or Tenement by the said Bill of
Complaint specified to be in Mary Stoake and to be parcell of the said Manor of
Taunton Deane And these defendants each answering for himselfe and her selfe as
aforesaid doe further say that they respectively believe it to be true that the said Robert
Browne was in his life tyme and at the tyme of his death interested and estated for the
terme of one thousand years or for some other longtyme of years and yet indureing
and not expired of and in tow Tenements and certaine lands thereunto respectively
belonging called Middleton and lieing within the parish of Huish Champflower in the
said County of Somersett each Tenement being of the Clear yearly value of
seaventeen pounds and not above which two Tenements are as the said defendants
doe respectively conceave the messuage or tenement or lands in the said Bill of
Complaint mencioned to be called Middleton But these defendants doe respective
Denye that said Robert Browne was to these defendants respective knowledge at the
tyme of his said Death possessed of soe much ready money Creditts Plates Bedding
lynen or other goods or household stuffe as were worth three thousand pounds and
upwards as by the said Bill of Complaint is most vainely furnished neither doe the said
defendants certainely know of what value the said personall Estate of the said Robert
Browne is as at the tyme of his death But these defendants doe respectively say that it
is true that the said Robert Browne had issue living onely the Complainant and this
defendant Elizabeth being both at the tyme of his death very young and that the said
Robert Browne intending to make some provision for a reasonable maintenance for
the Complaynants and for this defendant Elizabeth dureing theire Mynorities and that
a Convenient porcion might be raised out of his reall and personall estate not settled
in Joynture on his said wife the said other defendant Elizabeth Browne for this
defendant Elizabeth being not otherwise in any sort provided for according to the
discrecion of his said wife whome hee entrusted in of behalfe and according to the
defects of the Complaint and this defendant Elizabeth the said Robert Browne to that
end leaveing an overawing power in the said other defendant Elizabeth touching the
same did on or about the second day of August which was in the year of our Lord
God one thousand six hundred and thirty seaven made his last Will and Testament in
writein and thereby amongst divers other thinge did expresse and declare that as for
his personall both reall As his Lease at Stoakehill aforesaid for three lives and this
Lease for one thousand years of the land called Middleton as aforesaid and his plate
Lynen Bedding and all house hold stuffe and other goods whatsoever hee did give to
his said wife Elizabeth in trust for this defendant Elizabeth and the Complainant but
that the defendant Elizabeth Browne should have the use of them dureing her
widdowhood estate and alsoe dispose of them for the behoofe and preferment of his
said Children as shee should see fitt and as they should merritt And as for the office of
Clerke and Porter of the castle of Taunton which shee held of the Bishopp of
Winton for his one life and for the life of John Browne one other of the defendants
in the said Bill of Complaint named hee did by his said Last Will give the same in the
same Manor to his said wife dureing her widderhood for the use of his said Children
to maintaine them and proferr them and raise up porcions for them as in her

discreccion should be thought fitt and with the advise of his overseer and that
instantly after his death the said office should be bought of the Bishopp for any other
life to be added to the said Defendant John Brownes in trust for his <wife>[34] and
children And of his said last Will did make his said wife sole executrix and one John
Porter Gentleman his Overseere of the same as by his last Will to which these
defendants doe for more certaintie thereof in all things respectively referr themselves
may more plainly appeare And the said defendants each answering as aforesaid doe
further say that they respectively believe it to be alsoe true that the name of <the>
other defendant John Browne was used only by the said Robert Browne in trust for
the said Robert Browne benefitt and of such to whome hee should assigne the
advantage there of and that they the said Roberte Browne and John Browne were in
the life tyme of the said Robert Browne lawfully seised for the Termes of their
<lives> and for the life of the longest liver of them in trust as aforesaid of and in the
said Office of Clerke and Porter of the said Castle of Taunton as by the said Bill of
Complaint so alleadged but these defendants doe respectively <denye> that to their
respective knowledge the said Office at any tyme was or is of the yearly value of One
hundred and eighty pounds beyond all reprises as by the said Bill of Complaynt is
vainely suggested or above the clear yearly value of One hundred pounds But doe
respectively believe that it is likewise true that the said Robert Browne died Shortly
after the making of his said Will and that after his death the other defendant Elizabeth
Browne in due forme of Lawe proved the said Will and tooke upon her the Burden
not only of the execucion of the same but of the severall trusts in the said Will
mencioned and by the said Robert Browne in her reposed as by the said Bill of
Complaynt is further alleadged And this defendant Thomas for himselfe that it is very
falsely <and Continually> alleadged by the Complainant as by his Bill of Complaint
that hee this defendant was a servant unto Doctor Palmer in the same Bill named and
living then in Taunton aforesaid neare the then habitacion of the said Elizabeth
Browne and this defendants said wife and a person of noe Value or that hee this
defendant by any his Interest in the men of Power in the late distracted tymes or by
any false or insinuateing wayes or courses or by threats or without the knowledge or
consent of the Complainant Married with the Complaynants said Sister for this
defendant sayeth that hee this defendant being very young and under the Tuition and
disposeall of Sir Henry Sambourne Knight this defendants unkle was by him
recommended to the said Doctor Palmer with and Intent to gaine knowledge and
experience in the profescion of Phisick by this defendant findeing that prosecucion to
bee of great difficultie and not to be suddenly attained unto by this defendant soe as
this defendant might conscienciously practice the same hee forthwith declared the
same both unto the said Sir Henry and the said Doctor having a good regard for this
defendant and observeing this defendants inclinacion and abilities to tend an
otherwayes did make this defendant Steward and Surveyor of all the lands belonging
to a Colledge within the Universite of Oxon where of hee was then warden and
afterwards this defendant was imployed by severall other persons of great worth and
authority in matters of the like nature and by his …re and industrie therein made a fair
addicion to a Competent estate left this defendant by his father and thereupon Married
with the daughter <of> one James Godwyne late of Wells in the said County of

Somersett Esquire deceased a person of great worth and reputacion and qualitie by whome this defendant had a considerable estate and by the disbursment of some moneys a farme worth One hundred and ffifty pounds by the yeare after whose death and tenn years after that the said Doctor Palmer made his abode at Taunton then and not before did this defendant become intimately acquainted with the Complaynants said mother and sister dureing which acquaintance an overture or proposall of marridge with this defendant said now wife and the Complaynant said sister <was> made unto this defendant by the Complainants said mother which this defendant persued with noe great eagernesse being diverted and disheartned therein by[35] the great differences that were then and long before depending betweene the Complainant and his said mother and sister accasioned as this defendant hath beene credibly informed by his stoubernesse and greate aversness to be advised by his said mother in matters Inducing to his proferment and good and by his insatiableness and covetousnes of his said mothers and sisters estate But this defendant hopeing that there might bee a better understanding and full reconciliacion betweene them <Hee> this defendant did endeavour the same before his Marridge which the Complaynants said sister and to that end this defendant did advise the Complainants said mother to write unto one Mr Gollopp whose daughter the Complaynant had lately married to give some considerable portion with his said daughter thereby to enable the Complainant said mother to settle on the Complaynant some part of the estate of the said Robert Browne and <to> raise a Competent porcion for the Complaynants said Sister with in the Intencion of her husbands said Will But the said Mr Gollopp utterly refused to give any porcion with the said daughter unles the defendant Elizabeth Browne would <seise> upon and assure unto the Complainant all the said reall <and personall> estate given unto her on the Trust aforesaid and the said Mr Gollopp refused likewise <then> to give any greatter porcion then ffoure hundred pounds which the Complaynants said mother did conceave as shee did declare unto this defendant to bee noe competent porcion for her said daughter the quantitie of her porcion being left by the Complainants fathers Will to the discrecion of the Complainants said mother especially since the Complainants said sister had by her evidence meritted much and on the Contrary the Complainant had merrited from his said mother very little for the reasons aforesaid with proposalls of porcion were as this defendant is induced verily to believe most malitiously opposed by the Complainant out of a desire to hinder whatsoever might tend to an assurance of some thing on the Complainants said Sister in pursuance of the true meaning of his fathers said will whereupon the Complainants said mother by the advise of the said John Porter councell learned in the Lawe who upon view and perusall of the severall Writeings then in the Custody of the said John Porter touching the said Intrusted estate and of the last Will of the said Robert Browne did under his hand in writeing declare his opinion what part thereof as hee conceaved might within the intencion of the said Will be settled on this defendant by the Complaynants mother as a porcion in marriage with his said sister which said opinion of counsell being afterwards sent <and> delivered unto this defendant hee this defendants thereupon did acquaint the Complainant with the said Treaty of a Marridge to be had Betweene him this defendant and the Complainants said sister and communicated to him the particulers thereof to which the Complainant gave this answer That hee heard of it and was very glad of it and wished that this defendant were accordingly married unto her saying that hee the thought she would never marry better and used words to that effect inducing the defendant to marridge with the Complaynants sister and this defendant Thomas Spigurnell doth denye that hee did at any tyme design to gaine the whole estate both reall and personall late of the Complaynants said father and the office aforesaid or to deprive the Complaynant of any benifitt or advantage intended into him by his said Fathers Will out of the same by any unworthy false indirect meanes or courses or suggestions or that hee this defendant did at any tyme labour to bring the defendants said mother into an ill opinion of him or suggested unto her that the Complaynant was an Enimye to the then Government or an undutifull sonne or by any unworthy infamous or false aspercions or otherwise caused the Complaynants said mother to withdraw any of her affeccion from him as by the said Bill of complaynt is most falsely suggested but on the contrary hath and ever did endeavoure to his utmost to settle a peace and to compose the manye great differences and discores betwene him the Complaynant and his said mother and sister that were begune and continued long before this defendants relacion to them <to them> And this defendant doth likewise denye that hee prepared or did bring prepared to the Complaynants said mother in her very great Sicknesse when she did not neither could understand the Tenor or design of a Conveyance any writeing whatsoever to be sealed by the Compaynants sayd mother to this defendant or to this defendants now wife or to any other person or persons to the use <of> or ~~for~~ in trust for them the said defendants or either of them as by the said of Complainants further most falsely and scandolously pretended But this defendant sayth that the Complaynant having lands to the Value of Five thousand pounds descended unto him from his faid father and having alsoe obstructed and within him lay most malitiously hindred all other wayes for Raysing a porcion for his said sister the Complaynants said mother did by the consent and approbacion of the said John Porter and advise of counsell and when shee was of a perfect memorie and in a reasonable strength of Body good health and disposeing minde by heer Indenture bearing date on the second day which was in the yeare of our Lord God One thousand six hundred fifty and nine in Consideracion of the Love and affeccion which she then did beare unto unto[36] this defendant who had then lately marryed this other defendant her only daughter and for their better mainteynance and livelyhood in present and for the future and in consideracion of the summe one Thousand and two hundred pounds promised by the Complaynants said mother to this defendant in Marriage with her said daughter did give graunt and demise unto this defendant all the said messuages lands and Tenements respectively lying and being in Huish Chamflower called Middleton and on Stoke hill aforesaid together with the said Office of Clerke and Porter of the said Castle of Taunton To have and to hold the said Tenements and Lands in Huish Chamflower with thappertenances unto this defendant Thomas Spigurnell his executors Administrators and assigned during all the then Remainder of the said Terme of a thousand yeares And to have and to hold the said Lands and Tenements on Stoke hill with their appertenances unto this defendant his heires Administrators and assignes for the Terme of ninetynine yeares of the said Thomas Browne and George Browne or either of them shall soe long Live And to

27

have and to hold the said office of the clerk and porter of the said Castle unto this defendant and his assignes in payment and satisfaccion of and for the said One thousand and two hundred pounds promised as aforesaid And the Complainants said mother did by the said Indenture Warrant the same and this defendants enjoyment thereof accordingly against her selfe and her heires and against all persons whatsoever as by the Last mencioned Indenture <to where this defendant> fore more certeinty thereof in all things doth referr himselfe may more playnely And this defendant further saith that this Indenture was drawne by the advise of the said John Porter and of the Complainants said Mothers counsell and afterwards openly and distinctly read unto her and by her thereupon sealed and delivered and wittingly and deliberately executed and when she was of a perfect and disposeing mind and in performance (as by this defendant by counsell is advised) and not violacion of the Trust in her reposed by the Complainants said father as aforesaid And in regard of the of the Contingenses and great uncertaineties of the said Lands at Stoke hill, the offices being held by the life of an aged person and profitt out of the said Lands called Midleton untill the death of <five>[37] persons yet in being wherefore the said Elizabeth was further pleased by another writeing under her hand and seale in the like manely duely expected to graunt <and> assure her Tenement <at> Sherford in the parrish of Wilton and after her decease the Residue of her goods not before delivered unto and possessed by her daughter this other defendant Giving and graunting unto this defendant full power and authority to nominate lives unto Sir William Portman when hee should bee of age to Graunte confiremth the same as by the said last mencioned deed or writeing and the[38] answer of the said Elizabeth to the former Bill of Complaint of the said George Browne exhibited in the Court of Exchequer may more fully appeare And this defendant doth denye that hee hath possessed himselfe or disposed, of any other part whatsoever of the estate either reall or personall of the said Robert Browne or hath made any Entries on any part of his reall estate or lands not in Joynture or received any the profitts of the same or of the office aforesaid other then such and in such manor as by his said Answer are hereafter set forth and with as this defendant humbly conceaves was lawfully for him to take and receave And although this defendant as hee is advised is not compellable to discover what rents or profitts hee this defendant hath received out of the premisses in regard the same were conveyed into him in consideracion of this marridge aforesad yet for the Complainants satisffaccon therein if hee will receave any hee this defendant further sayth that the said messuages and lands called Middleton were heretofore either by the Complainants said Father or mother or by some other under whom hee or she clayme or had the same demised for a Terme <of yeares> determinable upon sive Lives yet in being under the yearly rent of about tenn shillings whereof this defendant hath not to this day received any penny therof nor looked thereafter the said lands lying at a great distance from this defendants place of aboad and and the yearly sume soe[39] in considerable neither can that or the Remainder of the said Terme of one thousand yeares after the said fives Lives determined to bee thought or esteemed to be only considerable Benefitt unto this defendant the same being upon improved value yearly worth thirty five pounds by the yeare and noe more and touching the said Tenements and lands on Stoake hill the present <estate> therein doth depend upon the Lives of the said Thomas Browne

28

and George Browne and will in few yeares be clearly worth fifteene pounds by the
yeare and noe more out of which this defendant to this day hath not likewise one
penny profitt but the rents and profits thereof have beene and are received and taken
from the defendant by the Complainant although most uniustly and as concerning the
Office although the Complainant by his said Bill of complaynt doth pretend the same
to bee yearly worth One hundred and eighty pounds yet really and in truth was not
worth above One hundred pounds by the yeare any of the profitts whereof this
defendant received <to his owne use> untill about the sixteenth day of March 1659
but the whole profitts thereof before that tyme since the death of the said Robert
Browne have beene imployed for the use of the Complaynants said mother as by an
acknowledgement in writeing under her hand and seale ready to be produced and to
which this defendant for more particuler certainely doth <referr himselfe and> more
playnly appeare And the defendant further sayth that it doth appeare by accompts of
the said John Porter deputie Clerke fo the said Castle that there hath Beene since the
said six month day of March <about> the sume of fiftysix pounds <more Charged>
on the profitts of the said office by the Complaynants said mother <by her occasion
to supply her greate necessityes> soe as in such and really there hath beene nothing
received by this defendant out of the profitts of the said office for his owne use or
Benefitt, and ffor the goods and plate being furthere all of the intrusted estate of the
said Robert Browne as aforesaid of the Value of one hundred <and tenne> pounds
noe more in the posseccion of this defendants wife before marriage and soe bound by
this defendant and deteyned and kept with the approbation of the Complainants
mother all which being duly considered and that the Complaynant hath forcibly gotten
from this defendant the possession of the said lands on Stokehill and doth still
deteyne it from him This defendant can safely <In truth> sweare that hee hath as yet
actually received in portion with his said wife only trouble vexation and defence As in
perticuler hee this defendant hath beene at a Vast charge and expences near three
hundred pound at the request and for the Content of the said Elizabeth mother of the
Complainant in building repaireing furnishing a house at long sutten for their intended
habitation and to discharge Severall Debts due to severall persons from the said
Elizabeth all which this defendant is ready to prove to this honourable court and
further the said Elizabeth with her sister and three more servannts constantly for more
than two full yeares did live at ready charge of this defendant which amounted unto
far more than the profits of the offiice dureing the said tyme More over this
Defendant hath beene necessitated to make chargeable defence to a multitude of
causlesse malitious persecutions in divers and sundry Courts and places where the
Complaynant hath prosecuted this defendant and his wife the only sister to the
Complainant It being the constant unchristian and unnaturall practice of the
Complainant very Grossly to abuse reproach and most basely vilifie his sister and
perposely provoke her to passionate words in her weaknesse and the prosecute her and
this defendant her husband for the same and thereby to give great somes of money
from this defendant upon pretence of Damages by the words when in truth he
suffered not a penny of Damages thereby. And these defendants answering for
himselfe and herself as aforesaid doe respectively <Deny> that the Complainant hath
beene allowed litte or noe portion or maintence out of the said estate of his said

father as by the said Bill of Complaint is most vainly suggested for these defendants do respectively hope sufficiently to prove to this Honourable Court that there hath beene yearly ever since the death of the said Robert Browne allowed expended on or unto the Complainant out of the said intrusted estate by the Complainants said mother the summe of eighty pounds and upwards towards his maintenance and educacion And this defendant Elizabeth doth further say that that the said Complainant was the Chiefe cause of the expence of the moneys and yearly revenew left by her father ffor that the Complaynant hath ever lived a most idle life and exspensive and would never endeavour or undertake any studdy or prosecution but by force violence and threats extort what money hee pleased from his mother and carry himselfe most rebelliously towards her from his youth upwards even as his father by the observation of his ilnature did foresee and with great griefe expresse By which frowardnesse and the unhappy marridg of the Complaynant with the defendants mother in the opinion of her Phisicians by greife brought into that sad disease and sicknesse of which she is nownow dead And dureing that her sickness while this defendant did live with her and attend <her> Did this Complainant violently rush into the house where his mother lay swearing God Damne him hee would stick this defendants like a toad up against the Wall if shee did not depart the house whereupon this defendant for feare of her life did leave her mother and her goods and house at Sherford which the Complaynant yet wrongfully hold in his possession without the least shewing a pretence of Tytle thereunto being indeed before settled on this Defendant and her children before mentioned

Bill cum as res Michaelmas 1660. Longville.

[END OF DOCUMENT]

6.

Description: The answer of John Browne, 24 April 1661
Reference: T.N.A., C 8/191/30
Note: Filed with George Browne's complaint in T.N.A., C 8/191/30, George's
document is dated 14 November 1660, John's is dated 24 April 13 Charles II,
1661.

The severall Answer of John Browne Esquire one of The defendants
To The Bill of Complaint of George Browne Esquire[40]

The said defendant now and att all times hereafter saving unto himselfe all advantages
and exceptions to be taken unto the manifold untruths inperfections and incertenties
of the said complainants bill for answer to as much thereof as doth any way concerne
this defendant to answer unto he saith that he believeth it to be true that Robert
Browne Esquire deceased the complainants father did make his last will and testamant
in sich manner and to such purporte as is contained in the complainants bill and he
farther saith that the said Robert Browne did in his life time puchase from the Bishop
of Winton a grant or pattent of the office of Clerke of the Castle Ville and Lordship
of Taunton in the county of Somersett expressed in the complainants bill for the
severall lives of him the said <Robert> Browne and of him this defendant and of the
fees and profitts to the same office belonging which is now of about the yearly valew
of one hundred and twenty pounds and he doth acknowledge that the name of him
this defendant was made use of by the said Robert Browne onely in trust for the said
Robert and such person or persons as he should direct and he this defendant believeth
that the same Robert Browne did make such disposicon of the said office by his said
will as the complainant in his bill hath expressed and did make such direccions in his
said will for the adding of another life to this defendant in the said office as in the said
bill is conteyned and this defendant farther saith that after the death of the said Robert
Browne his this defendant did make a deputacion unto one John Porter for the
execucion of the said office he the said John Porter being imployed therein by the said
Robert in his life time and particular directions being given by the said Robert Browne
in his said will for the continuance of the said John Porter in the same imployment
and this defendant did likewise give direction unto the said John Porter to pay the
profitts of the said office unto the defendant Elizabeth Browne that for the same
profitts might be imployed according to the intention of the same <same> will but
this defendant doth deny any combination or confederacye with the defendant
Thomas Spigurnell towching his receiving the profitts of the said office neither hath
this defendant made any grant or assignment of the said office to any person or
persons whatsoever except what deputation or deputations he hath made to the said
John Porter who is to receive twenty pound per annum for execution of the said office
which was allowed him by the said Robert Browne in his life time and this defendant

doth deny that he did ever claime a peculiar right or interest in the said office without any trust as the complainant hath wrongfully suggested in his bill neither did this defendant ever give out to his best rememberance that he hath or will grant or assigne the same to the said defendant Thomas Spigurnell but although this defendant hath ben requested to make such assignment yett hath this defendant refused soe to doe and if the said defendant Thomas Spigurnell hath received the profitts of the said office yett was not the same by any order or direction of this defendant he this defendant having appoynted the said John Porter to pay the profitts of the said office to the said defendant Elizabeth Browne as hearein he hath before expressed and this defendant further saith that he believeth that noe farther estate can be bought in the said office without this defendants surrender which he is willing and ready to doe to the intent another life may be added to this defendant for the benefitt of the complainant and the defendant Elizabeth his sister according to the intention of the said will and this defendant acknowledgeth that he hath ben sollicited by the complainant to make surrender of the said office to the use of him the complainant onely which this defendant conceiveing he could not doe without manifest breach of trust refused to doe and <And> this defendant saith that very lately by the consent of the complainant and the defendants he hath appointed the said John Porter to pay the profitts of the said office unto him this defendant to be by him received and disposed of to the uses contained in the said will and this defendant acknowledgeth that he hath ben informed that the defendant Elizabeth Browne hath made some deed of guift or grant of the said office to the defendant Thomas Spigurnell but the same was contrary to the goodliking of this defendant and against his expresse direction and this defendant denyeth that he hath to his knowledge in any thing broaken the trust in him repossed by the said Robert Browne as is untruely charged against him in the said bill but saith that he will endeavour to his utmost to performe the said trust and <without> that that any other matter or thing in the said complanants bill contained materiall or effectuall in the law to be answered unto by this defendant and herein before not particularly answered unto traversed avoyded or denied by this defendant is true to the knowledge of this defendant all which matters and things this defendant is and still will be ready to aver and prove in such manner and forme as this honourable Courte shall award and there for humbly prayeth to be dismissed out of this Honourable Courte with his costs and charges in this behalfe wrongfully susteyned. John Browne[41]

The response to the defendant was made on 24 April 1661 before the commissioners Robert Williams Willia: Coker[42]

[END OF DOCUMENT]

7.

Description: Further answer of Thomas Spigurnell gentleman in the case of George Browne v Elizabeth Browne widow, Thomas Spigurnell gentleman and Elizabeth his wife, 11 May 1661
Reference: T.N.A., C 6/167/18
Note: This is an additional answer to the joint one submitted by Thomas and Elizabeth Spigurnell on 11 April 1661 at C 8/167/18.

16 die July 1661
per sacramentum Georgii[43] *Spigurnell generosis*
W Glascock[44]

And this Defendant Thomas Spigurnell for himselfe doth further say that hee doth denye all or any Combinacon of the Confederacy by the said Bill of Complaint most falsely ……[45] to this chardge or that hee this Defendant or the sayd other Defendant John Browne to this Defendants knowledge have or hath made any graunt or assissment of the Office to any person whatsoever or that the said John Browne to this Defendants like knowledge did at any tyme the trust of the said office as aforesaid or doth or ever did …..[46] to have any peculier right or interest to himselfe in <the same> without any trust whatsoever as by the said Bill of Complaynt is Surmised And if the said John Browne hath at tyme given out that hee either hath or will graunt and assigne the same to this Defendant as by the said Bill of Complaynt is further produced the same is not either will bee as this defendant is advised Contrary to the Trust reposed in him as aforesaid but in pursuance there of and according to the intent of the said Robert Browne And this Defendant saith that hee beleiveth that the personall estate of the said Robert Browne were duly inventoried by which it will and doth appeare of what Value the said personall estate was and this defendant hath been Credibly informed that the Complainants said mother was dureing the late Troubles and since the death of her said Husband plundred of a Considerable parte of the said Estate left unto her by her said husband, and the said defendants each answering severally as aforsaid doe denye that they or either of them have or hath or doe or doth Clayme any other right tytle Interest or Clayme to all or any other part of the Reall or personall estate late of the Complaynants sayd fathers or to the said Office then as aforesaid But this defendant Thomas Spigurnell doth <say> that the above menconed Indenture and demise made by the Complaynants said mother unto this Defendant and bearing date on the second day of May aforesaid was as by her sealed and delivered in the presence of Samuell Whetcombe Thomas Harvey and Jo. Goddard (without that &c any matter or thing that is here in or hereby traversed <or denyed)> all which the said Defendant doe averr and are ready to proove as the Honorable Court shall Award humbly desireing to bee hence dismissed with their reasonale Costs in this Behalfe moste wrongfully susteyned.
This answeare was taken at Mr Christofers house in Taunton <in the County of

Somersett> the xi[th] day of May Anno Domini 1661 uppon the oathes of the said
Thomas Spigurnell and Elizabeth his wife before

   Mr Philip Lissant
   Sam: Whetcombe[47]

[END OF DOCUMENT]

8.

Description: The answer of John Browne in the case of Thomas and Elizabeth Spigurnell v John Browne esquire, 14 June 1662 with amendments 14 February 1662/3

Reference: T.N.A., C 8/192/102

Note: This is slightly unusual in that the date of the amendments is recorded.

[*Endorsed*] After the amendments taken 14 February 1662[/3][48]

The severall answer of John Browne Esquire one of the defendants to the bill of Complaint of Thomas Spigurnell and Elizabeth his wife Complainants

The said defendant now and at all tymes hereafter saveing unto himselfe all advantages and excepcions to be taken unto the untruths incertenties and manifold Imperfections of the said Complainants bill for answer thereunto and as much thereof as doth any way concerne this defendant to answer unto he this defendant sayth that true it is that Robert Browne Esquire deceased father of the Complainant Elizabeth did about the tyme in the Complainants bill mencioned purchase of the the Lord Bishop of Winton the Offices of Clerke of the Castle and Lordship of Taunton in the Complainants bill expressed and likewise of the porter of the said Castle for the terme of the lives of him the said Robert Browne and of this defendant and the survivor of them which purchase was made with the proper money of him the said Robert Browne and in trust for him the said Robert his executors and Administrators And he this defendant farther sayth that he beleiveth it to be truse that the said Robert Browne by his last will and testament in writing did make such limitacion and appoyntment of the said office with directions for the purchasing of another life therein as the Complainant in his bill hath expreseed And this defendant sayth that he was not privy to the traty of Mariage that was betweene the Complainants nor to what agreement was made betweene the Complainant Thomas and Elizabeth Browne widdow deceased the relict and Executrix of the said Robert Browne but sayth that in persuance of the Trust in him this defendant reposed by the said Robert Browne and according to the intencion of the said Robert Browne expressed in his last will and testament he this defendant did after the decease of the said Robert graunt a deputacion of the said office unto one John Porter overseer named in the said will who did accompt to this defendant for what profitts he received of the said office But this defendant Received noe parte thereof but the profitts thereof were by this defendant ordered to be paid to the said Elizabeth Browne the executrix who accordingly received the same Save that by the accompt of the said John Porter it doth appeare that he paid unto the Complainant Thomas Spigurnell the summe of threehundred ffifty and three pownds out of the profitts of the said office by the direction of the said Elizabeth the executrix And this defendant believeth that there was such bill Exhibited in the Courte of Exchequer by the defendant George Browne and such answer thereto made as the Complainant in his bill hath expressed And he farther sayth that there was a bill <exhibited> in this Honourable Courte against him this defendant and Elizabeth Browne the executrix by the other defendant George Browne as the Complainant in his bill hath expressed to which bill this defendant did answer and conceiveth that the said Elizabeth the executrix did likewise answer thereunto and that he this defendant had Copies if her said Answers to which answers being on Record this defendant referreth himselfe And this defendant farther sayth that after the death of the said Elizabeth the executrix the defendant George Browne having <had> some treaty with the late Lord Bishop of Winton for the adding of his owne life after this defendants in the severall offices of Clerke and porter of the said Castle as he pretended repaired to this defendant and acquainted him therewith And uppon his the said defendant George Browne his promise to let this defendants life continue in the said offices according to the will of the said Robert Browne and to ad onely his owne life in the said Graunts which were thereof to be taken he this defendant did deliver to the said ~~Robert~~ <George> Browne the patents of both then said offices that uppon Surrender of thise patents he might take new Graunts there of but he the said ~~Robert~~ <George> Browne finding that the delivery upp of the said patents was noe avoydance of the former graunts without a Surrender made by this defendant one John Gollop gentleman brother in law of the said defendant George Browne repaired to this defendant and acquainted him this defendant that he the said Gollop had received from the said George Browne a letter wherein he desired him to repaire to this defendant to procure him to selae a writing which the said Gollop then brought with him and produced to this defendant being an instrument whereby the Graunt of the said offices made to him this defendant by the said patents was to be Surrendred up into the hands of the then present Lord Bishop of Winton And this defendant uppon the assurance of the said John Gollop that it was the intencion of the said George Browne to take the new graunt of the said offices to him this defendant and the said Defendant George Browne he this defendant hopeing that the same would have ben accordingly performed did Seale such writing or instrument of Surrender But this defendant is Since informed that the said defendant George Browne hath taken new patents or graunts of the said offices to himselfe and to the said John Gollop for their lives contrary to the intencion of the said Robert Browne menconed in his will and the promise and Agreement of him the said George Browne And this defendant doth deny that he hath confederated or combined with the defendant George Browne to defraud and deceive the said Complainant Thomas Spigurnell of any appoyntment made by the said Elizabeth the executrix of the monies to be raised for the Complainant Elizabeths porcion out of the profitts of the said office of Clerke of the said Castle and Lordshipp or of any parte of the said monie And without that any matter or thing in the said Complainants bill materiall or effectuall in the law to be answered unto traversed avoyded or denied by this defendant and herein before not sufficiently answered unto traversed avoyded or denied is true to the knowledge of this defendant All which matters and things this defendant is and still will be ready to aver and proove in wuch manner and forme as this Honourable Courte shall award and therefore humbly prayeth to be dismissed out of the same with his Costs and

charges in this behalfe susteyned &c.
[*signed*] John Browne[49]

This response was taken at Dorchester in the county of Dorset on 14 June in the 14th
year of the reign of Charles king of England Scotland France and Ireland *fidei defensor*
held under a commission before the commissioners

    Joseph Derbie
    John Bartlett

[*Endorsed*] *28 die Octobris 1662*
promanus Josephi Derby generosis

[END OF THE DOCUMENT]

9.

Description: The complaint of Thomas Spigurnell in the case of Thomas
Spigurnell v George Browne, 14 February 1662/3
Reference: T.N.A., C 10/78/62
Note: This action is Spigurnell's attempt to recover a debt of £31 from George
Browne. George Browne's reply of 25 May 1663 is in T.N.A., C 10/78/62 and
transcribed as number **11** in this volume.

Hillary 17 Charles the Second S:3:
14 February 1662 Wilkinson
To the Right Honourable Edward Earle of Clarendon Lord Chancellor of England
Complayning shoeweth unto your Lordshipp your Orator Thomas Spigurnell of Long
Sutton in the County of Somersett gentleman That Elizabeth Browne Late of Wilton
in the County of Somersett deceased being the executrix of Robert Browne her
husband and entrusted with the disposeall of some part of his estate by his Last will
and Testament as is hereafter expressed in these words viz As for my personall estate
both reall as my lease att Stokehill for three Lives with the Coppiehold of Taunton
Deane held sometimes in the possession of one Collins and my lease for a thousand
years of the land Called Middleton in the parish of Huish Champfflower, and
personall Chattells as my plate Linnen bedding and all householdstuffe and other
goods whatsoever I give to my wife Mrs Elizabeth Browne in trust for my Children
and my meaning is that she shall have the use of them for her widdowes estate and
also dispose of them for the behoofe and preferment of her Children as she shall see
fit and as they merit And though I am very confident of the entire Love and affection
that my said wife beareth to her Children and that she will doe them all the good She
can yet my will and meaning is that if my said wife should marrie againe that then she
shall relinquish all her right to my goods and Chattells aforesaid and content her with
her Joynture and such goods onely as are necessarie for her person according to her
ranke And that she shall make them <over to> Overseers hereafter to be named or his
assigns to an four the use of my Children to be distributed to them as he or thay shall
in their discretion thinke fitt requiering him her or them to deale faithfully with them
and for the office of Clerke and Porter of the Castle of Taunton which I hold under
the Bishopp of Winton and for my one life and the life of my Cosen John Browne I
give the same in the same manor to my wife dureing her widdowhood to the use of
my Children to maintaine them and preferre them and raise portions for them as in
her discretion shall be thought fitt and with the advice of my Overseeres and my will
is that instantly after my death the said office shall be bought of the Bishopp for
another life to be added to my Cosen John Browne in trust for my wife and Children
and the said Robert and Elizabeth haveing issue onely George Browne and Elizabeth
nowe the Wife of your orator she the said Elizabeth Browne the mother in pursuance
of the said will and directions of her said husband did assigne the office of porter and
Clerke of the Castle of Taunton and Lordshipp thereof held by Pattents from the

Lord Bishopp of Winton and as alsoe some leasehold Lands at Stokehill and Huish Champfflower to your Orator in recumpence of a marriage Portion with the said Elizabeth <her daughter> there being freehold Lands and other estates before settled uppon the said George her sonne, And your orator further sheweth That although the said Elizabeth the mother had a faire estate in Joynture moreover and besides the said offices and Leasehold Lands yet by the reason of the Late unhappie warrs her longe sicknesse and some unnaturall deportment of her said sonne shee the said Elizabeth was reduced to poverty and was constreyned to borrow and take up money from your orator and severall other persons and in particuler from John Porter the then agent or deputy Clerke in the said office <out> of the profitts thereof but the said John Porter understanding and well knowing that the revenewes of the said office were to bee accounted for and paid to your orator hee the said John Porter refused to supply the said Elizabeth Browne any further without order from your orator who finding her necessityes increasing and other supplyes fayleing your orator <in tender consideration of her distress> directed the said John Porter to supply her the said Elizabeth as her necessityes or occations should require But the said John Porter refused soe to do unlesse your Orator should allow of what the said Porter had before payd the said Elizabeth Browne upon his owne motions and without the privity or direction of your Orator which was one and thirty pounds and furthermore give caution in the case the said Elizabeth should dye and not leave an estate wherewithall to pay they said thirty one pounds as by the said writeing herein incerted doth more att Large appeare whereupon your Orator in tender compassion and respects unto the said Elizabeth Browne (her estate being detayned from her by the said George Browne her sonne and not able to recover it being bedridden and greveously oppressed with a Palsey) to give incouragement to the said John Porter to give a further supply unto the said Elizabeth for the future as her necessityes should require your Orator was contented to signe a paper to this effect viz Whereas John Porter gentleman deputy Clerke of the Castle of Taunton hath disbursed Laid out and paid out of the profitts of the office of the Clerkeshipp of the Castle aforesaid to the use and by the order of Elizabeth Browne Widowe my mother in Law the sume of thirty pounds of lawfull money of England since the profitts of the said office were conveyed and graunted unto me Thomas Spigurnell of Taunton in the County of Somersett gentlemen by they said Elizabeth Browne in consideration of my marriage with Elizabeth her daughter which said sume of thirty one pounds the said John Porter layd out to supply the present necessity of the said Elizabeth Browne who is to repay the said thirty one pounds unto the said John Porter being due unto him upon his accompt I the said Thomas Spigurnell doe hereby declare my allowance thereof and do alsoe <heerby> acquitt and discharge the said John Porter his Executors and Administrators of and from all demands of the set thirty one pounds by me my Executors and administrators and whereas the said John Porter att my request is contented to expect and receive the said thirty one pounds from the said Elizabeth Browne if it may be received from her I doe hereby covenant promise and agree for me mine executors and Administrators to and with the said John Porter his Executors and administrators to recover the said thirty one pounds from the said Elizabeth Browne her executors or Administrators in some short time and if the same cannot be recovered in law or equity from the said Elizabeth Browne hair executors or Administrators Then I doe hereby oblige my selfe my Executors and Administrators in threescore pounds of lawfull money of England for the true payment of thirty and one pounds unto the said John Porter his Executors Administrators or assignes with interest for soe longe time as the same shall be forborne and unpaid in witnesse whereof I have here unto sett my hand and seale the fifth day of October In the yeare of our Lord God one thousand six hundred and sixtye But the said Elizabeth Browne suddenly after dyed soe that the said John Porter never after the said writeing was made (as your orator believes) payd anymore money to the said Elizabeth Browne and the said Porter since the subscription of the said paper sent to your Orator for to take it up either because he had sufficient in his hands to give himselfe satisfaction for the said thirty one pounds or else because there was noe danger of a further Losse and not regarding this thirty one pounds being lent to a person to whom he had a great respect <and> under whom he had beene imployed in the said office many yeares to his great Creditt and advantage And your Orator further sheweth that the said John Porter made his will and thereby appointed one Robert Procter of Taunton in the County of Somersett merchant <and [*blank*] Procter> his executors and dyed haveing in his Custody at the time of his death severall summes of money of a considerable value accomptable to your Orator and besides severall Pattents deeds Leases and other conveyances belonging to the estate of the said Elizabeth Browne settled on your Orator upon consideration of marriage with her daughter as aforesaid And your Orator further sheweth that the said Robert Proctor <and [*blank*] Procter> executors of the said John Porter conbineing with the said George Browne and minding to make a prey upon your Orator have disposed of the profitts of the said office amongst them selves and delivered up the Pattents Leases conveyances and other writeings unto the said George Browne by meanes whereof your Orator is not onely disappoynted of his expectation of his intended office in Leiu of his marriage portion but likewise made subject and left lyable to the payment of the said thirty one pounds, And your orator further sheweth that the said George Browne at the death of the said Elizabeth possessed him selfe both of the reall and personal estate of the said Elizabeth Browne worth above five thousand poundes where of your Orator hath as yet no parte or share wherefore your Orator humbly Conceaves the said George Browne ought in right and equity to discharge the said debt of thirty and one pounds being lent at severall times to preserve his one mother from perishing yet althought there be scarce any other debt due from her to any other person the said George Browne doth incite and stirr up the said executors of the said John Porter to sue your Orator at Common Lawe one the said paper for the said one and thirty pounds All which Practizes are very mutch contrary to all equity and good conscience In tender consideration whereof and for that your Orator hath noe remedy <by> the Common Law of this nation but is properly and onely releaveable before your Lordshipp in this Honorable Court of Equity And to the End that the said Confederates may sett forth what money they or either of them have received out of the profits of the said office since the date of the said writeing being the fifth of October one thousand six hundred sixtie and how the same is paid or disposed of as alsoe what deeds leases Pattents or conveyances or writeings concerneing the estate aforemencioned came to their or either of their hands and that the said George

40

Browne may by the decree of this Honourable Court make payment of the said thirty one pounds and your orator discharged from the same and further relieved herein according to equity and good conscience may it please your Lordshipp to graunt unto your Orator his Majestyes gratious writt of subpena out of this Honourable Court of Chancery to the said George Browne and the executors of the said John Porter <said Robert Procter and [*blank*] Procter> commanding them thereby at a certayne day and under a certayne payne therein to be limited personally to be and appeare before your Lordshipp in the honourable Court of Chancery then and there to answere all and singuler the promises and further to stand to and abide such further and other order and directions there in as to your Lordshipp in your wisdome shall seeme meete convenient and agreeable to equity and good conscience.
[*signed*] John Farwell

Before Aldred Seaman, John Sowthey and Robert Leigh

[END OF DOCUMENT]

10.

Description: The depositions taken at Taunton in the case of Browne v
Spigurnell, 31 March 1663
Reference: T.N.A., C 22/767/33
Note: This is the longest and most detailed document in this dispute.

31 March 1663 Browne v Spigurnell

[*m.1r*[50]] **Interrogatories** to <be> minstred unto wittnesses to bee produced on the
parte and behalfe of George Browne Complainant against Thomas Spigurnell and
Elizabeth his wife defendants

1. **Imprimis** doe you knowe the parties Complainant and defendents or any or either
and which of them? how longe have you knowne them?
2. **Item** did you knowe Robert Browne Esquire and Elizabeth his wife deceased late
father and mother of the Complainant and of the defendant Elizabeth? how longe did
you knowe them? how longe since did they respectively dye?
3. **Item** are the notes or writings now shewen unto you or any or either and which of
them, or is the note or writinge now shewen you true coppyes, or a true coppy, of
what they or it purport to bee coppyes or a coppy? when, and wherewith, did you
examine the same?
4. **Item** whether or noe did you knowe the defendant Thomas Spigurnell when he
came first to live as a servant in Taunton unto one Mr John Palmer? or whiles hee
lived with him in Taunton before the yeare one Thousand six hundred ffourty and
foure? whether or noe was hee then a very meane person and did hee serve the said
Mr Palmer with Condicion of a Groome, and usually dresse saddle water and
otherwise order the horses of the saide Mr Palmer, and cleanse his stable? expresse the
truth of your knowledge with all circumstances?
5. **Item** whether or noe was the saide Mr Palmer chosen to serve as a Burgesse in
parliament for the Towne of Taunton in the yeare 1640? Whether was the said
defendant Thomas Spigurnell at that tyme a servant to the saide Mr Palmer and for his
forwardnesse and activity against the late Kinge Charles the first, preferred to be a
surveyor of lands directed by that parliament to bee solde? whether or noe did the
saide defendant Thomas Spigurnell act as such a Surveyor? was he active in that
service and afterwards a very busie person in intermedlinge with sequestred
parsonages and tythes? and thereby gott monyes, putt himselfe unto a good habitt and
had a good esteeme from those ingaged against the saide late Kinge, and his Majestie
that now is? expresse what you knowe beleive or have heard with all circumstances ?
6. **Item** whether or noe was the saide defendant Thomas Spigurnell after his
intermarriage with the other defendant a greate and earnest purchaser of lands
appointed by the late usurped powers to bee solde for the Loyaltie of those that
owned them? and in particular of the lands late of Sir John Stawell deceased? to what

yearely value did the Lands hee soe bought amount? expresse what you knowe beleive or have heard with all circumstances?

7. **Item** whether or noe did the saide defendant Thomas Spigurnell upon the Accompt of his purchasinge the lands mencioned in the former Interrogatorie, and of the interest hee had in those who late usurped the Royall power, and of his beinge reputed one much concerned in that party, about the tyme of his marriage with the other defendant assume much state, and looke very high, as if hee had bene indeed a person of an estate and quality? whether or noe was hee by many of that party soe reputed? whether did hee on that Accompt make his addresse unto and afterwards marry the other defendant? expresse what you knowe beleive or have heard with all circumstances?

8. **Item** to what value in gold, ready moneys, plate, clothes, linen, woollen, utensells of household, household stuffe, or other personal or Testamentary estate, did the saide Robert Browne dye possessed? what were the particular natures quantityes qualityes and full values of the same respectively? whether did the same uppon or after his death come to the hands use custody or possession of the saide Elizabeth Browne his relict and executrix? was she in the late wars plundered or dispoyled of the same, or of any considerable, and what parte thereof, were the said gold ready moneys plate Jewells and the principall and best parte of the residue of the said clothes and goods in her custody, or at her commande, untill and after the defendants marriage? expresse what you knowe beleive or have heard with all circumstances?

9. **Item** whether was the said Elizabeth Browne att the tyme of the death of her late husband Mr Robert Browne, and until she fell sicke of the Palsie whereof she afterwards dyed, a discreete, prudent, and a provident woman, and soe esteemed by those who very well knew her? or was she a weake foolish and improvident person? did she in this tyme live thriftily, and within the compasse of her owne joynture, or beyond it? expresse what you knowe beleive or have heard, and what family she usually kept?

10. **Item** what somme or sommes of money in particular belonginge to the saide Mr Robert Browne at his death, or to the saide Elizabeth Browne his Relict at any tyme in her life tyme were there in the Exchequer of the Castle of Taunton, or in the hands of John Porter deceased Deputy Clerke of the saide Castle, in his life tyme, to bee desposed of at interest for his or her use or benefit, or was or were there rent out at interest by the saide John Porter, or any other and who, and to whome, for his or her use? to whome was the same soe lent? for what tyme? to whome hath the same or any and what parte or parts thereof, and when bene since delivered out? whether was the same intended by the saide Elizabeth Browne for the marriage porcion of the defendant Elizabeth? what is now become of the saide monyes? Declare what you knowe beleive or have heard or by any acquittances Accompts receipts surrenders discharges or other papers or writings remayninge in the saide Exchequer or in the hands of the saide Mr Porter at his death, or elsewhere, have discovered, found, or can declare, touchinge any the matters in this Interrogatorie.

11. **Item** whether or noe had you any intencion or thoughts of beinge a suitor for marriage to the defendant Elizabeth before her intermarriage with the other defendant? whether did you upon any such Accompt, or otherwise, at any tyme and

when repayre to Mr John Porter then Deputy Clerke of the Castle of Taunton or any other and who, and inquire of him or them what porcion the defendant Elizabeth had or was like to have? what answere did the said Mr Porter or such other of whome you soe inquired give you touching the same? how much ready money did hee or they affirme or assure you that Mrs Elizabeth Browne her mother had then for her towards her porcion? where or in whose hands did hee or they affirme that the same then was? expresse the particulars and what you knowe beleive or have heard touching the premises.

12. **Item** how longe before the death of the saide Elizabeth Browne, and about what certaine tyme did she fall sicke of the palsie whereof she afterwards dyed? how longe after that disease seised on her was she soe able to manage and governe her owne Joynture, and the eastate left to her by her husband in trust for her children, as she was before that disease seized on her? about what certaine tyme was she by reason of that disease soe disabled in her person speech parts and understandinge that she could not, or did not, in her owne person manage or governe the same? whether did the defendants at that tyme live with her? did they or either and which of them thereuppon take uppon them him or her to manage order and governe both the saide Elizabeth Browne, and her ioynture, and the saide estate left to her by her husbands will in trust for his children? Did the defendants or either and which of them in order thereunto take into theire keepinge her keyes and personall estate in gold, monyes, plate, securityes for monyes, clothes, and goods and Chattles in and about her house, and receive the Rents and profitts of her ioynture and the estate left to her by her husband for her childrens use and dispose of the same as hee shee or they please and thought fitt? whether was the saide Elizabeth Browne in such her weaknesse free to direct or doe, and did she direct and doe what she pleased with and in and about her said Jointure, and the saide estate soe left unto her by her husbands will for his childrens use? or had the defendants or either and which of them an awinge power over her and did she soe much feare or was she <soe> subordinate to them or either and which of them, that she durst[51] doe noe more or other then what they hee or she pleased? whether did the defendants or either and which of them in such the weaknesse of the saide Mrs Browne, tender to her or obtrude upon her any deeds or writings to bee sealed or signed by her? did she uppon such tender or obtrudinge of the same, ever question or consider of, or was by advice satisfyed touchinge the same, or did she forthwith without any dispute or consideracion signe seale and deliver what was so obtruded on her? what words or speeches have you at any tyme and how often heard the saide Mrs Browne use touchinge such writings as the defendants or either of them soe gott her to signe seale or deliver, or touchinge the defendants themselves or either of them for pressinge or obtrudinge writings on her in such manner? whether was the said Mrs Browne in her judgement and affeccion for the late Kinge and the Royall interest? and of what Judgment was the defendant Thomas Spigurnell and how did he act?

13. **Item** whether did the defendants or one of them or some other and who by the order of them or either of them, or for theire or either of theire use, under colour or by pretence of some deeds and writings, or some deed or writinge, signed or sealed or delivered or supposed to bee signed sealed or delivered by the said Mrs Browne in her

sicknesse, and very greate weaknesse, and how longe before her death, or otherwise, seize uppon or possesse themselves him or herselfe, or otherwise dispose of all or the greatest best and most considerable parte or of some and how much of the gold, silver, ready monyes, plate, Jewells, Rings, clothes, goods, housholdstuffe, Cou…, corne, Cattle, and reall and personall eastate of the saide Mrs Browne and the reall and personall estate and offices left to her by her late husband as aforesaide for his childrens use? and receive the profitts thereof, and dispose of the same, as hee shee or they thought fitt, and convey away what parte thereof was to bee conveyed away from the saide Mrs Browne, and out of her house, and from the places where, the same then were, to places unknowne? expresse the particular natures, qualityes, quantityes and full worth and values of the same respectively? when the saide Mrs Browne had knowledge and notice given her of the defendants carryinge and conveyinge away of the same, what did she expresse say or declare touchinge it? or concerninge the defendants or either of them for soe doeinge? Declare what you knowe beleive or have heard with all circumstances?

14. **Item** what somme or sommes of money or other profitts of all or any the offices messuages Lands Tenements or hereditaments late of Robert Browne Esquire desceased late father of the Complainant, and of the said defendant Elizabeth, or of Elizabeth Browne theire late mother deceased, did the defendants or either of them or any other person or persons of the order of them or of either of them, or to or for the use of them or either of them, in the life tyme of the saide Elizabeth Browne deceased, or since take receive or dispose of? expresse the particulars and what you knowe beleive or have heard touchinge the same with all circumstances?

15. **Item** how longe have you knowne the defendant Thomas Spigurnell, by all the tyme of your knowledge of him hath hee bene or is hee reputed a person of honesty and inte….[52] and one that made or maketh conscience of what hee did doth and speaketh? if nay, under what other Character or reputacion hath the saide defendant Thomas Spigurnell passed and doth hee passe? and how hath hee bene and is hee reputed?

16. **Item** are you and how longe have you bene well acquaynted with the handwritinge of the defendants or of either and which of them? are the writings or any or either of the writings, now shewen unto you and which of them or is the writinge now shewen unto you or the names of the saide defendants or the name of either and of which of them? expresse what you knowe or, beleive with the reasons of your soe knowinge or beleivinge .

17. **Item** did you see the sealinge and delivery of the deed or writing now shewen unto you? by whome was the same sealed and delivered? is your name or marke subscribed thereto or indorsed theron your owne handwritinge?

18. **Item** for what estate was the saide Robert Browne deceased in his life tyme and at his death seized or possessed of a certaine messuage and Tenement with Thappurtenances att Stokehill within the parish of Stoke Mary in the County of Somersett, did hee enioy the same? have you seene or perused the conveyance thereof made by a late Bishopp of Winchester unto the saide Robert Browne, by virtue of which hee claymed and enioyed it? whether was it a ffreehold estate in the said Robert Browne for lives, or an estate for yeares, and by the said conveyance granted or

mencioned to bee granted To hold to him and his heires and assignes, or to him and his assignes, or how else? is the Complainant the only sonne and next heire of the said Robert Browne? was the said conveyance a good conveyance in the law or not? expresse what you know beleive or have heard with the reasons of your beleife.

19. **Item** what and how much value doe you knowe or beleive, or have you heard by the acknowledgment or expresseions of the said Mrs Browne deceased in her life tyme, or of the defendants or either of them or of any other and of whome that the saide defendants or either of them or any other person or persons to or for his her or there ...[53] <his her or the> direccion have had or received out of the reall and personall estate of the said Robert Browne and Elizabeth Browne ...[54] his marriage with the defendant Elizabeth, as or in his or[55] her marriage porcion or by meanes or reason of the saide inter marriage?

20. **Item** whether or noe did the said Elizabeth Browne deceased keepe and mayntayne the defendant Elizabeth accordinge to her degree and quality from the tyme of the death of the said Robert Browne untill her intermarriage with the other defendant? declare what you knowe beleive or have heard and at what extraordinary costs and charges the said Elizabeth Browne was att, in the educacion or marriage of the defendant Elizabeth if she were at any?

21. **Item** whether or noe did the saide Elizabeth Browne in her life tyme and after the intermarriage of the saide defendants for a longe tyme till little before her death, manifest or declare such kindnesse or respect to the saide Complainant, or take such care of him, as she did manifest unto and take of him before that marriage had, and since the happy restauracion of his Majestie that now is? if nay, whether was the cause thereof because the defendant Thomas Spigurnell was against the Kinge, and Complainant for the Kinge, and she durst not or thought it not safe for her to shew him kindnesse <in those times> or what else was the cause thereof? how did she manifest her love and respect to the saide Complainant uppon the happy restauracion of the Kings Majestie that now is? whether did shee then receive the saide Complainant and his family into her house and manifest her utter dislike and disaffeccion to the defendant Thomas Spigurnell, and the courses hee had taken? expresse what you knowe or beleive or have at any tyme heard the saide Elizabeth Browne in her life tyme expresse, say, or declare touchinge the same, or touchinge the condicion and hazard she lived in for feare of the saide Thomas Spigurnell.

[*m.1v*] 22. **Item** whether or noe did the defendants or either of them soe much prevayle with the saide Mrs Browne in her saide weaknesse, that she at the request of the defendants or one of them did by morgages or a morgage of any and what parts or parte of her estate, secure the payment of monyes borrowed and received by the defendants or one of them, or disposed of by them or for theire owne use, uppon the faithfull promisses of the defendants or one of them to pay the same at the tymes lymited in the same morgages or morgage for payment thereof? how much monyes did the saide Mrs Browne soe devize? to whome? what promise or promises did the defendants or either of them make to the saide Mrs Browne touchinge the payment thereof by them or either of them? was the same accordingly paide by the defendants or either of them or not? Did the lands soe morgaged for the same remayne charged with the saide monyes and the interest thereof at the tyme of the death of the saide

Elizabeth Browne? to whome are the saide lands now come or conveyed? expresse what you knowe beleive or have heard?

23. **Item** whether or noe did the defendant Thomas Spigurnell after his intermarriage with his now wife, labour to sett and keepe greate distance and differencies betweene the said Elizabeth Browne and the said Complainant? reproach the saide Complainant for beinge a Cavilier and labour to insinuate to the saide Elizabeth Browne in her weakenesse, that it was very perillous for her to shew any kindnesse to him, hee beinge an enemy to the state or to some such effect? and did the saide Mrs Browne in those tyme seeme to neglect and shew little or noe favour or Countenance to the said Complainant? Declare what you knowe beleive or have heard?

24. **Item** what was the true and full yearely value ultra reprizes comminibus Annis of the messuages lands Tenements hereditaments and offices respectively which uppon the death of the saide Robert Browne were enioyed and the Rents and profitts of the same received by the saide Elizabeth Browne and for some tyme since the defendents intermarriage, by the defendant Thomas Spigurnell?

25. **Item** to how much doth the yearely profitts of the office of Clerke and Porter of the Castle of Taunton yearely amount, comminibus Annis as a medium thereof ultra reprizes, and beside the execucion of the same? what is the same office worth to bee solde for the life of John Browne of Frampton in the county of Dorset Esquire by whose life the same was in the life tyme of the saide Elizabeth Browne held? of what age is hee? expresse what you knowe or beleive?

26. **Item** whether were you at any tyme heretofore and about what tyme, present at and a wittnesse unto the signinge sealinge or delivery of any writing or writings deed or deeds by Elizabeth Browne widdow deceased in her life tyme unto or to the use of the defendents or of either of them or unto or to the use of any other person or persons and who in trust for them or either of them or for theire or either of theire benefitt or advantage? were, or were not such writinge or writings deed or deeds distinctly and plainely reade unto the saide Elizabeth Browne in your presence or were the same by herselfe perused or reade over before they were soe sealed and delivered by her? or were the same signed sealed or delivered by her without any solemne reading or perusinge of the same? whether was it the Common use of the defendents or either of them when they brought writings to her to bee signed sealed or delivered by her to reade over the same distinctly to her, or only to tell her that the same were to such or such a purport or <except>[56] as hee shee or they thought fitt, and soe to gayne her hand or seale to them, and delivery of them? expresse what you knowe beleive or have heard

27. **Item** in what Condicion of health was the saide Elizabeth Browne at the tyme of the signinge or executinge of the writinge or writings deed or deeds mencioned in the former Interrogatories? was she then uppon her sicke bedd very weake or in what other posture and Condicion? was she then by reason of her sicknesse much impaired and decayed in her memory and parts? was she then able well to understand and comprehend the full contents draft and designe [of the said][57] writing or writings deed or deeds if read unto her was she then able to speake or declare herselfe soe playnly and articulately that any but those that were in …[58] conversant with her and did with much attention lay theire eare very nereby could understand what the saide intended or

47

desired was that then done by the defendents or either of them? declare what you knowe beleive or have heard.

28. **Item** whether or noe did the defendent Thomas Spigurnell and the said Complainant since the death of the saide Elizabeth Browne and how long since, by mutuall consent referr all differencies betweene them to the finall end and determinacion of John Browne of Frampton Esquire and enter into bonds of greate penalty to each other to performe what award hee should make touchinge the same? what Relacion had the saide John Browne to the Complainant and to the defendent Elizabeth? did the saide John Browne examine the saide differencies and thereuppon make his award betweene the saide parties touchinge the same? what was the effect and substance of the saide award? what in particular was the saide Complainant thereby ordered or awarded to doe pay or performe to the said Thomas Spigurnell? and what was the saide Thomas Spigurnell by the saide award ordered to doe pay or performe to the saide Complainant? expresse what you knowe beleive or have heard.

29. **Item** in whose hands or custody were the said bonds of award when soe entered into left or deposited? whether did the saide Mr John Browne upon makinge of the saide award deliver or refuse to deliver to the Complainant the bond to him entered into by the defendent Thomas Spigurnell for performance of the saide award?

30. **Item** is the writinge now shewen unto you the Award which the saide John Browne soe made betweene the defendant Thomas Spigurnell and the said Complainant for the finall endinge of all differencies betweene them? is the name of John Browne subscribed to the writinge now shewen to you his owne hand writinge? were you present when hee signed sealed and published the same? did the defendent Thomas Spigurnell and the Complainant upon perusuall of it, respectively declare theire consent, and submitt thereunto? and promise to performe the same?

31. **Item** whether or noe were you present in the Exchequer of the Castle of Taunton uppon the foure and Twentyeth day of June in the yeare one Thousand six hundred sixty and one, with the Complainant and the defendant Thomas Spigurnell? whether or noe did the Complainant att that tyme in your presence tender and pay to the defendant Thomas Spigurnell the somme of Three hundred pounds, which by an Award made by John Browne Esquire between the Complainant and the defendant Thomas Spigurnell, the saide Complainant was att or before that day to pay to the saide defendant <Thomas Spigurnell?> whether did the saide defendant count all or any parte of the saide Three hundred pounds and receive all the saide three hundred pounds into his custody? whether or noe did the saide Complainant Thereuppon demaund or request the saide defendant Thomas Spigurnell to deliver to him the deeds writings and evidencies which by the saide award hee was uppon payment of the saide three hundred pounds to deliver to the saide Complainant? and whether or noe did the Complainant then and there alsoe z . z . z . z .[59] tender to the said defendant Thomas Spigurnell a writinge to bee executed by him whereby hee was to relinquish and release to the Complainant all his clayme and title to the severall estates and offices of Robert Browne Esquire and Elizabeth Browne widdow late ffather and mother of the Complainant and defendant Elizabeth? was the saide writinge then distinctly reade over unto the saide defendant Thomas Spigurnell and in his hearinge? did hee dislike or take away any exepcions to the same, or to any parte thereof?

whether did the defendant Thomas Spigurnell uppon the Complainants saide demaund deliver up unto him the saide deeds writings and evidencies, and seale and deliver the said writinge accordinge to the desire of the saide Complainant, and the tenor and direccions of the saide Award? or did hee absolutely refuse to deliver upp the writings by the saide award directed to bee delivered up unto the saide Complainant by him and to execute the writinge surrendered to him and thereuppon express himselfe that the Complainant might if hee pleased sue him for not performinge the Award or to that effect? whether or noe did the Complainant thereuppon tell the saide defendant in respect hee had not the defendants bond of award to force his performance of the same, that hee should bee unwillinge to suffer him to carry the saide three hundred pounds thence unlesse hee would performe that parte of the saide award which on his parte was to be performed, or to that effect? whether did you or any other and who then and there use any arguments to persuade the saide defendant Thomas Spigurnell for setlinge of peace and quietness betweene the Complainant and him, to performe soe much of the <saide> Award as was on his parte to bee performed? was the saide defendant thereuppon drawne or prevailed with to performe the same? or was hee soe positive in his refusall, that he persisted in it, and went thence without doeinge any thinge in order to it, and left the saide Three hundred pounds in the saide Exchequer? about what houre of the day did the saide defendant Thomas Spigurnell soe depart and leave the saide three hundred pounds behinde him? Did the Complainant thereuppon withdraw himselfe alsoe thence, or continue the remayning parte of the saide day in the saide Exchequer, in readinesse to performe the things by him to bee performed by the saide award? Did the Complainant expresse his readinesse, and was hee in truth ready on his parte to performe the saide award, if the defendant Thomas Spigurnell would performe soe much thereof as was on his parte to bee performed? Declare what you knowe beleive or have heard with all circumstances?

32. **Item** whether was the saide Robert Browne att the tyme of his death interested in Certaine messuages tenements and lands called Middleton lyinge in the parish of Huish Champflower in the County of Somersett for a longe terme of yeares then and yet enduringe? for how many yeares? what is the yearely value of the saide messuages and premisses ultra reprizes, did the saide Elizabeth Browne after his death and in her lifetyme and how longe before her death grante any estate therein? what estate? to whome? for what consideracion? to whome was the mony for which the saide estate therein was soe sold, payde? and how and to what use was it disposed of? expresse what you knowe beleive or have heard, and what estate is now in beinge uppon the premisses?

[*end of membrane signed by the commissioners*] Tho: Dyke, Will: Doble, H Plucknett

[*m.2r*] Interrogatories to bee ministred as witnesses on the parte and behalfe of the suite of George Browne Esquire Complainant.

1) Doe you knowe the Lands att Benfield and Graston, or either of them in the county of Dorset late in the Tenure of Elizabeth Browne the Mother of the Complainant,

and the defendant Elizabeth what Rent did the Lands or either of them yeeld her yearely whiles shee lived enjoyed them, and what Rent doe they yeeld now and to whome is the said Lands descended and the Rent paid or hath been paid ever since her death, speak what you know, have heard, or believeth, and the reason of such your knowledge or beliefe herein.

2) Have you any acquittance from the defendant Thomas Spigurnell for any Rents or profitts of the said Lands att Benfeild, or did you ever pay, or know to bee paid any of the Rents or profitts of the said Lands at Benfeild or Graston unto the hands of the said Thomas Spigurnell, or to his use or direcions were not much of the said Rents paid unto the hands of the said Elizabeth Browne the Mother, and hath you not her receipts and Acqittances for the same, and was it the residue paid unto George Browne the Complainant towards his mayntenance by directions of the said Elizabeth his Mother dureing her life, speake what you know, have heard believeth, and the reason of such your knowledge or beliefe.

3) Was there not a Mannor, either at Benfeild, or Graston of the Estate of Elizabeth Browne; to whome is the same now descended, doth the Complainant George Browne receive the auncient and accustomary Rents thereof, and howlong hath hee received them, and what are they yearely; How many Coppie holders and Lease holders are there in the said Manor weare there not severall Lands and Tenements in the said Mannor att the death of Elizabeth the Complainants Mother which were held onely by one very old life, or two very olde lives, soe that much money might have been made then, or may now bee raysed by the Complainant in graunting farther Estates therein? speake what you know, have heard, or beleiveth, and the reason of such your knowledge or beliefe herein.

4) Was not the Inn called the Bull at Bridport of the Estate of Elizabeth Browne the Complainants Mother; to whome is the same discended since her death; and what is the yearely value of the said Inne; speake what you know, have hard, or beleeve, and the reason and cause of such your knowledge, or beliefe herein.

5) Were not you (or who was a Tenant) to some Lands or Lymekilns in Stoakehill by the graunt of Elizabeth Browne, and were you not, or was the Tenant in Covenant to pay the Rent, thereof to her yett; why did hee or you not pay itt to her; was it not because the Complainant threatned to hurt you or your goods, or the Tenant or his goods, and carry away his, or your Corne, And in regard the said Elizabeth lay sick and weake, and not able to defend you; Howmuch Rent did you pay, or was paid the Complainant for the Rent of those Lands; speake what you know have hard, or beleeve &c.

6) How long since did Robert Browne the father of the Complainant and defendant dye; what ready money was hee possessed of att his death (name the sume) and in whose hands was itt; what Creditts did hee dye possessed of, and wheare; what particuler peices of Plate, and the value of them; What bedding, what Lyning, or other goods and Chattles, household stuffe and the true value of the same, and what in particuler thereof came to the hands or possession of the defendant Thomas; speake what you know, have hard of the same, and the reason of such you knowledge herein.

7) Was not Elizabeth Browne the widdow and Executrix of the said Robert forced to hide, convey away, and disperse; and thereby loose great parte of the said household

stuffe, plate goods and Chattles by reason of the Warrs, dureing which tyme was shee not divers tymes plundred by Souldiers, especially whiles the Seiges were att Taunton; how farr did shee live from the Towne dureing the Warrs, speake what you know, have hard, or beleeve; and the reason of such your knowledge and beleife.

8) Did not the Complainant (some tyme after the Warrs) accompanyd with one John Gollop his Brother in Law, breake open a door of a Roome in the house of the said Elizabeth Browne his Mother att Sherford, Therein enter and did not the said George and John take and carry away divers things that …[60] secured dureing the Warrs, and was not the Complainants Mother very much grieved and troubled there att and greatly offended with the Complainant for his soe doeing; speake what &c.

9) How long after the death of the said Robert Browne, and after the late Warrs and plundering did the defendant Thomas marry with Elizabeth the Complainants Sister, was itt not possible that much of his goods and Chattles might bee lost, sould, and disposed of before that tyme; did not Elizabeth the Mother of the Complainant desire the defendants to live with her, and would shee nott have had them continue with her till death, might shee had her will, x x and did not the Complainant force them out of the house against the consent, and to the greate greife of his Mother; speake &c.

10) Did you knowe what particuler goods, and the value of them that were carryed from the house of Elizabeth Browne att Sherford unto the house of the defendants at Sutton, weare they nott carryed by her Consent then Intending to remove thither and live with the defendants at a farther distance from the Complainants, But afterwards shee being soe weake as not able to remoove, were not the goods brought back againe from Sutton[61] and settled as before att her house att Sherford, soon after the returne of the said goods did not the Complainant force the defendants out of the said house att Sherford, and secure the said goods himselfe, and doth hee ……[62] keepe them in his possession, speake &c.

11) Weare you present att the house of Elizabeth Browne the Mother when the Complainant did enter, and force out his Sister the defendant; did hee not then stand by and view all the defendants owne proper goods shee Carryed forth and secure such other goods as hee pretended did belong to his Mother, And did not the Complainant the next day or some few days after come to the place where the goods of the defendants were lodged, and take annother view of them, ……[63] if there were any parte of his Mothers goods carried away by the defendants; And did not hee the Complainant then confesse that there noe other, but the proper goods of the defendants; speake &c.

12) How long did the defendants after Marryage live with Elizabeth Browne their Mother, att whose charge was the housekeepeing defrayd, dureing that tyme what doe you gues it may cost the defendant to maynteyne the servants, sister, and dependants yearely, for <her> condicion of sicknesse, and many Attendants considered.

13) What manner of life did the Complainant take up dureing his minority, and what yearely charge might it bee to his Mother to maynteyne him; doe you not beleeve shee did expend her whole revenue yearely from the tyme her husband dyed; And moreover runn in order to maynteyne her Children, famely, and poore relacions, And did shee not send goods and household stuffe to the Complainant att and after his Marryage ……[64] bound for moneyes to supply occasions.

51

14) Did not the Complainant George Browne come to you and desire you to testifye that the defendant Thomas was a Groome, and did dresse the horses of Doctor Palmer, and ~~xxxx~~ to encourage you thereunto; did not hee the said Browne tell you one James King had sworne it already; and therefore you might doe it more safely, did you not reply to the said Browne the qualityes, conversacions, and reputacion of the said James King, and the whole truth of the businesse.

15) Was not Doctor Palmer Warden of Alsoules Colledge in Oxford for many yeares until his death, And was not the defendant Thomas, Steward and Surveyor of the Mannors and Lands belonging to the said Colledge for the tyme hee aboade with the said Doctor. And was there ....[65] for Groomes, and Coachmen allowed him att the charge of the said Colledge &c.

16) Was not the Complainants Mother much greived, and became weake and sickly with the conceite and thoughts that the Complainant has Marryed a wife against her consent and brought noe portion to proferr his sister the now defendant, And did shee never complayne thereof to you, or in your hearing, how much shee was troubled to consider how shee might finde out a way to rayse a porcion for her daughter; was not her daughter very ......[66] diligent, and carefull of her in her in her sicknesse and did not the said Elizabeth the Mother often confesse that her said daughter had merrited much love, and that shee resolved to live and dye with her, and continued that desire whiles shee had any life or sence.

17) Wherein doe you know the Complainant did ever any thing that was dutyfull or meritorious towards his Mother, speake the particulers &c.

18) Were you ever directed by Elizabeth Browne the Mother to sell, or did ever sell a Gold chayne, or any parts thereof, which was suppos'd to bee left by Robert Browne her husband, or doe you know who did sell the same, and to whome &c.

19) Doe you know the Customary Lands att Stockehill in the possecion of the Complainant or his Tenants, whats ......[67] value, and who receives the Rents thereof.

20) What Interest doe you know the defendant had in men of power in the late Warrs, was the defendant ever a Souldier under those powers, did hee not some way oppose those powers, was hee not ymprison'd by Desbourrow, did you ever see him Ride in Armes under that power, did not the Complainant ride with sworde and pistalls in those tymes when the Kings Souldiers and adherents were dissoulv'd, And did hee ever take ....[68] either Milletary or Civell under his Majestie since his restoracion.

21) What Estate profitt, or benifitt, hath the defendant Thomas Spigurnell had by the Intermarryage ...[69] is hee not damadged by that match.

22) What other matter or things doe you know, have hard, or can say touching the matters in question of the defendants.

[end of membrane signed by the commissioners] Tho: Dyke, Will: Doble, H Plucknett

[m.2v is blank, m.3r]

Deposicions of Wittnesses taken att Taunton in the County of Somersett the last day of March In the ffifteenth yeare of the Raigne of our soveraigne Lord Charles the second by the grace of god of England Scotland France and Ireland Kinge Defender

of the fayth xc Anno domini 1663 by Thomas Dyke William Doble and Henry
Plucknett gent by vertue of a Commission yssued out of the high Court of Chancery
unto them and unto John Stocker gentleman or any three or two of them directed for
the examinacion of the witnesses in a cause there dependinge betweene George
Browne Esquire Complainant and Thomas Spigurnell and his wife defendants (as
followeth

James Kinge of Taunton Magdalen in the County of Somersett carpenter aged
threescore yeares or there abouts produced on the parte and behalfe of the
Complainant to the ffirst and ffourth Interrogatory and there upon sworne and
examined
1. To the first Interrogatory this deponent saith That he doth well know the parties
Complainant and defendants and hath knowne them all by the space of Twenty yeares
last past or thereabouts
4. To the ffourth Interrogatory this deponent saith That he did well knowe the
defendant Thomas Spigurnell when he first came to live in Taunton in the County of
Somerset as a servant with Mr John Pallmer in the Interrogatory named sithence
deceased and whiles he lived with the said Mr Pallmer as his servant in Taunton
aforesaid which was as this deponent remembreth about Twenty yeares sithence and
this deponent further saith That the said defendant Thomas Spigurnell was at that
tyme in this deponents accompte but a very meane person and this deponent alsoe
saith That he was and is induced soe to judge for that he this deponent was before and
untill that tyme a servant in the nature of a Groome unto the said Mr Pallmer unto
whome the said defendant Thomas Spigurnell did succeed in that service and
employment and did usually dresse saddle water and otherwise order the horses of the
said Mr Pallmer and cleanse his Stable but for how longe tyme the said defendant
Thomas Spigurnell soe lived as a Groome with the said Mr Pallmer this deponent now
remembreth not And more he saith he cannott depose.

Henry Tymewell of Taunton Magdalen in the County of Somersett Vintner aged
ffortie ffive yeares or there abouts produced on the parts and behalfe of the
Complainant to the ffifth and sixth Interrogatoryes and thereuppon sworne and
examined.
5. To the ffith Interogatorie this deponent saith that Mr John Palmer in the
Interrogatorie named was chosen a Burgesse to serve in the Parliament for the Towne
of Taunton in the County of Somersett in or about the yeare of our Lord one
thousand six hundred and ffortie <and foure> and this deponent saith that he
beleeveth the defendant Thomas Spigurnell lived at that tyme as a servant with the said
Mr Palmer And this deponent saith That the said Thomas Spigurnell was imployed
and did acte <as a> Surveyer of Lands directed to be sould by that Parliament but
whether he was proferred to that inployment for his activitie against the late Kinge this
deponent knoweth not and this deponent saith he hath heard that the said defendant
Thomas Spigurnell did afterwards intermeddle with sequestrated Parsonages and
Tythes and beleeveth that the said defendant thereby and by actinge as a Surveyer as
aforesaid hath raysed a greate part of his estate and saith that the said Thomas

Spigurnell kept himselfe in a good habbitt and was at that tyme well esteemed of by those who werre engaged against the said late Kinge And more to this Interrogatory he deposeth not.

6. To the sixth Interrogatorye this deponent saith That the said defendant Thomas Spigurnell did heretofore Purchase of this deponent and divers others persons some parte of the Lands of Sir John Stawell deceased appoynted to be sold by the late usurped powers but of what yearly value the Lands by him soe bought were this deponent knoweth not and more to this Interrogatory he deposeth not.

Osemond Spreete of Taunton in the County of Somersett Butcher Aged ffitie yeares or thereabouts produced on the parte and behalf of the Complainant to the ffourth ffith sixth and seaventh Interrogatoryes and thereupon sworne and examined.

4. To the ffourth Interrogatory this deponent saith That he did knowe the defendant Thomas Spigurnell when he came first to live in Taunton as a servant with Mr John Palmer in the Interrogatory named but how longe since it was this deponent knoweth not And this deponent saith that in his repute or apprehension the said Thomas Spigurnell was a meane person when he came first to serve the said Mr Palmer and saith that the said Thomas Spigurnell did usually ride his said masters Horses to water and more to this Interrogatory this deponent deposeth not.

[5.] To the ffifth Interrogatory this deponent saith That Mr Palmer in the Interr named was chosen to serve as a Burgesse in Parliament for the Towne of Taunton in or about the yeare One thousand six hundred and ffortie Att which tyme the said Thomas Spigurnell was a servant to the said Mr Palmer and the saith that the said Thomas Spigurnell was inployed by that Parliament as a Surveyor of Lands by that Parliament then directed to be sold And beleeveth that he was thereunto profered for his forwardnesse and Activity against the late Kinge Charles the first and beleeveth that the said Thomas Spigurnell did acte as such a Surveyor And alsoe beleeveth that the said Thomas Spigurnell did afterwards intermeddle with sequestrated Parsonages and tythes and did gett monyes thereby And therewith putt himselfe into a good habitt and saith he was in good esteeme with such persons as were engaged against the late Kinge and his majestie which now is.

6. To the sixth Interrogatory this deponent saith That the said Thomas Spigurnell did Purchase Lands late of Sir John Stawell deceased appoynted by the late usurped powers to be sold butt whether it were before or sithence his Entermarryage with the other defendant this deponent knoweth not neither doth hee knowe of what yearly value that lands soe by him bought were but hath heard that he paid unto George Treagle the summe of Thirty pounds And unto one Henry Tymewell the summe of Twenty pounds for Lands soe by him bought And beleeveth that the said Lands were better worth.

[7.] To the seaventh Interrogatory this deponent saith That the said Thomas Spigurnell about the tyme of his marriage with the other defendant did assume much state and looke very high as if he had binn indeed a person of greate Estate and qualitie And beleeveth that the said Thomas Spigurnell did the same upon the Accompt of his purchasinge of the Lands in the former Interrogatory mencioned and of the interest which he had in those late usurped Regall Powers and of his beinge of greate repute amongst that partie And more to this Interrogatory this deponent deposeth not.

John Rowland of Taunton in the County of Somersett Whitebaker aged ffifty two yeares or thereabout produced on the parte and behalfe of the Complainante to the ffourth sixth and seaventh Interrogatoryes and thereupon sworne and examined.
To the ffourth Interrogatory this deponent saith that he knoweth that the defendant Thomas Spigurnell did heretofore live in Taunton with one Mr John Palmer in the Interrogatory named and as his servant as this deponent beleeveth but how longe sithence it was this deponent doth not now certainely can remember And further saith that he hath many tymes seene the said Thomas Spigurnell [*m.3v*] To ride the said Mr Palmers horses to water bare ridged and in a Canvas frocke and more to this Interrogatory he deposeth not.
To the sixth Interrogatory this deponent saith That he knoweth That the defendant Thomas Spigurnell was heretofore a Purchaser of some of the Lands late of Sir John Stawell deceased and appoynted to be sold by the late usurped powers for which he agreed to pay twenty pounds and upwards unto to one Henry Tymewell but of what yearly value the Lands by him soe purchased were this deponent knoweth not neither can he materially answere further to this Interrogatory.
To the seaventh Interrogatory this deponent saith that he cannot materially depose.
Thomas Harvey of Taunton in the County of Somersett gentleman aged six and thirtie yeares or thereabouts produced on the part and behalfe of the Complainant to the sixteenth nineteenth five and twenteth and one and thirtieth Interrogatoryes and there upon sworne and examined.
To the sixteenth Interrogatory this deponent saith that he is and hath benn by the space of seaven yeares last past or thereabouts very well acquainted with the hand writing of the defendant Thomas Spigurnell and saith that he verily beleeveth that the name or words Tho: Spigurnell written or subscribed in ffoure severall places at the ffoote of severall Accompts mencioned in the booke of Accompts now shewed forth unto him this deponent at the tyme of this his examinacion uppon the first page whereof are written these words (vizt) (A booke of ffees in the exchequer court and out of the Courts from the second day of July 1658 for one whole yeare then next followinge) were of the proper hand writing of the said Thomas Spigurnell And saith that he verily beleeveth also that the name or words Tho: Spigurnell written or subscribed in ffoure severall places at the ffoote of severall Accompts mencioned in an other Booke of Accompts now likewise shewed forth unto him this deponent uppon the first Page whereof are written these words (vizt) (A Booke of ffees in the Exchequer Courts and out of the courts from the second day of July 1659 for one whole yeare then followinge) were likewise of the proper hand writing of the said Thomas Spigurnell.
To the Nineteenth Interrogatory this deponent saith that he cannot materially depose.
To the five and twenteth Interrogatory saith that the yearly profitts of the office of Clerke and Porter of the Castle of Taunton beyond reprises and besides the charge of the execucion thereof due Comminibus Annis yearly amount to One hundred pounds or neere there abouts And saith that the said Office is worth to be sold for the life

John Browne Esquire in the Interrogatory named the summe of three hundred pounds or there abouts in this Deponents Judgement the said Mr Browne being an aged man and more to this Interrogatory he deposeth not.

To the Thirtieth Interrogatory this deponent saith that he was present in the Exchequer of the Castle of Taunton with the Complainant and the defendant Thomas Spigurnell uppon the ffoure and twentieth day of June which was in the yeare of our Lord one thousand six hundred sixtie and one And saith that the Complainant did then and there in this deponents presence tender to pay unto the said Thomas Spigurnell the summe of three hundred pounds in Pursuance of an Award made by John Browne Esquire betweene the Complainant and the defendant Thomas Spigurnell directing the payment thereof as was affirmed which Three hundred Pounds was counted by this deponent but this deponent did not see the defendant Thomas Spigurnell to Count any part thereof and this deponent further saith that at <that> tyme a writeinge purportinge a Release to be given by the said Thomas Spigurnell was read over in the presence of the said defendant who refused to seale and Execute the same neither did he at that tyme deliver upp any writeinges to the Complainant for ought this deponent now remembreth And this deponent saith that the Complainant then told the defendant Thomas Spigurnell that he the said Complainant was unwillinge to suffer the said Defendant to carry away the said three hundred Pounds from thence unlesse the defendant would performe that parte of the Award then <in> question betweene them which was by the <said> defendant to be performed or to that effect to this deponents best remembrance And saith that the said defendant went away thence and left the said three hundred Pounds in the said Exchequer in the eveninge of the day before remembred And saith that the said Complainant did then expresse his readynesse to the best of this deponents remembrance to performe the Award then in question on his parte to be performed and more to this Interrogatory he deposeth not.

John Spencer of Netherbury in the County of Dorsett husbandman aged threescore and ffourteene yeares or thereabouts produced on the parte and behalfe of the Complainant to the second eighth ninth thirteenth one and twenteth and ffoure and twenteth Interrogatory and there upon sworne and examined.

To the second Interrogatory this deponent saith that he did very well knowe Robert Browne Esquire and Elizabeth his wife the deceased ffather and mother of the Complainant and Defendant Elizabeth and did know them by the space of Twenty yeares and upwards before theire severall deathes And was a servant unto the said Robert Browne <who> dyed about Eighteene yeares sithence and the said Elizabeth his wife dyed about two yeares sithence.

To the eighth Interrogatory this deponent saith That the said Robert Browne was possessed of soe much plate at the tyme of his death as was worth five hundred Pounds in this deponents Judgement And he rather he doth judge it to be soe worth because this deponent beinge a servant unto the said Mr Robert Browne did use many tymes to make cleane the said Plate the same <being> three greate two Parnddle fflasketts full and this deponent saith That uppon a tyme when this deponent had made cleane the said plate and was dryinge it in the Garden of the said Mr Browne he the said Mr Browne he the said Mr Browne then cominge into the Garden asked this deponent what he thought the same - Plate to be worth And this deponent then told the said Mr Browne that he Judged it to be worth ffoure hundred pounds but acknowledged that he had noe skill in valuinge of plate for that he had neither bought or sold or exchanged any And the said Mr Browne then replyed that he this deponent had well spoken for that he the said Mr Browne would not parte with the said Plate for ffoure hundred and ffifty pounds And this deponent further saith that the Beddinge lynnen Pewter brasse household stuffe and other utensills of household whereof the said Mr Robert Browne dyed possessed were in this deponents judgement worth Three hundred Pounds or neere thereabouts And this deponent further saith That the said Mr Robert Browne did likewise dye possessed of a chayne of Gold and of a Gold Ring which said chayne of Gold was of the value of Three hundred pounds and the said Ring was worth Two hundred pounds as Mrs Elizabeth Browne deceased late wife of the said Mr Robert Browne affirmed unto this deponent All which plate Goods and Householde stuffe chayne of gold and Gold Ring uppon and after the death of the said Robert Browne came unto the hands of the said Elizabeth Browne his Relict and Executrix to his this deponents knowledge And this deponent saith that the said Mrs Elizabeth Browne was not Plundred or dispoyled thereof or of any part thereof in the late wars that this deponent ever knew or heard of but the same remayned in the custody and possession of the said Mrs Elizabeth Browne untill the enter marriage of the ....[70] which this deponent the better knoweth because he lived a servant with the said [Mrs Browne][71] and the said Mrs Elizabeth Browne.

[end of membrane signed by the commissioners] Tho: Dyke, Will: Doble, H Plucknett

[m.4r] To the Ninth Interrogatory this deponent saith That the said Mrs Elizabeth Browne at the tyme of the death of her said late husband Mr Robert Browne and untill she fell sicke of the Palsie whereof she afterwards dyed was a discreete Prudent and provident woman And was soe generally reputed And saith that the said Mrs Browne did in those tymes live thriftyly and within the Compasse of her Joynture and kept but a small ffamylye.

To the thirteenth Interrogatory this deponent saith that in the tyme of the sicknesse of the said Mrs Elizabeth Browne whereof she dyed Two Cowes of the goods of the said Mrs Browne were taken out of her custody and possession by the defendants or theire Order and as this deponents was informed it was in the might season which Cowes were of the value of nine pounds or thereabouts And further saith that about the same tyme the said Mrs Browne complayned unto this deponent that the defendants had taken and carryed away a greate parte of her Plate and some other parte of her goods and the greatest parte of her wearinge Apparell and had left her scarcelly wherewith all to change for a woman in her condicion And thereupon sent this deponent unto the defendants at Drayton where they then lived to demannd of them her Plate Goods and Clothes before menconed which this deponent did accordingly And spake with the said defendant Elizabeth touchinge the same who told this deponent shee had heard that her husband the other defendant had sold the same away and saith That he this deponent being shortly afterwards sent by the said Mrs

Browne unto the defendants at Drayton aforesaid of the same message and errand this deponent did speake then with both the defendants And <then> told the said defendant Thomas Spigurnell that the said Mrs Browne had sent him this deponent to demannd of him her Plate goods and Clothes before mencioned And this deponent asked the said Thomas Spigurnell what was become of them who thereuppon replyed and acknowledged that he had sold the same though at first he said they might be forth comeinge and more to this Interrogatory he deposeth not.

To the one and twenteth Interrogatory this deponent saith That the said Elizabeth Browne in her life tyme after the Entermarryage of the said defendant for a longe tyme and untill a little before her death did not manifest or declare such kindesse or respect to the said Complainant or take such care of him as she did manifest unto and take of him before that maryage had and since the happy restauracon of his Majestie that now is and the cause of such disrespect of the Complainant was as the said Elizabeth Browne said in this deponents heareinge because the defendant Thomas Spigurnell was against the Kinge and the Complainant for the Kinge And she durst not nor thought it not saffe for her to shew him the said Complainant respect or kindnesse in those tymes but after such tyme as the defendant Thomas Spigurnell was gon from the said Elizabeth Browne to live as aforesaid and after the happy restauracon of his Majestie that now is the said Elizabeth Browne did manifest Love and shew respect to the Complainant and did receive him and his famyly into her house and then did manifest dislike and disrespect to the defendant Thomas Spigurnell and the courses which he had taken And this deponent had heard the said Elizabeth Browne Expresse and say that she lived in feare least the said Thomas Spigurnell would doe her some discurtisie in regard her sonne the Complainant was for the Kinge and the said Thomas Spigurnell of the countrary partie.

To the foure and twenteth Interrogatory this deponent saith that uppon the death of the said Robert Browne the said Elizabeth Browne his widdow and Relict had held and enjoyed the Offices of Clerke and Porter of the Castle of Taunton of the cleare yearly value one yeare with an other of One hundred Pounds And also divers Lands and tenements in the County of Dorsett of the yearly value of one hundred and five or six pounds by the yeare And also enjoyed and tooke the profitts of a certaine tenement at Stoake Hill in the County of Somersett of the cleare yearly value of ffifteene pounds. And also enioyed and tooke the profitts of a messuage and tenement at Sherford in the said County of Somersett of the cleare yearly value of tenn pounds or thereabouts And also tooke and enioyed the profitts of a meadow lyinge neere a place called French Weare neare unto Taunton of the cleare yearly value of ffive pounds or thereabouts And saith that the said defendant Thomas Spigurnell did receive and take the profitts of the said offices for some tyme since his marryage with the other defendant how longe this deponent knoweth not and more to this Interrogatory this deponent deposeth not.

Amye White of chedon ffitzpayne in the County of Somersett single woman aged thirtie yeares and upwards produced on the parte and behalfe of the Complainant to the ninth Twelveth thirteenth one and twentieth Three and twenteth six and twenteth and seven and twenteth Interrogatory and thereupon sworne and examined.

To the ninth Interrogatory this deponent saith that Mrs Elizabeth Browne the Complainants mother untill she fell sicke of the Palsie whereof she afterwards dyed was a discreete and provident woman and a neere woman for the world and soe generally reputed And saith that she kept but a little famyly (to witt) ordinaryly but two men servants and two maide servants and sometymes one Mrs Capon her Sister was liveinge and abidinge with her And saith that the said Mrs Browne lived thriftilly and within the Compase of the yearly revenue of her estate as she this deponent believeth.

To the Twelveth Interrogatory this deponent saith That the said Mrs Browne about ffive yeares sithence fell sicke of the Palsie whereof she dyed about three yeares thereafter And saith that after that disease seised uppon her she was not able to manage and governe her Joynture and estate And saith that the defendants lived with the said Mrs Browne duringe the tyme of her sicknesse untill about ayeare before her death And saith that the said defendants duringe the tyme that <they> soe lived in house with the said Mrs Browne did take uppon them to manage order and dispose of her Joineture and estate and the affaires and her house and ffamyly And tooke into theire Custody and keepinge the key of the said Mrs Browne and her Personal estate Plate Clothes And other the goods of the said Mrs Browne in and about her house And saith that the said Mrs Browne told this deponent that the said defendants had likewise taken into theire Custody and keepinge the Gold moneys Jewells Ringes a Gold chayne and a border of [*blank*] Gold for Gentlewomen to wear on there Heads of her the said Mrs Browne Which said Jewelles Rings Gold chayne and border of Gold the said Mrs Browne also told this deponent she had with much care and difficultie preserved in the late Warrs And did Complaine with teares unto her this deponent being then a servant in house because the defendants as she the said Mrs Browne affirmed carryed the same away and would not lett her have have them againe they being worth foure hundred pounds as the said Mrs Browne said And this deponent further saith that the said defendants or one of them dureing the tyme they soe lived with the said Mrs Browne did receive and take the Rents and profitts of her Jointure and estate and disposed thereof as they thought fitt and for the maintenance of the said Mrs Browne and her servants And saith that the said Mrs Browne duringe that tyme did noe more or other then what the defendants pleased least she might offend them and this deponent further saith that duringe the tyme of such the sicknesse of the said Mrs Browne the defendant Thomas Spigurnell did bring and tender unto her a writinge touchinge the profitts of the office of Taunton [*sic*] which he desired the said Mrs Browne to seale who beinge then very weake told him she was not able to hold the seale and thereupon the said Mr Spigurnell putt on the seale unto the said writinge <and> tooke the said Mrs Brownes hand and put it uppon the seale and[72] soe the seale was taken off the said Mrs Browne by reason of the weaknesse of her hand beinge unable to use it And saith that after the defendant was gon out [*m.4v*] of her Chamber the said Mrs Browne wept And Complayned much that the said defendant had made her to doe that she never intended to keepe quietnesse aleadgeing the said defendant by that writing would have her Acknowledge that the profitts of the office by him received had been imployed for her use which she denyed And saith that the said Mrs Browne was in her Judgement and Affection for the late Kinge and his interest and wished she might live to see the tyme of his now Majesties returne and restauracion but of what Judgement the defendant Thomas Spigurnell <was> or how he acted this deponent knoweth not.

To the thirteenth Interrogatory this deponent said that the said Mrs Browne told her this deponent that the defendants in the tyme of her sicknesse had taken and carryed away her Plate and Clothes and would not lett her to have them againe though she had sent for them for which she was much grieved And more to this Interrogatory she cannot Answere further or otherwise then she hath already deposed in her Answer to the next precedent Interrogatory.

To the one and twenteth Interrogatory this deponent saith that the said Elizabeth Browne in her life tyme and after the Intermaryage of the said defendants did not in outward Appearance manifest or shew such kindenesse or respect to the Complainant in the sight and presence of the said Thomas Spigurnell as she did manifest and shew unto him the said complainant before the marryage had but this deponent believeth that the said Elizabeth Browne did very well love and Affecte the said Complainant in <her> heart though she durst not manifest or openly shew the same for displeaseing the said Thomas Spigurnell And this deponent further saith That after the happy restauracion of the Kinges Maieste that now is And after the said Thomas Spigurnell was gon to live from the said Mrs Browne she the said Mrs Browne did openly manifest great love and respect to the said Complainant And did then receave him and his famyly in to her house And did manifest her dislike with the cuurses of the said Thomas Spigurnell And said shee could not contentedly live with hime and more to this Interrogatory this deponent saith she cannot depose.

To the three and twenteth Interrogatory this deponent saith that the said Thomas Spigurnell after his Entermarage with his now wife would usually Jeere the said Complainants for being Cavaleers and told the said Mrs Browne that it was dangerous for her to shew kindnesse to the said Complainant he beinge an enemy to the State by means whereof the said Mrs Browne did shew little or noe respect or Countenance to the Complainant in the presence of the said Thomas Spigurnell.

To the sixe and twenteth Interrogatory this deponent saith That she was never a witnesse unto the signeinge sealing and delivery of any deed or deeds signed and sealed by the said Mrs Elizabeth Browne unto or to the use of the defendants or either of them neither did she ever set her hand or marke to any such deed or writinge to her now best remembrance neither did this deponent ever see any other writinge brought by the defendants or either of them to be sealed by the said Mrs Browne other then the writinge formerly mencioned in these her deposicons which writinge was not read in this deponents hearinge.

To the seaven and twenteth Interrogatory this deponent saith that when the writinge formerly menconed in these her deposicons was tendred by the said defendant Thomas Spigurnell to be sealed by the said Mrs Browne she was very weake in body and much in paired in her memory And this deponent beleaveth the said Mrs Browne could not then have understood the said writinge if the same had been reade unto her And saith that the said Mrs Browne could not then speake but <with> soe Low a voice that none could understand her but such as were much conversant about her and laid theire Eare very neare unto her when she spake And saith the said defendant Thomas Spigurnell did lay his eare very near unto the said Mrs Browne when he

Tendred the writinge aforesaid to be sealed by her but believeth that he could not understand what she then said And more she saith not.

George Golloppe of Northboard in the County of Dorsett gent aged seaven and twenty yeares or thereabouts produced on the parte and behalfe of the Complainant to the one and thirtieth Interrogatory onely and thereupon sworne and examined saith That he was present with the Complainant and defendant Thomas Spigurnell in the Exchequer of the Castle of Taunton uppon the ffoure and twenteth day of June which was in the yeare of our Lord One thousand six hundred sixtie and One And saith that the Complainant at that tyme in this deponents presence did tender and pay unto the defendant Thomas Spigurnell the summe of three hundred pounds which by an Award made by John Browne Esquire betweene the Complainant and Defendant Thomas Spigurnell (as this Deponent hath ben credably informed) the Complainant was at or before that day to pay unto the said defendant Thomas Spigurnell and saith that the said defendant did Count part of the said Three hundred pounds and did say that he did accept of the whole for Three hundred pounds in Bagges and directed a Minister then of his Company to receive the same into his Custody on his the said Defendents behalfe And saith the Complainant did thereupon demand or request the said Defendant Thomas Spigurnell to deliver unto him the said Complainant such deeds and writings as the said Complainant then affirmed were by the Award before mencioned to be delivered unto him on payment of the said Three hundred pounds And this deponent saith that the Complainant did then and there also tender unto the said Defendent Thomas Spigurnell a writinge to be sealed and executed by him the said Defendent whereby he was to relinquish and release to the Complainant all his clayme and interest in the offices and estates of Robert Browne Esquire deceased and Mrs Elizabeth Browne the Complainants late ffather and mother And saith that the said writinge was then distinctly read over in his heareinge of the said Defendent who then stood at the doare and leaned and looked into the roome where the said writing was then read And saith that to the best of this Deponents now remembrance the said Defendent did not dislike or take any exceptions to the same or any part thereof And saith the said Defendent Thomas Spigurnell did not seale and execute the writing soe tendred unto him neither did he then deliver upp the deeds and writinges which the Complainant did then request him to deliver upp unto him though he was severall tymes thereunto requested by the said Complainant the said Defendent Thomas Spigurnell sayinge that the Complainant might if he pleased sue him for not performing the Award and saith that the said Complainant did thereuppon tell the Defendent that in respect hee had not the Defendents bond of Award to inforce his performance of the same he should be unwillinge to suffer the Defendent to carry away the said Three hundred pounds thence unlesse he would performe his parte of the Award or used words to that effect And this Deponent further saith that he this Deponent and one Mr Procter did then and there persuade the said Defendant for quitnesse sake to accept of the said Three hundred pounds and to performe his parte of the Award which the Defendent notwithstandinge refused and went away and left the said Three hundred pounds behinde him in the said Exchequer about seaven of the Clocke in the after noone of that day to the best of this deponents remembrance and saith the Complainant did afterwards continue there until neare Nine of the Clocke and did afterwards tender the said monyes and declare his readynesse to performe the[73] [m.5r] Parte of the Award on his parte to be performed And this deponent veryly beleeveith the Complainant was in truth ready to performe the Award on his parte if the said defendant would have performed soe much thereof as was on his parte to be performed and more he saith not.

Alice Capon of Wilton in the County of Somersett Widdowe Aged ffifty yeares and upwards produced in the parte and behalfe of the Complainant to the second sixth seaventh Eighth ninth Twelveth Thirteenth ffourteenth ffifteenth nineteenth twenteth One and Twenteth Two and twenteth three and twenteth ffoure and twenteth and ffive and twenteth Interrogatory and thereupon sworne and examined.

To the second Interrogatory this deponent saith that she did very well knowe Robert Browne Esquire and Elizabeth his wife deceased late father and mother of the Complainant and defendent Elizabeth many yeares before theire respective deathes And saith the said Robert Browne dyed above sixteene yeares sithence And that the said Elizabeth Browne dyed about two yeares sithence.

6. To the sixth Interrogatory this deponent saith That she hath heard and veryly beleeveth that the defendant Thomas Spigurnell was a Purchaser of some parte of the Lands late of Sir John Stawell deceased which were appointed to be sold by the late usurped powers but of what value this deponent knoweth not and more to this Interrogatory she deposeth not.

7. To the seaventh Interrogatory this deponent saith that the defendent Thomas Spigurnell uppon the account of his purchaseing of the Lands mencioned in her deposicion in Answere to the next precedent Interrogatory and of his interest in the late usurped powers and of his beinge reputed one much concerned in that parte as this deponent verily beleeveth did about the tyme of his marryage with the other defendent Assume much estate uppon him and looked very high as if he had beene indeed a person of an estate and qualitie And was as she beleeveth soe reputed by many of that partie And upon that account as she veryly beleeveth made his Addresse unto and afterwards marryed the other Defendent

8. To the eighth Interrogatory this deponent saith that Robert Browne Esquire deceased the Complainants father dyed possessed of a very good personall Estate which after his death came unto the hands and possession of Mrs Elizabeth Browne his widdow and executrix And saith that the said Mrs Elizabeth Browne was plundred and dispoyled but of a very little thereof in the late Warrs which she this deponent the better knoweth for that she was Sister unto the said Elizabeth Browne and lived in house with her dureinge the tyme of the late Warrs And saith that the Plate Jewels goods and household stuffe or the principall and best parte thereof which came unto the hands of the said Mrs Browne as executrix of her said husband were remaininge in her Custody and at her Command and disposinge untill and after the Intermarriage of the defendents which she the better knoweth for that she then lived with her said sister Mrs Browne.

9. To the ninth Interrogatory this deponent saith that the said Mrs Elizabeth Browne the Complainants mother at the tyme of the death of Mr Robert Browne her late

husband and untill she fell sicke of the Palsie of which she afterwards dyed was a very discreet Prudent and a provident woman and soe estemed by those which very well knew her And saith she lived in those tymes very thriftylie and beleveth she lived within compasse of the yearly income of her estate and kept but a small famyly.

12. To the twelveth Interrogatory this deponent saith that the said Mrs Elizabeth Browne about two yeares before her death fell sicke of the Palsie of which she afterwards dyed And saith that duringe the space of One yeare and halfe before her Death she was (by reason of her said sicknesse) soe disabled in her person speech parts and understandinge that she could not in her owne person manage or govern her estate And saith that at <that> tyme the defendents lived with her who thereuppon tooke uppon them to manage and governe her said estate And saith that the defendent Elizabeth did take into her keepinge her said mothers Keyes Plate Jewlles Clothes and goods and Chattles in and about her house but doth not knowe of any ready moneyes or securityes for moneyes which the said defendent Elizabeth then tooke into her keepinge of the said Mrs Brownes And saith that dureinge that tyme she hath seene the Tenenants of the said Mrs Browne to pay some of theire Rents unto the said defendents Thomas Spigurnell and Elizabeth his wife or one of them but Whether they afterwards payd or otherwise accounted for the same unto the said Mrs Browne this deponent knoweth not And this deponent further saith that the said Mrs Elizabeth Browne in the tyme of this her weaknesse and dureinge the tyme the defendents lived with her stood in soe much awe and feare of them <that> she durst not doe any more or otherwise in or about <the managinge of>[74] her estate then they liked And this deponent saith to the best of her remembrance she did never see the defendents or either of them to tender any deed or deeds to be signed and sealed by the said Mrs Browne neither hath she heard the said Mrs Browne to Speake any thinge touchinge the same for ought she can nowe remember And this deponent saith that the said Mrs Browne was in her Judgement and affection for the late Kinge and the Royall interest And that the said defendent Thomas Spigurnell was of the countrary parte and acted accordingly.

13. To the thirteenth Interrogatory this deponent saith That the defendents did take[75] and carry any out of the said Mrs Brownes house her Plate Jewelles Ringes Gold a Gold chayne and a border of Gold and Clothes to a very greate value without the knowledge or consent of the said Mistris Browne as she the said Mrs Browne then told this deponent And saith that the said defendents did cause two Cowes and one Mare of the goods of the said Mrs Browne to be given away without her consent or knowledge as the said Mrs Browne likewise told this deponent And this deponent saith that when the said Mrs Browne had notice of the defendents carryinge away of the said Plate and goods she said unto this deponent that if she had knowne the defendents <have served her soe she> would before that tyme have sold the same away and disposed of the money at her pleasure.

14. To the ffourteenth Interrogatory this deponent saith that the defendent Thomas Spigurnell and after the tyme of his maryage with the other defendent Elizabeth dureinge the life tyme of the said Mrs Browne did take and receive the profitts of the Offices of Clerke and Porter of the Castell of Taunton and more to this Interrogatory this deponent deposeth not.

15. To the fifteenth Interrogatory this deponent saith That she hath knowne the defendent Thomas Spigurnell by the space of three yeares and upwards And saith that he is and hath been reputed an unwise man and more to this Interrogatory she deposeth not.

19. To the nineteenth Interrogatory this deponent saith That she doth not know what porcion the defendent Thomas Spigurnell hath had with or by reason of his maryage with the other defendent either by the acknowledgement of the said Mrs Browne or of either of the said defendents and more to this Interrogatory she deposeth not.

21. To the one and twenteth Interrogatory this deponent saith that the said Elizabeth Browne did not manifest or show soe much[76] kindnesse or respect to the said Complainant after Intermarryage of the said defendents as she did before that maryage had and since the happy restauracion of the Kings Majestie which now is And this deponent conceveth the cause thereof to <be> because she stood in some feare of the defendent Thomas Spigurnell And further saith that after the happy restauracion of his majestie which now is shee the said Elizabeth Browne did manifest greater love and affeccion to the said Complainant then formerly she had done And did then receive him and his famyly into her house and manifest her dislike and disaffecion to the defendent Thomas Spigurnell and the courses which he had taken and more to this Interrogatory this deponent saith she cannot depose.

22. To the two and twenteth Interrogatory this deponent saith That the said Mrs Browne in the tyme of her sicknesse did tell this deponent that she had morgaged parte of her Estate (vizt) <a> meadow and a close of land to secure the payment of some monyes borrowed and received by the said Thomas Spigurnell but what the certaine summe was this deponent knoweth not which morgage was so made by the said Mrs Elizabeth Browne at the request of the said Thomas Spigurnell as this deponent veryly beleeveth [m.5v] And the said Mrs Browne did likewise tell this deponent that the said Thomas Spigurnell did promise her to pay the money soe borrowed att the tyme lymittes in the <same> morgage for the payment thereof which the said Thomas Spigurnell fayled to performe by meanes whereof the Lands soe morgaged was forfeited and lost And saith that the monyes for which the said Lands were soe morgaged was borrowed of one Oateway And further saith that the Land soe morgaged did remaine charged with the monyes and interest thereof at the tyme of the death of the said Elizabeth Browne And the said Lands are now come unto the said Oateway and doe remaine in his hands or to some person by his appointment for any thinge this deponent knoweth to the contrary.

23. To the three and twenteth Interrogatory this deponent saith That the defendent Thomas Spigurnell after the intermarryage with his said wife did labour to <sett> and keepe distance and differences betweene the said Elizabeth Browne and the said Complainant and more to this Interrogatory this deponent saith she cannot depose other then she hath expressed in her former deposicion.

24. To the ffoure and twenteth Interrogatory this deponent saith That she hath heard and beleeveth that the messuage Lands tenements Hereditaments and offices where upon the death of Mr Robert Browne the Complainants father were enioyed by the said Mrs Elizabeth Browne his mother were of the yearly value of three hundred pounds And saith that the said defendent Thomas Spigurnell did take the profitts of

the said Offices for some tyme after his Intermarage with the other defendent.
25. To <the> five and twenteth Interrogatory this deponent saith she cannot materially depose.

William Lane of Totnis in the County of Devon gentleman aged nineteene yeares or thereabouts produced on the parte and behalfe of the Complainant to the eight and twenteth nine and twenteth thirtieth and one and thirtieth Interrogatoryes and there upon sworne and examined.
28. To the eight and twentieth Interrogatory this deponent saith that the defendent Thomas Spigurnell and the Complainant about a quarter of a yeare after the death of Mrs Elizabeth Browne the Complainants mother did <as this deponent beleeveth> referr all differences betweene them by the finall end Award and determinacion of John Browne of Frampton in the County of Dorsett Esquire <but was not present at such submission, And likewise beleeveth they> entered into bonds each to other of the penalty of Two Thowsand pounds to performe what Award he should make touchinge the same <or otherwise Mr Browne would not have made an Award therein and taken paynes about the same> which said Mr John Browne is Uncle to the Complainant and the defendent Elizabeth as this deponent hath credably heard and beleeveth And saith he believeth the said Mr John Browne did examine the said differences and he knoweth that the said Mr John Browne did make his Award touchinge the same but for the effect and purport of the said Award and what in particular was thereby ordered to be don paid or performed by the Complainant and defendent Thomas Spigurnell respectively this deponent refereth him selfe to the same Award.
29. To the nine and twenteth Interrogatory this deponent saith that he beleeveth the said bonds of Awards when soe entered into were left in the hands of the said John Browne and more to this Interrogatory he deposeth not save only that he beleeveth the said Mr John Browne did not refuse to deliver unto the Complainant the bond of Award Entred into by the defendent Thomas Spigurnell if it were demaunded of him.
30. To the thirtieth Interrogatory this deponent saith that the writing now shewed unto him at the tyme of this examinacion purporting an Award and heareinge date the sixteenth day of May in the Thirteenth yeare of the Raigne of our Soveraigne Lord Kinge Charles the second is the same Award which the said John Browne soe made betweene the Complainant and defendent Thomas Spigurnell for the finall endinge of all differences betweene them And saith the name John Browne thereunto subscribed was of the proper hand writing of the said Mr John Browne And saith that he this deponent was present when the said Mr John Browne did signe seale and Publish the same and that the name William Lane subscribed as witnesse to the signeinge sealeinge and publishing thereof is of the proper hand writing of him this deponent And this deponent beleeveth that the defendent Thomas Spigurnell and the Complainant uppon perusall thereof did respectively declare theire consent and submission thereunto and promised to performe the same.
31. To the one and thirtieth Interrogatory this deponent saith that he was present with the Complainant and the defendent Thomas Spigurnell in the Exchequer of the Castle of Taunton uppon the foure and twentieth day of June which was in the yeare of our

Lord One thousand sixe hundred and one And saith the Complainant at that tyme in the presence of this deponent did tender and pay unto the defendent Thomas Spigurnell the summe of three hundred pounds which by an Award made by John Browne Esquire between the Complainant and Defendent Thomas Spigurnell the Complainant was at or before that day to pay to the said Defendent Thomas Spigurnell And saith he doth not now remember whether the said Defendent did count any parte of the said money but saith that he did receive into his Custody and accept of the whole summe in Baggs for the summe of Three hundred pounds and saeth he beleeveth the Complainant did thereupon demaund and request of the said Thomas Spigurnell to deliver unto him the deeds writings and evidences which by the said Award he was uppon the payment of the said Three hundred pounds to deliver to the said Complainant And this deponent saith that the Complainant did then and there tender unto the said defendent Thomas Spigurnell a writinge to be sealed and executed by him whereby he was to relinquish and Release to the Complainant all his clayme and title to the severall Estates and offices of Robert Browne Esquire <and Mrs Elizabeth Browne> the Complainants ffather and mother And further saith that the said writinge was then destinctly read over in the presence and hearinge of the said defendent Thomas Spigurnell who dyd not to this deponents best remembrance dislike or take any exceptions thereunto And this deponent saith that the defendent Thomas Spigurnell did not seale and execute the writinge soe tendred unto him neither did he then deliver up unto the said Complainant the said deeds and writings soe demaunded of him alleadgainge that he woold first carry away the said moneys and dispose of it as he pleased and that the Complainant might if he pleased sue him for not performeing of the <said> Award or used words to that effect and this Deponent saith that he beleeveth that the Complainant did thereupon tell the said Defendent that in regard he had not the defendents bond of Award to force his performance of the same hee should be unwillinge to suffer the said defendent to carry away the said three hundred pounds thence unlesse he would performe that parte of the Award which was on his parte to be performed or used words to that effect to the best of this deponents remembrance And saith that the said defendent went away from thence about sixe or seven of the Clocke in the Eaveninge of the same day and left the said Three hundred pounds behinde him in the said Exchequer but saith the Complainant did continue and remayne there untill after sunnsetting in readynesse as he expressed to performe his parte of the said Award And this deponent verily beleiveth the Complainant was then in truth ready to have performed the said Award on his parte if the defendent[77] [m.6r] Thomas Spigurnell would have performed soe much there of as was on his part performed.

John Mare <of> Nettlecombe in the County of Somersett yeoman age ffortie <two> yeares or thereabouts produced on the parte and behalfe of the Complainant to two and thirteth Interrogatory only and thereupon sworne and examined saith That Mr Robert Browne in the Interrogatory named was at that tyme of his death Interressed in certaine messauges tenements and lands called Middleton within the parish of Huish Chamflower in the said County of Somersett for a longe terme of yeares then and yett indureinge but for how many yeares this deponent knoweth not and saith that

the said messuages and Lands are worth ffortie pounds by the yeare beyond reprises
And saith that Mrs Elizabeth Browne the widdow and Relict of the said Robert
Browne in the yeare one thousand sixe <hundred> fortie nine did graunt one
tenement with the appurtenances parcell of the premisses unto Sibble Mare mother of
this deponent for Ninety nine yeares if Joane Mare the elder and Joane Mare the
younger and Thomas Mare or either of them should fortune to live soe longe And
saith that the said Sibble Mare paid the summe of two hundred sixtie and seaven
pounds for the same which money was paid unto one Mr John Porter since deceased
to the use of the said Elizabeth Browne And this deponent further saith that in the
last mencioned Tenement there is an estate yet remaineinge for divers of the said
nintye nine yeares yf Joane Mare the younger and Thomas Mare or either of them
shall live soe longe the said Joane Mare the elder beinge dead since the said Estate was
graunted And saith that there is an estate in beinge in the residue of the said
messuages and Lands for divers yeares if this deponent and one Joane Webber or
either of them shall live soe longe.

Robert Hucker of Hilbishopps in the County of Somersett Woollstapler Aged sixe and
ffifty yeares or there abouts produced on the parte and behalfe of the Complainant to
the Fifth Sixth Fifteenth and Sixteenth Interrogatory and thereuppon sworne and
examined
To the ffifth Interrogatory this deponent saith That Mr John Palmer in the
Interrogatory named was about the yeare of our Lord one thousand sixe hundred
ffortie three chosen to serve as a Burgesse <in Parliament for the Towne> of Taunton
<in> the County of Somersett And this deponent saith That he hath heard that the
defendent Thomas Spigurnell was then a servant to the said Mr Palmer and likewise
hath heard that he was and acted as a surveior[78] of Lands directed by that Parliament
to be sold And hath likewise heard that the said defendent ~~was~~ was a very <unkind>
person <in> intermedlinge with sequested parsonages and tythes and hath heard him
very much Complayned of touchinge his actinges therein.
To the Sixth Interrogatory this deponent saith that the defendent Thomas Spigurnell
did heretofore buy and purchase of severall persons severall parcells of Lands which
were the Lands of Sir John Stawell late deceased and appointed to be sold by the late
usurped powers and more to this Interrogatory he deposeth not.
To the ffifteenth Interrogatory this deponent saith That he hath knowne the
defendent Thomas Spigurnell by the space of ffifteene or sixteene yeares last past And
saith that he is a person of noe good repute but he is a man that hath been much
Complayned of neither hath this deponent ever looked uppon him as a person that
made conscience of what he said and more to this Interrogatory he deposeth not.
To the sixteenth Interrogatory this deponent saith That he hath been acquainted with
the hand writing of the said Thomas Spigurnell by the <space of> ffoure or fives
yeares and upwards and veryly beleeveth that the name or words Thomas Spigurnell
written or subscribed in ffoure severall places at the ffoote of severall Accompts
mencioned in the booke of Accompts now shewed fourth unto him this deponent at
the tyme of this his examinacion upon the first Page whereof are written these words
(vizt) A Booke of ffees in the exchequer and out of the Courts from the second day

of July 1658 for one whole yeare then next followinge, were of the proper hand writing of the said Thomas Spigurnell And saith that he veryly beleeveth also that the name in words Thomas Spigurnell written or subscribed in foure severall places at the foote of severall accompts mencioned in an other booke of Accompts now likewise shewed forth unto him this deponent upon the first Page where of are written these words (vizt) A booke of ffees in the Exchequer and out of the Courts from the second day of July 1659 for one whole yeare then ~~next~~ followinge were likewise of the proper hand writing of the said Thomas Spigurnell And this deponent veryly beleeveth also that the acquitance for ffifteene pounds bearinge date the three and twenteth day of October 1660 now likewise shewed fourth unto this deponent together with the words or name Thomas Spigurnell thereunto subscribed was of the proper hand writing of the said Thomas Spigurnell And he veryly beleeveth also that the Letter now shewed fourth unto him dated the ffourth of January 1660 beginninge with these words Mr Porter and subscribed with the name or words Thomas Spigurnell was likewise of the proper hand writing of the said <defendent> Thomas Spigurnell and more he deposeth not.

Robert Procter of the parish of Taunton Magdalen in the County of Somersett merchant aged fortie five yeares or there abouts produced on the parte and behalfe of the Complainant To the sixteenth and one and thirteth Interrogatory and thereupon sworne and examined.

To the sixteenth Interrogatory this deponent saith that he hath been well acquainted with <the hand writing of> the defendent Thomas Spigurnell by the space of eight or nine yeares <last past> or thereabouts and saith that the Acquitance now shewed unto him at the tyme of his examinacion beareinge date the three and twenteth day of October 1660 and the name in words Thomas Spigurnell subscribed thereunto were of the proper hand writing of the said defendent Thomas Spigurnell And also beleeveth that the Letter now shewed unto him at the tyme of this his examinacion dated the 4th of January 1660 and beginninge with these words Mr Porter and endninge with the words or name Thomas Spigurnell is likewise of the proper hand writing of the defendent Thomas Spigurnell and he also veryly beleeveth the name or words Thomas Spigurnell written or subscribed in ffoure severall places at the ffoote of severall Accompts mencioned in the booke of Accompts now shewed forth unto this deponent at the tyme of his examinacion on the first Page whereof are written these words (vizt) A booke of ffees in the exchequer and out of the Courts from the second day of July 1658 for one whole yeare then next following, were of the proper hand writing of the said Thomas Spigurnell And saith that he also veryly beleeveth that the name in words Thomas Spigurnell written or subscribed ffoure severall places at the ffoote of severall Accompts mencioned in an other booke of an Accompts now likewise shewed unto this deponent upon the first Page whereof are written these words (vizt) a booke of ffees in the exchequer and out of the Courts from the second day of July 1659 for one whole yeare then followinge, were of the proper hand writing of the said Thomas Spigurnell.

To the <one and> Thirteth Interrogatory this deponent saith That he was present with the Complainant and defendent Thomas Spigurnell in the exchequer of the

Castle of Taunton upon the foure and twenteth day of June wh………… in the yeare of our Lord one thousand six hundred sixtie and one And saith that the Complainant did [*m.6v*] and there tender unto the defendent Thomas Spigurnell the summe of three hundred Pounds which he the said Complainant affirmed he was to pay unto the said defendent by an Award made betweene them by John Browne Esquire And saith the said defendent did count some parte of the said monyes and[79] Mr Harvey then present affirming he had counted over the whole summe the said defendent did accept of and receive into his Custody the whole summe in Baggs for the summe of Three hundred pounds And saith the Complainant Did then tender to the said defendent Thomas Spigurnell a writinge to be sealed executed by him in pursuance of the said Award as the Complainant then aleaged which writinge was distinctly read over in the presence and hearinge of the defendent Thomas Spigurnell the certaine contents whereof this deponent doth not now well remember <neither doth he remember> that the said defendent did dislike or take any exceptions thereunto but saith the said defendent did absolutely refuse to seale and execute the writing soe tendred unto him sayinge that he doubted they would take away the money from him againe or not suffer him to carry it away or to that effect but said he would not seale the said writinge untill those monyes were saffe in one Mr Whetcoms house in Taunton and saith the said complainant did then say he should be unwillinge to suffer the defendent to carry away the said monyes from thence unlesse he would seale the said writinges and performe that parte of the Award which was on his parte to be performed And this deponent saith that he this deponent for removeinge the feare and jealosie of the defendent touchinge his saffe carryinge away of the said mony did offer the said defendent to morgage all his this deponents Taunton Deane Lands worth neare two thousand pounds to secure the safe payment and delivery thereof that day to the defendent at the said Mr Whetcombs house But saith the defendent neverthelesse was not thereupon prevayled with all but departed thence with out doeinge any thinge at all in order to the performance of the said Award leaveinge the said three hundred pounds behinde him in the said exchequer in the eaveninge of the same day And this deponent saith he verily beleeveth the Complainant was then in truth ready to have paid the said monyes and performed the said Award on his parte if the defendent Thomas Spigurnell would have performed his parte of the said Award and more he deposeth not.

John Bridle of the parish of Burton in the County of Dorsett yeoman aged Threescore yeares or there abouts produced on the parte and behalfe of the Complainant to the ffourteenth Interrogatory only and there upon sworne and examined saith That he did hold at an Agistment rent from Mrs Elizabeth Browne in the Interrogatory named certaine Lands at Benfield and Graston in the said County of Dorsett for the which this deponent did pay unto Elizabeth one of the defendents halfe a yeares rent for the said Lands at Benfield amounting to the summe of sixteene pounds and tenn shillings and one quarter of a yeares Rent for the said Lands at Graston amounting to the summe of nineteene pounds And saith that he also paid to the defendent Elizabeth Three pounds and eight shillings for <a> head Rent for halfe a yeare for a house commonly called the Signe of the Bull in Bridport and two and thirty shillings for one halfe yeares head rents reserved and payable fourth of certaine tenements in Graston then stated out which moneyes this deponent soe paid unto the said defendent Elizabeth in the life tyme of the said Mrs Elizabeth Browne her mother and more he saith not.

John Bartlett of Frampton in the County of Dorset gentleman aged three and thirty yeares or there abouts produced on the parte and behalfe of the Complainant to the eight and twenteth nyne and twenteth and thirteth Interrogatory and thereupon sworne and examined.

To the eight and twenteth Interrogatory this deponent saith That about two yeares sithence the Complainant and defendent Thomas Spigurnell did referr all differences betweene them to the finall end and determinacion of John Bartlett of Frampton Esquire in the Interrogatory named as was manifest unto this deponent by theire Entringe into bonds or Ingagements each to other in the penalty of Two thousand pounds for performance of what Award the said Mr John Browne should make touchinge the same And saith that he this deponent hath heard and beleeveth That the said Mr John Browne is Cozen german[80] to the Complainant and defendent Elizabeth And the deponent saith that the said Mr John Browne did make his Award in writinge under his hand and seale betweene the said parties touchinge the same where unto this deponent referreth himselfe for what was to be performed thereby by the Complainant and defendent Thomas Spigurnell.

To the nyne and twenteth Interrogatory this deponent saith That he veryle beleeveth that the said bonds of Award or Ingagments when soe entred into as aforesaid were best in the hands of the said Mr John Browne And saith the same are yet remaininge in his the said Mr John Brownes hands and more to this Interrogatory he deposeth not.

To the thirteth Interrogatory this deponent saith that the writing or Award now shewed forth unto him this deponent at the at the the tyme of this his examinacion beareing date the sixteenth day of May in the thirteenth yeare of his nowe Majesties Raigne is the Award which the said Mr John Browne made betweene the Complainant and defendent Thomas Spigurnell for the endinge of all differences betweene them And saith the same was signed sealed and Published by the said John Browne in the presence of this deponent whose name subscribed as <a> witnesse thereunto is of the proper hand writinge of him this deponent And saith he beleeveth one parte of the said Award was forthwith after the makinge thereof delivered to the Complainant and the other parte thereof delivered to the defendent Thomas Spigurnell and more he deposeth not.

John Gollopp of North Bowood in the County of Dorset gentleman aged Thirtie yeares or there abouts produced on the part and behalfe of the Complainant to the eight and twenteth nine and twenteth and thirteth Interrogatorys and there upon sworne and examined.

To the eight and twenteth Interrogatory this deponent saith that the Complainant and defendent Thomas Spigurnell since the death of Elizabeth Browne in the Interrogatory named did by theire mutuall consent referr all differences betweene them to the finall end and determinacion of John Browne of Frampton Esquire And did enter into bonds of the penalty of two thousand pounds each to other to performe such Award as the said John Browne should make touchinge the same as the said Complainant and defendent Thomas Spigurnell did both of them acknowledge in the heareinge of this deponent And saith that the said John Browne is Cozin German to the Complainant and defendent Elizabeth And saith that the said John Browne did make his Award betweene the said parties touchinge the same And saith that this deponent was present att and did see when the said John Browne did signe and seale the said Award and delivered the same to the said Complainant and the said Thomas Spigurnell but touching what the Complainant was thereby ordered to doe pay or performe to the said Thomas Spigurnell and what the said Thomas Spigurnell was there by to pay doe or performe to the said Complainant this deponent referreth himselfe to the said Award whereunto he was a witnesse and more he deposeth not. To the nine and twenteth Interrogatory this deponent saith that when the said Award was delivered as aforesaid to the said Complainant and defendent Thomas Spigurnell the said Mr John Browne did acknowledge he had in his Custody the said bonds of Award and saith that the said Mr Browne beinge requestred to deliver the bond entred into by the defendent Thomas Spigurnell to the Complainant for performance of the said Award he did refuse to deliver upp the same and this deponent beleiveth he doth still detayne it in his hands.

[*end of membrane signed by the commissioners*] Tho: Dyke, Will: Doble, H Plucknett

[*m.7r*] To the thirteth Interrogatory this deponent saith that the writinge now shewed forth unto this deponent at the tyme of his examinacion purporting an Award and beareing date the sixteenth day of May in the thirteenth yeare of his now Majesties Raigne is the Award which the said John Browne soe made betweene the Complainant and defendent Thomas Spigurnell for ending all differences betweene them And saith that the name John Browne thereunto subscribed was of the proper hand writinge of him the said John Browne and that the said Award was signed sealed and published by the said John Browne in this deponents presence who subscribed his name as <a> witnesse thereunto and more to this Interrogatory he deposeth not.

Richard Jeane of Middlezoy in the County of Somersett gentleman aged Thirtie three yeares or thereabouts produced on the part and behalfe of the Complainant to the fifth sixth seaventh and ffifteenth Interrogatoryes and there upon sworne and examined.
To the fifth Interrogatory this deponent saith that he beleeveth that Mr John Palmer in the Interrogatory named was chosen to serve as a Burgesse in Parliament for the Towne of Taunton <in> or about the yeare 1646 and saith that the defendent Thomas Spigurnell was then or about that tyme a servant unto the said Mr Palmer as this deponent hath heard And further saith That the said defendent Thomas Spigurnell did act as a Surveyer of Lands directed to be sold by that Parliament namely the Lands of Sir John Stawell and others and was very active in that service especially in Sir John Stawells and not only in surveyinge but also endeavouringe to have his house att Cothelston pulled downe And doth also knowe that he Entermeddled very much with

parsonages and Tythes whereof some were sequestred and others were seized on because the Leases thereof made by the Deane and Chapter of Wells and others as this deponent hath heard were dated after the tyme mencioned in a pretended act order or Ordinance of that Parliament made to avoide the same And did receive the Tythes for one or more yeares of Salt Moore which Tythes were graunted under the seale of the Deane and Chapter of Wells to or for the use of the now wife <of> Richard Atwey of Weston and did nominate this deponent a Comissioner on the behalfe of Sir John Thurrogood and others named Trustees by <the> said Parliament touching such Parsonages and tythes to examine Witnesses in a cause there dependinge in the then Court of Exchequer betweene the said Trustees and some of the parishoners of Burnham in the County of Somersett for tythes and after witnesses were examined some of the parties compounded and gave securitie for payment of the money compounded for the said tythes and cost of suite to the said defendent Thomas Spigurnell And doth believe that he did gett much mony by Entermeddlinge with such Parsonages and Tythes and procureinge Augmentacions for unworthy Ministres and saith that he was much ymployed and intrusted by Collonel Pyne and others who were at the tyme of his imployment enemies to his Royall Majestie that now is and had binn to his late ffather the blessed memory and more to this Interrogatory he deposeth not.

To the sixth Interrogatory this deponent saith that the defendent Thomas Spigurnell was a Purchaser of some of the Lands of Sir John Stawell appoynted to be sold by that Parliament for the Loyalty of the said Sir John Stawell and more to this Interrogatory he deposeth not.

To the seaventh Interrogatory this deponent saith That for some tyme before the Entermarryage of the said defendent Thomas Spigurnell with his now Wife by[81] reason of the estate which he then enjoyed and his interest in those who usurped the Royall power and his imployment under them did carry himselfe very high both in words and accions as if he had bin a person of a Reall estate good quallytie and well descended and believeth thereuppon and his declaracion of his Emnitie to his Majestie and the Royall partie did make his addresse unto <and> afterwards marryed the other defendent his now wife and more to this Interrogatory he cannott depose.

To the ffifteenth Interrogatory this deponent saith that <he> hath knowne the defendent Thomas Spigurnell by the space of twelve yeares last past and upwards dureinge which tyme the said Thomas Spigurnell was reputed to be dishonest in many of <his> accions And this deponent hath heard some Ministres and divers other persons declare and say that the said Thomas Spigurnell had deceived and abused them and <he> alwaies passed under the Character of an Enemy to his Majestie untill his happy restrauracion and for manifestacion of his disloyalty brought an accion for words alleadged by him to be spoaken whereby he might be preiudiced in his reputacion with the late usurped powers and thereupon was Awarded great damages as by the Records of his Majesties Court of Common Pleas may appeare and more he saith not.

Robert Leigh of Milverton in the County of Somersett gentleman aged Twenty five yeares or there abouts produced on the parte and behalfe of the Complainant to the third Interrogatory only and thereupon sworne and examined saith that the note or writinge now shewed forth unto this deponent at the tyme of this his examinacion touchinge the tyme of the Babtizme of John Browne Esquire is a true Coppie of what it doth purport and was examined by this deponent with the Register booke of Frampton in the County of Dorset and is agreeable thereunto and more he deposeth not.[82]

[m.7v blank; m.8r]

parte Deft.

Tristrum Lane of Taunton in the County of Somerset husband[man] Aged Thirtey and Five yeares or thereabouts produced and examined for and on the behalfe of the defendents, To the ffourteenth and ffifteenth Interrogatorys only deposeth as followeth:

To the ffourteenth Interrogatory this deponent saith that hee cannot depose.

To the ffifteenth Interrogatory this deponent saith that Doctor Palmer in the Interrogatory named, was Warden of Allsoules Colledge in Oxford for five yeares togeather, And that the defendent was, or att least was reputed Steward and Surveyor of the Mannors and Lands belonging to the said Colledge for the tyme hee aboade with the said Doctor And this deponent saith that there was a groome allowed unto the said Doctor Palmer in Oxford by the said Colledge, namely one John Prew, and farther deposeth not.

Henry Tymewell Gentleman formerly produced and sworne on the parte and behalfe of the Complainant and now examined on the behalfe of the defendents deposeth as followeth.

20. To the Twenteeth Interrogatory this deponent saith that the defendent had greate acquaintance with Collonell Pyne, and one Collonell or Lieutenant Collonell Bovett in tyme of the late Warrs, But whether hee weare ever a Souldier under those powers this deponent knoweth not, yet beleeveth hee ever opposed those powers; And saith hee hath seene him ride with a sworde in those tymes: But never sawe the Complainant ride with a Sworde or Pistalls in his life. And this deponent saith that the Complainant hath not taken any Comaund, Milletary or Civill under his Majestie since the resteracion to this deponents knowledge; Howbeitt beleeveth the Complainant is, and wilbee ready to spend his Estate and blood for his Majestie.

21) To the One and Twentieth Interrogatory this deponent saith that he knoweth nothing of this Interrogatory.

Osmond Spreete formerly produced and sworne on the parte and behalfe of the Complainant and now Examined on the behalfe of the defendents deposeth as followeth

15) To the ffifteenth Interrogatory this deponent doth not depose.

21) To the One and Twentieth Interrogatory doth not depose.

Thomas Harvey of Taunton Gentleman produced sworne, and Examined on the parte and behalfe of the Complainant and now Examined on the behalfe of the defendents deposeth as followeth.

12) To the Twelfth Interrogatory this deponent saith that the defendents lived with Elizabeth Browne the defendent Elizabeths Mother by the space of one yeare or thereabouts after their Marryage as this deponent conceiveth dureing which tyme the said Elizabeth the defendents Mother was sick as this deponent hath hard and beleeveth, And hath also hard and beleeveth that a sister of the defendent Elizabeths Mother lived with her some parte of that tyme, but what servants or other Attendants the defendent Elizabeths Mother then had dureing her said sicknesse, or who defrayed the charge of the house keepeing this deponent knoweth not.

21) To the One and Twenteith Interrogatory this deponent saith that hee cannot materially depose.

Richard Carpenter of Taunton in the County of Somersett Upholsterer, Aged Thirtey and Two yeares or thereabouts produced sworne, and examined on the parte and behalfe of the defendents to the Eleaveth Interrogatory only deposeth as followeth:

11) To the Eleaventh Interrogatory this deponent saith, that the Complainant with his Aunt Capon did stand by, and view some parte of the defendents goods which were carryed forth of the house of Mrs Elizabeth Browne the Complainants mother by the defendents and claymed as there [were] none proper goods, which this deponent bought, and to which the Complainant layd noe clayme, hee farther saith that after such the goods soe bought by this deponent were layd up in this deponents Custody, the Complainant reviewed the same and layd noe clayme thereunto.

John Spenser husbandman formerly produced and sworne on the parte and behalfe of the Complainant, and now examined on the behalfe of the defendents deposeth as followeth.

1) To the ffirst Interrogatory this deponent saith that hee knoweth the Land att Benfield and Graston in the County of Dorset In the Interrogatory mencioned, late in the tenure of Mrs Elizabeth Browne the Complainants Mother which Lands did yeld one hundred and ffive or Six pounds per Annum or thereabouts which Lands are discended and come to the hands of the Complainant, who now receives the Rents thereof.

2) To the Second Interrogatory this deponent saith that much of the Rents of the Lands at Benfield and Graston in the Interrogatory mencioned, were paid to Mrs Elizabeth Browne the defendents Mother, and some parte thereof was paid or allowed by the said Mrs Browne and the Complainant towards his mayntenance.

3) To the Third Interrogatory this deponent saith, that there were some Tenements stated forth of Lands in Dorsetsheare late the Inheritance of Robert Browne esquire deceased, which discended to the Complainant; But what the Auncient and accustomed Rents thereof were this deponent knoweth not. But saith that some parte of those Estates fell into hand but of late.

4) To ffowerth Interrogatory this deponent saith that the Inn called the Bull in Bridport in the Interrogatory mencioned was the Estate of Elizabeth Browne the Complainants Mother in her life tyme. And that the same is since her death discended unto the Complainant. But what the yearely value thereof is, this deponent knoweth not.

6) To the Sixth Interrogatory this deponent saith that Robert Browne the

Complainants ffather dyed about Eighteene yeares sithence. But what ready money hee dyed possest of this deponent knoweth not, neither doth this deponent knowe of any debts or Credits due or payable to him, for thother parte of this Interrogatory this deponent referreth himselfe to his deposicion formerly taken on the parte of the Complainant.

7) To the Seaventh Interrogatory this deponent saith that hee cannot otherwise depose to this Interrogatory then what he hath already deposed to the effect Interrogated on the behalfe of the Complainant.

8) To the Eighth Interrogatory this deponent cannot depose.

13) To the Thirteenth Interrogatory this deponent saith that the Complainant lived in as good faishon in his Minorety as any Gentleman of his quallity in the County of Somerset; And this deponent doth beleeve that it cost his Mother neer thirty pounds per Annum to maynteyne him, But saith shee did not spend her whole revenue, nor runn in to debt to maynteyne her Children, famely, and relacions; neither did she send Goods or household stuffe to the Complainant att, or after the Marryage, or become bound for moneyes to supply occasions for ought this deponent overhard.

21) To the One and Twenteith Interrogatory this deponent saith that hee knoweth not, what Estate proffitt or benifitt the defendent Thomas Spigurnell hath had by the Intermarriage of the Complainants Sister, but in al things referreth himselfe to what hee hath formerly deposed on the behalfe of the Complainant, and farther hee is not Examined.

Amy White formerly produced sworne and Examined on the parte and behalfe of the Complainant, and now Examined on the parte of the defendents deposeth as followeth.

2) To the Second Interrogatory this deponent saith that shee remembreth that when the Rents of the Lands of Benfield and Graston were brought by the Tenants unto Elizabeth Browne in the Interrogatory named, the Defendents or one of them did receive the same but what was soe paid them, this deponent knoweth not, But doth not know that any parte thereof was paid to the Complainant.

6) To the Sixth Interrogatory this deponent saith that shee knoweth not how long since Robert Browne in the Interrogatory named father of the Complainant and defendent Elizabeth dyed, neither doth shee know what ready money hee was possest of att his death, nor in whose hands it was (if any were) nor doth this deponent know what Credits the said Mr Robert Browne dyed possest of And father this deponent saith that shee cannot tell what particuler peeces of Plate, or the Value of them[83] lyning Beding or other goods and Chattles or household stuffe of the said Robert Browne came to the hands of the defendent Thomas Spigurnell.

8) To the Eight Interrogatory this deponent saith that shee did never see, nor hard that the Complainant accompanyed with one John Gollopp did breake open a dore in the house of his Mother att Sherford, or ever carry away any thing there once, which shee beleeveth shee should have seene, or hard (if any such thing had been done) shee haveing lived there as a servant divers yeares.

9) To the Nynth Interrogatory this deponent saith that shee knoweth not the precise tyme of the Intermarriage of the defendents, But hath hard and beleeveth it was about

five yeares since.

12) To the Twelth Interrogatory this deponent saith, that the defendents after there Marryage did live with Elizabeth Browne the Mother, for the space of Two yeares or there abouts, and in that tyme did take the Income of the Estate and defrayed the charge of the house keepeing; and more shee deposeth not.

John Hewes of Hill Bishopps in the County of Somerset Wostard Comber, Aged two and fforty yeares or thereabouts produced sworne and Examined for and on the parte and behalfe of the defendents, deposeth as followeth.

7) To the Seaventh Interrogatory this deponent saith that Elizabeth Browne in the Interrogatory named the widdow and Executrix of Robert Browne in the interrogatory likewise named, did as shee told this deponent hide, convey away, dispurse and thereby, and by plundring, and troubles of the tymes, did loose greate parte of the household stuffe Plate Goods and ......[84] to the value (as shee said) of One thousand pounds, more especially while the Seiges were att Taunton, shee liveing but Three quarters of a Mile from the Towne.

13) To the Thirteenth Interrogatory this deponent saith, that the manner of the Complainants liveing dureing his minority was very high, and like a Gentleman, and this deponent doth Judge it did cost his Mother Three or ffowerscore pounds per Annum to mainteyne him But whether shee did expend her whole revenue yearely from the tyme her husband dyed, or runn in debt hee knoweth not.

18) To the Eighteenth Interrogatory this deponent saith that Elizabeth Browne in the Interrogatory named did tell this deponent that the Gold Chayne in the Interrogatory mencioned which was left by Robert Browne her husband was soald long before the Intermarryage of the defendents, But to whome this deponent knoweth not.

[m.8v] 22) To the Two and Twenteith Interrogatory this deponent saith, that Mrs Elizabeth Browne the Complainants Mother told this deponent Tenn tymes at least, that shee would her daughter Elizabeth the now defendent worth ffifteene hundred pounds in money and goods, if she liked the man shee should Marry with. And this deponent farther saith that he beleeveth that the said Elizabeth Browne did give her consent for her daughter to Marry the now defendent Thomas Spigurnell, or else itt had never been done; and farther hee doth not depose.

Alice Capon widdow formerly produced sworne, and examined on the parte and behalfe of the Complainant and now also Examined on the behalfe of the defendents deposeth as followeth.

6) To the Sixth Interrogatory this deponent saith that Robert Browne Esquire in the Interrogatory named, dyed about Sixteene years sithence, but what ready money hee dyed possest of this deponent knoweth not, neither doth this deponent know what Credits hee dyed possest of, And this deponent saith that the said Robert Browne dyed possest of the severall peeces of Plate following, One Silver Ewer, two silver Basons, two silver Candlesticks, two silver fflaggons, a greate silver Skillett, a silver Warming pann, three silver Tankards, a silver Chafeingdish, a silver paire of Saussers, two silver Beare Boles, one silver Wine Bole, a silver Candle Capp, two Silver sugar dishes, two silver Colledge potts, two other broad silver Boles, two great silver Salts,

two silver Trencher Salts, one dozen of silver spoones, one gilt Bole covered, one lesser gilt Bole covered, two other silver dishes with covers, a silver Ladle, but what the value of them were this deponent knoweth not, neither doth shee knowe of any Beding, Lyning, or other household stuffe that come to the hands of the defendents, But the Plate and such other things as are mencioned in her deposicions on the parte of the Complainant came to the hands of the defendents.

7) To the Seaventh Interrogatory this deponent saith that Elizabeth Browne in the Interrogatory named by reason of the Warrs did hide away some parte of the plate, But this deponent beleeveth shee lost noe parte thereof, and shee that shee was very little plundred by the Souldiers dureing the Seiges against Taunton, And that she lived within one Mile of the Towne, and farther saith not.

8) To the Eighth Interrogatory this deponent saith that shee cannot depose.

9) To the Nynth Interrogatory this deponent saith that shee cannot depose.

10) To the Tennth Interrogatory this deponent saith that shee knoweth not the particuler value of what goods were carryed from the house of Elizabeth Browne in the Interrogatory named neither doth shee knowe what goods were carryed from her house att Sherford, unto the defendents house att Sutton but saith that some goods were there carryed, and she the said Mrs Browne had a purpose to goe to Sutton, but not to live there as she beleeveth. And she saith that she hath heard that some of those goods were returned againe.

11) To the Eleaventh Interrogatory this deponent saith shee cannot depose.

12) To the Twelth Interrogatory this deponent saith that the defendents after there Marryage did live with Mrs Browne there Mother for the space of Two yeares or thereabouts, and the charge of housekeepeing during that tyme was defrayed by Mrs Elizabeth Browne for any thing this deponent knoweth to the contrary.

16) To the Sixteenth Interrogatory this deponent saith that shee cannot depose.

18) To the Eighteenth Interrogatory this deponent saith that shee was never directed by Mrs Browne to sell a Gold chayne of hers, neither did shee this deponent sell any such, nor can shee tell who solde the same, unless the defendents or one of them did sell it.

Mary Fry the wife of Thomas Fry of Hilbishopps in the County of Somerset Taylor, Aged Seaven and Twenty yeares or thereabouts, produced, sworne and Examined on the parte and behalfe of the defendents deposeth as followeth.

7) To the Seaventh Interrogatory this deponent saith that shee this deponent was useing in and out to the house of Mrs Elizabeth Browne in the Interrogatory named whiles shee lived, and that shee the said Mrs Browne did declare in the heareing of this deponent (being at the side of her Bed) that shee did lose goods in the tyme of the late Warrs, And she saith that the house of this deponents ffather was searched for some of the goods of the said Mrs Browne, shee also saith that the said Mrs Browne was plundred by Souldiers whiles the sieges were against Taunton, as she the said Mrs Browne told this deponent, And that the said Mrs Browne lived a Mile from the Towne of Taunton.

18) To the Eighteenth Interrogatory this deponent saith that shee hath been sundry tymes ymployed by Mrs Alice Capon sister to Mrs Elizabeth Browne, and who lived

then in house with her, to sell sundry parcells of a Gold chayne devided into broken links, small Rings, Corall, broken peeces of Gold, one necklace of Pearle, and other things of value, which shee this deponent on request did sell; And that one Jane Towers, as the said Mrs Capon told this deponent made sale of parte of a Gold chayne, wherein the said Mrs Capon said shee was wronged by the said Jane Towers; This deponent also saith that shee had charge from the said Mrs Capon to conceale the name of the partie whose goods they were But should declare it to bee a Gentlewomans of the Country, and sometymes directed her to say that it was one Mrs Tyderleighs. Howbeitt this deponent beleeveth that it was not the goods of the said Mrs Capons, because it was sold in hugger mugger.[85] And this deponent saith that att a tyme when shee brought some moneys to the said Mrs Capon for some of the things soe sold, The said Mrs Capon told her shee had sold a greate deale more then she was willing to sell, to give her daughter content.

William Mantle of Hill Bishopps in the County of Somerset Taylor, Aged Threescore and ffower yeares or there abouts is produced sworne and Examined on the parte and behalfe of the defendents deposeth as followeth:

7) To the Seaventh Interrogatory this deponent saith that the house of Mrs Elizabeth Browne was some tymes plundred by Souldiers whiles the Seiges were before Taunton, And that there were Clothes taken away, for which this Deponents house was searcht (but there were none found). Howbeitt this deponent saith that hee hath hard that those Clothes were conveyed into St James parish and there sould, but by whome, or for what, this deponent knoweth not.

9) To the Nynth Interrogatory this deponent saith, that the defendents hath been Marryed togeather for the space of ffower yeares last past and upwards. And saith that Mrs Elizabeth Browne did desire the defendents to live with her in her house att Sherford, And did declare content in there Company (hee this Deponent haveing been sundry tymes att the house and seen, and hard the same) And this deponent saith, that hee verily beleeveth the said Mrs Browne would have had the defendents to have continued with her till death, might shee have had her will. Hee also saith that the Complainant did force the defendents out of their said Mother against her consent, and to the greife of his Mother as this Deponent verily beleeveth by his threatning words towards the defendents, affirming in those words, that if shee would not leave the house, hee would prick her against the wall like a Toade, as hee hath hard the said defendent Elizabeth reporte, or words to such effect.

10) To the Tennth Interrogatory this deponent saith, that some particuler goods of Mrs Elizabeth Brownes the Complainants Mother were carryed from her house att Sherford unto the Defendents house att Sutton by the Consent of the said Mrs Browne shee then Intending to live there herselfe, But afterwards shee being disappoynted in a Conveayency for her removeall thither, did settle herselfe att her house att Sherford, whereupon some parte of the goods soe carryed away, were returned backe againe unto her said house att Sherford.

21) To the One and Twenteith Interrogatory this deponent saith that hee doth not know of any benifitt or profitt that the defendent Thomas Spigurnell hath had by his Marryage with the Complainants sister, But verily beleeveth the said Thomas

Spigurnell is a Thousand pounds the worse for that Match.

Robert Procter of the parish of Taunton Magdalen in the County of Somerset
Merchant formerly produced and sworne on the parte and behalfe of the Complainant
and now Examined on the parte and behalfe of the defendents, to the one and
twenteth Interrogatory only deposeth as followeth.
21) To the One and Twenteith Interrogatory this deponent saith, hee knoweth not
what the Complainant had by the Intermarriage of the Complainants Sister, and
farther hee is not Examined.

John Bridle of the parish of Burton[86] in the County of Dorset yeoman formerly
produced and sworne on the parte and behalfe of the Complainant and now
Examined on the parte and behalfe of the defendents deposeth as followeth:
1) To the ffirst Interrogatory this deponent saith that hee doth know the Lands of
Benfield and Graston in the County of Dorset, and that the Lands att Benfield were
lett for Three and Thirtey pounds per Annum, the Tennament discharging Rates and
Taxes, And that the Lands att Graston were also lett for Threescore and Sixteene
pounds per Annum the Landlady discharging Rates and Taxes, And that the now
Complainant doth receive the Rents for the same, and hath ever since the death of
Elizabeth Browne his Mother, But saith one Mrs Keymore hath lately made clayme to
the Lands att Benfeild. To the second Interrogatory this deponent saith[87] [m.9r] that
this Deponent hath no Acquittance from the defendents Thomas Spigurnell for any
Rents or profitts of the Lands of Benfield or Graston, neither did ever this Deponent
pay, or know to bee paid any of those Rents unto the hands of the Defendent Thomas
Spigurnell, But saith that hee paid the Rents mencioned in his deposicion taken on the
parte and behalfe of the Complainant to the said Elizabeth, And this deponent saith
that one tyme hee this deponent by order and direction of Mrs Elizabeth Browne the
Complainants Mother did pay unto the Complainant the sume of Twelve pounds and
Tenn shillings, and farther hee deposeth not.
To the Third Interrogatory this deponent saith that hee this deponent did in the life
tyme of the said Mrs Elizabeth Browne collect and receive the head Rents of the Inne
called the Bull in Bridport, being Eight pounds per Annum Includeing Rates and
Taxes, and paid the same severall tymes unto her, and since the death of the said
Elizabeth Browne hee this deponent hath Collected and paid those Rents unto the
Complainant, And farther hee is not Examined.

Alexander Hill of Taunton in the County of Somerset Gentleman Aged ffifty yeares
or thereabouts produced sworne and Examined for and on the parte and behalfe of
the defendents deposeth as followeth.
13) To the Thirteenth Interrogatory this deponent saith, That the Complainant in the
tyme of his Minority did take up a course of life suteable to a gentleman of his Ranke;
And that his Mother did maynteyne him Equevilent thereunto as this deponent
beleeveth; And this deponent saith that hee hath hard and doth beleeve that the
Complainants Mother did spend the whole revenue of her Estate from the tyme of
her husbands death in housekeepeing and otherwise, and more he deposeth nott.

16) To the Sixteenth Interrogatory this deponent saith that the Complainants Mother did declare a dislike, and complayne in this deponents heareing, that her sonne the now Complainant had Marryed against her good will; And this deponent saith that the defendent Elizabeth was carefull of her Mother in the tyme of the sicknesse whereof shee dyed, And this deponent beleeveth the said Elizabeth Browne did very well love and affect her said daughter.

21) To the One and Twenteith Interrogatory this deponent saith that hee never knew of any Estate, proffitt, or benefitt, the defendent Thomas Spigurnell had by his intermarriage with the Complainants Sister, and farther deposeth not.

Jane Tower wife of William Tower late of Wilton in the county of Somersett Carpenter aged ffortie ffive yeares or thereabouts produced on the behalfe of the defendent to the twelveth and Eighteenth Interrogatoryes and thereupon sworne and examined.

12) To the twelveth Interrogatory this deponent saith that she this deponent after the marage of the defendents was imployed in and about the house of Mrs Elizabeth Browne divers tymes and that she did receive severall sumes of money by appoyntement of the defendent Elizabeth from <her> ~~the~~ husband the defendent Thomas Spigurnell towards the discharge of some necessaryes in house keppinge And she also saith that she hath heard the said defendent Thomas Spigurnell say that it cost him Two hundred and ffifty pounds by the yeare in house keeping whiles he lived with his mother in Lawe.

To the Eighteenth Interrogatory this deponent saith That she was directed by one Mrs Capon sister to Elizabeth Browne the Complainants Mother to sell some small peeces of Lincks of a Gold chayne which she this deponent sold to one Mr Reeves a gold smyth for ffifteene shillings or ffifteene shillings and six pence and saith That beinge questioned by the said Mrs Elizabeth Browne touchinge the same the said Mrs Browne told this deponent it was a part of her the said Mrs Brownes gold chayne and that the same cost about ffiftie or three score pounds and more she saith not.

[*end of membrane signed by the commissioners*] Tho: Dyke, Will: Doble, H Plucknett

[*m.9v, endorsements on the outside of the roll*] Wilkinson 6th Bundle
Browne v Spigurnell
Anno 15° Carolus 2di
C22⁸⁸
767
33

xxv die Mar 1662
per Sacrum - Robt Leigh ...
Walli - Littleton

[END OF DOCUMENT]

11.

Description: The answer of George Browne esquire, 25 May 1663
Reference: T.N.A., C 10/78/62
Note: Browne's answer to Thomas Spigurnell's complaint concerning a debt owing to
Spigurnell from Browne's deceased mother's estate.

The severall answere of George Browne Esquire one of the defendants to the bill of
Complaint of Thomas Spigurnell Complainant

The saide defendant now and att all tymes hereafter saivinge to himslefe the benefitt
and advantage of excepcion to the incertainties insufficiencies and imperfeccions of
the said bill of Complaint and the matters therein contayned for answere thereunto
sayth that at the tyme of the death of Robert Browne esquire this defendants late
father hee this defendant was very younge and uncapable of what was then or at any
tyme before in the life tyme of this defendants said late father by him done four or
about the settlement or disposing of his estate But this defendant sayth that hee hath
heard that his saide late father did in his life tyme make his will and thereof did
constitute Elizabeth his then wife this defendants late mother his Executrix and
thereby did intrust her with parte of his estate in such manner and in the words in that
behalfe in the said bill of Complaint sett forth and expressed and saith that it is true
that they had yssue at the tyme of the death of the said Robert Browne only this
defendant and Elizabeth his sister the now wife of the said Complainant but this
defendant doth not knowe or believe that this defendants said mother did ever assigne
the offices of Porter and Clerke of the Castle of Taunton and Lordship thereof and
the Leasehold lands att Stoke hill and Huish Champflower in the said bill of
Complaint mencioned or any or either of them or any parte or parcell of them or of
any or either of them unto the said Complainant in Recompence of a marriage
porcion with this defendants said sister or otherwise as the said Complainant in and by
his said bill of Complaint in that behalfe suggestseth But this defendant death
confesse that some lands heretofore entayled on the heires male of this defendants
said late Father did uppon the death of this defendants saide mother who had an
estate therein for her life for her joynture come to this defendant But this defendant
sayth that hee does not knowe or believe that this defendants said late mother was in
her life tyme reduced to poverty or constrained to borrow any somme or sommes of
money of the said Complainant or of any other person or persons whatsoever as in
and by the said bill of Complaint is in that behalfe most falsly alleaged However this
defendant hath heard and doth beleive that his saide late mother did in her life tyme
borrow some monies of one Thomas Oteway and others for repayment of which she
morgaged some lands she then had but this defendant has bene informed and hopes
to prove that the same was soe by her borrowed not out of any poverty or by
constraint but at and uppon the earnest desire of the said Complainant and for his
owne use and not for the use of this defendants saide late mother which monies this

defendant have heard and hopes to prove that the said Complainant did accordingly receive and did faithfully promise to repay at the tymes in the said morgage or morgages lymited for payment of the same which this defendant doth beleive hee never did And this defendant sayth that hee doth not knowe that his saide mother did at any tyme in her life tyme borrow any money of John Porter in the said bill of Complaint in that behalfe named out of the profitts of the saide office of Clerke of the Castle of Taunton or otherwise nor of any such agreement or agreements passages or transactions by or betweene the defendants said late mother the saide John Porter and the said Complainant or any of them touching any somme or sommes of money whatsoever borrowed Lent or secured by or betweene them or any of them as in and by the said bill of Complaint is in that behalfe sett forth And this defendant doth deny that hee ever kept or detayned from this defendants said late mother any estate belonging to her and saith that hee doth not knowe that the said Complainant did ever signe or seale any such paper to the said John Porter as the said Complainant in an by his said bill hath sett forth to bee by him signed to the said John Porter nor touching Thirty and two pounds supposed in an by the said bill of Complaint to bee by him lent to this defendants said late mother nor doth this defendant knowe that the saide John Porter did in his life tyme make his will nor who hee made his executors but confesseth it that hee about two yeares since died but whether hee att the tyme of his death had in his hands any somme or sommes of money for which hee was accomtable to the said Complainant or whether hee had at his death in his hands or custody any patent deed lease conveyance or other writing belonging to the estate late of this defendants saide mother setled on the said Complainante in consideracion of his marriage with this defendants said sister this defendant doth not knowe However this defendant sayth that hee never had or received of or from Robert Procter and [*blank*] Porter in the said bill of Complaint named any of the profitts of the said office or any patent deed lease conveyance or other writinge whatsoever belonging to any of the estate to which the said Complainant in or by his said bill of Complaint pretendeth any title But this defendant doth confesse that hee livinge with his said mother at the tyme of her death in the house wherein she lived and dyed that severall of the goods and householdstuffe in her possession att her death did uppon her death come to the hands of this defendant all which and all other her personall estate she havinge not longe before she dyed declared she would leave to this defendant hee this defendant did uppon her death take the same into his custody and did indeavour to have made such her declaration to amount unto a will and to have taken an Administracion of her goods but this defendant being therein opposed by the said Complainant and his saide wife this defendant hath not only hitherto bene therein hindered and obstructed by the said Complainant but an Inventary of the same goods and household stuffe hath uppon the Complainants speciall mocion and prosecucion bene by special Commission yssued forth of the Prerogative Court of Canterbury[89] by speciall Commissioners taken and returned into the said Court all which amount to the value of fourescore and tenn pounds or thereabouts which this defendant doth beleive was and is the full value of the same And this defendant sayth that hee hath not nor never had in his custody to his knowledge and best Remembrance any more or other goods of his saide late mothers then were produced or made knowne to the said

Commissioners at the taking of the said Inventary and doth deny that this defendants saide late mother did to his knowledge dye possessed of a reall and personall estate worth five thousand pounds or more then the somme the said Inventary did amount unto as aforesaid And this defendant sayth that hee is neither Executor nor Administrator to his said late mother and is and must bee accomtable for the goods of his saide late mothers in his custody to such as are or shalbee thereto lawfully intitled and further saith that the said Complainant himselfe hath claymed and as this defendant doth beleive death clayme the same as in right belonging unto him by virtue of some grante thereof to him made by the saide Elizabeth Browne this defendants saide late mother in her life tyme for which reasons this defendant hopeth under favour of this honourable Court and soe is advised by his Councell that hee is not nor of right ought either in law or equity to stand chargeable or to discharge any debt or somme of money due by the said Elizabeth Browne this defendants said late mother at her death and in particular the saide somme of Thirty and two pounds in an by the said bill of Complaint mencioned for which the said Complainant in and by the same bill of Complaint seeketh to bee relieved against this defendant And this defendant sayth that John Browne or Frampton Esquire was uppon the death of this defendants said late Father seized for the terme of his life in the said office of Clerke of the Castle of Taunton by vertue of a patent thereof granted by some late Bishopp of Winton, and beinge thereof soe seized did by Letter of Attourney and his hand and seale authorize this defendant to surrender the same to the end this defendant might buy and purchase a further estate therein in pursueance of which authority this defendant sayth that hee did about [*blank*] yeares since accordingly surrender the saide patent unto Brian then Bishopp of Winton who thereuppon granted the same office unto this defendant and one John Gollopp for theire lives and the longest liver of them by vertue of which grante or patent this defendant sayth that hee did shortly after the obtayning of the same enter into the said office and by his deputy ever since hath executed and doth still execute the same and hath received and doth receive the profitts thereof which hath in all ultra reprizes amounted unto the somme of two hundred foure and twenty pounds and noe more <to the best of this defendants knowledge or remembrance> and saith that hee never received any of the profitts of the said office before the obtayning of the said grante thereof and death deny all the practice and Combynacion in and by the said bill of Complaint layde to his charge and alsoe that hee ever had or hath in his hands custody or keeping any other deed lease patent conveyance or other writinge concerninge all or any the estate or the saide office claymed by the said Complainant in or by his said bill then this defendant hath herein before sett forth and expressed without that that any other matter or thinge clause sentence or allegacion in the said bill of Complaint contayned materiall or effectuall in the law for him this defendant to make answere unto and not herein and hereby sufficiently answered unto confessed and avoyded traversed or denyed is true all which this defendant is ready to averr justifye and prove as this honourable Court shall award and humbly prayeth to bee hence dismissed with his reasonable costs and charges in this behalfe and without just cause sustained.

25 May 1663 [*signed*] Ald: Seaman, John Southey, Ro: Leigh

[END OF DOCUMENT]

12.

Description: Complaint of Edward Chard of Long Sutton in the county of Somerset gentleman and Elizabeth his wife versus George Browne, date missing
Reference: T.N.A., C 6/176/18
Note: No date is written on the document but it is after June 1665 when Edward Chard married Elizabeth Spigurnell widow.

To the right honourable Earle of Clarendon Lord high Chancellour of England Humbly complaineing sheweth unto your Lordshipp your daily Orator and Oratrix Edward Chard of Long Sutton in the County of Somersett Gentleman and Elizabeth his wife the onely daughter of Robert Browne late of Taunton in the said County of Somersett Esquire deceased and late wife and relict of Thomas Spigurnell late of Long Sutton aforesaid gentleman deceased That whereas the said Thomas Spigurnell in his life tyme and your said Oratrix Elizabeth his then wife in or about the terme of St. Michaell which was in the yeare of our Lord 1661 Exhibited their Bill of Complaint unto this honourable Court against George Browne gentleman the onely brother of your said Oratrix Elizabeth and John Browne of Frampton in the County of Dorsett Esquire thereby setteing forth that the said Robert Browne your Oratrix said late father in his life tyme in or about the yeare of our Lord 1633 did purchase of Walter then Lord Byshopp of Wynton the office of Clarke of the Castle and Burrough and Lordshipp of Taunton in the said County of Somersett unto himselfe and unto the said John Browne (beinge the sonne of John Browne late of Frampton aforesaid in the said County of Dorssett Esquire deceased (who was your Oratrix fathers elder brother for the terme of their lives and the life of the longest liver of them, which was an office antiently grannteable by the Byshopp of Wynton for the tyme being who had power in right of his Bishoppricke to graunt the same, and as by the Instrument it selfe under the said late Byshopps seale (if it might be produced) would more plainely appeare which said purchase was contracted for and made by the said Robert Browne alone and the ffine or consideration therefore given was paid by the said Robert Browne your Oratrix said late ffather and with his proper moneyes, and the name of the said John Browne the younger was incerted in the pattent or Instrument of grannt of the said office by the direccion and appoyntment of the said Robert and in trust for him his Executors Administrators and Assignes and accordingly hee said Robert Browne entred in the said office alone and had took and commited to his own use all the rents and yearely profitte of the said office and premisses dureinge the then future terme of his life which was for six yeare and upwards dureinge all which tyme the said John Browne did not intermeddle in the said office or receave any rents or profitts thereof though the same was worth one hundred and fforty pounds per Annum And that the said Robert beinge soe there of seiced and having yssue by Elizabeth his then wife two children (vizt) George his onely sonne and your Oratrix Elizabeth his onely daughter made his last Will and Testament in writinge beareing date the second day of August which was in the yeare of our Lord <u>1637</u> and conceiveinge (as the truth was and is) that hee might Lymmitt and appoynt thereby the benefitt of the trust and after his death by the said pattent and grannt would rest in the said John Browne and intendinge to settle and appoynt howe the trust should be disposed of and imployed by his said last will did amongst other things give and appoynt the said office and premisses which he held under the Byshopp of Wynton for his owne life and the life of the said John Browne as aforesaid to his said wife Elizabeth dureing her widdowehood to the use of his Children to mayneteyne and proferr them and to rayse portions for them as in her discretion should be thought fitt with the advise of his Overseer and thereby was further appoynted that instantly after his death the said office should be bought of the Byshopp for an other life in trust for his said wife and children and of his said Will made his said wife whole and sole Executrix and John Porter gentleman overseer thereof as by the said Will relation thereunto beig and if produced would alsoe more plainely and att large appeare. And shortly thereafter the said Robert Browne dyed and the said John Browne him survived and became solely enstated in the said office but upon the trust aforesaid thereby farther setting forth that the said Thomas Spigurnell your Oratrix said late husband having an estate in Lands of neere two hundred pounds by the yeare in the said County of Somersett and else where to the knowledge of the said Elizabeth Browne widdow and Executrix of the said Robert Browne your Oratrix said late mother and after some treaty betweene the said Thomas Spigurnell and the said Elizabeth your Oratrix said late Mother touchinge a Mariage to be had betweene the said Thomas and your Oratrix And upon the said Thomas and your Oratrix her consent it was about fower yeares before the exhibiting of the said Bill agreed on betweene the said Thomas and the said Elizabeth the Executrix said Mother by and with the consent and approbacion of the said George Browne your Oratrix said Brother that a Marriage should be had between the said Thomas and your Oratrix and that the said Thomas should have as a Marriage portion with your said Oratrix the summe of one thousand pounds to be raysed out of the profitts of the said office by virtue of the said trust over and besides the porters office and other Lands to the vallue of about two hundred pounds being in all 1200^{li} And that the said Elizabeth Browne your Oratrix said late Mother and Executrix of the said Robert her father aswell in pursuance of the said Marriage Agreement as alsoe of the trust and power granted her by the said Will of her husband with the consent and knowledge of the said George Browne did by deed under her hand and seale charge the said office with the Rayseing of 100^{li} parte of the porcion of your Oratrix. And the said Elizabeth the Mother to further the raiseing of the said portion did give direction unto the said John Porter (who executed the said office and who had knowledge of the said appoyntment made by the said Elizabeth the Mother to passe an accompt with and pay the profitts of the said office as the same should be raysed unto the said Thomas Spigurnell in his life tyme which accordingly was donne by the said John Porter without any contradiccion of the said John Browne who had perfect notice of the said appoyntment And the said Thomas Spigurnell did thereby further sett forth that shortly after the said Marriage (to witt) in or about the year 1659 the said George

Browne did exhibite his bill into the Court of Excheqer against his said Mother to compell her to sett forth what estate she had settled on the said Thomas Spigurnell as a portion with your Oratrix to which Bill the said Elizabeth gave her Answeare that she had charged the said office with the payment of the said 1000^{li} which answeare beinge duely filed in the said Court and received by the said George Browne he forthwith wayved his proceedings in that Court and dismissing his Bill exhibited another Bill into this honourable Court of Chancery against his said Mother and the said George Browne the party trusted to the same to which she gave the like Answeare that she had for the said Thomas Spigurnells portion in Marriage which your Oratrix chardged the said office with the payment of the said one thousande pounds All which the said George Browne well knowne as alsoe the said John Browne party trusted he beinge party to the said suites and had coppes of the said Bills and Answears and gave in his owne Answeare thereunto and agreed to performe the said trust and likewise the said John Browne and George Browne very well knewe that there was noe other portion or maintenance to be raised for your said Oratrix but out of the profitts of the said office (besides those small things given to the said Thomas Spigurnell as aforesaid yet not with standinge the said George Browne allthought he well knewe that it was the direicion of the said Robert Browne his ffather by his said Will that the life of the said John Browne should bee continued and that at the first opportunity an other Life should be purchased and added to the said John Browne for the benefit of the said Robert as aforesaid and that the said George Browne was privy and consentinge to the Mariage agreement yet he had the said George by Combinacion had with the said John Browne, And to the ende to defraud the said Thomas Spigurnell in his lifetime of the said one thousand pounds and that the said trust and estate under the pretence of pursueinge of the direccions of the said Will of the said Robert Browne his father and upon promise that the life of the said John Browne should still be continued and stand in a newe Pattent or Graunt to be obteyned of the said Office to the use of the said last will of the said Robert Browne And that he would onely add his owne life and by other sinister meanes he the he the he the said George Browne soe far prevailed with the said John Browne that the said John Browne did deliver unto him the said George Browne the said first pattent or Graunt obteyned by the said Robert Browne with a lettre of Attorney or other power to surrender the same which he noe sooner had obteyned but contrary to his promise and the trust and direccions of the said Last Will of his said father in the name of the said John Browne, did surrender up the said pattent or Graunt and insteed of incertinge againe the name of the said John Browne accordinge to the trust and directions of the said Will he tooke and obteyned from the then present Lord Byshopp <of> Winton whose Grannt the said office was a newe Pattent or Grannt thereof to himselfe for two other Lives or names intendinge thereby to defraud the said Thomas Spigurnell of his trust and interest in the profitts of the said office and of the said 1000^{li} and dammages for the same whereas the said newe pattent or Grannt ought in Equite to be suiect to the trust or poynted by the will of the said Robert Browne And consequently chargeable with the said 1000^{li} to the said Thomas Spigurnell and the said trust for him and your said Oratrix And the said Thomas and your Oratrix did there by <alsoe> further shewe that they haveinge notice of this

86

greate fraud tendinge to the utter ruine of them did peticion the then Lord Bishopp of
Wynton thereby settinge forth their said right and title and the fraud committed by the
said George Browne which the said Lord Bishopp beinge sencible off, was pleased to
grannt upon the said peticion a lettre of prohibicion unto the then Deane and Chapter
of Wynton intimateinge his beinge surprized by the said George Browne and to desire
the saide Deane and Chapter to forbeare the confirmacion of the said newe pattent or
grannt but the said George Browne made such hast unto the Deane and Chapter that
he obteyned a confirmacion of the said newe pattent or graunt by the said Deane and
Chapter some fewe howres before the said Thomas Spigurnell had come to them with
the said Letter of prohibicion and soe the said George Browne haveinge thus
surrepticiously obteyned the said newe pattent or Graunt and confirmacion thereof as
aforesaid, hath made some secrett estate or estates thereof to some person or persons
unknowne to the said Thomas in his life tyme and after to your Oratrix in trust for
himselfe or upon some other trust and would not permitt or suffer the said Thomas in
his life tyme to receave the said portion of 1000^{li} and damages out of the said office or
the profitts thereof although the said George Browne had and hath an estate left him
by his said late father and Mother worth about six thousand pounds besides the said
office, there xxx beinge noe other children left by the said Robert but the said George
Browne and your Oratrix Elizabeth who hath received noething as yet of what was left
or intended for her by her said fathers will and appoyntment of the said Elizabeth her
Mother (to whome she was ever obedient serviceable and pleaseinge) Thereby alsoe
further settinge forth that the said George Browne has got into his custody or the
custody of some other by his delivry consent or privity the said last Will of the said
Robert Browne denying to let the said Thomas Spigurnell to have the same or the
sight or perusall thereof In tender consideracion whereof and for that the said
Thomas and your Oratrix had noe remedy by the strict Rules of the Common Lawe of
the Realme to compell the said George to suffer the said Thomas in his life time by
percepcion of the profitts of the said office to receive satisfaccion of the said 1000li
portion and damages he the said Thomas having never received above Thirty pounds
out of the profitts of the said office towards the said 1000li and dammages but the
said Thomas had h.. up and <in>deed only remedy before your Lordshipp in the high
Court of Chancery where breach of trust frauds and circumvencions are properly
examinable and remedyed neither could the said Thomas for want of the said old
pattent or graunt and last Will manifest or make out the trust or directions thereof or
other the transaccions aforesaid else where or otheerwise then un this honourable
Court upon the oathes of the said confederates many of the persons that should or
could prove the same beinge since dead or removed into partes beyond the seas far
remote and unknowne to the said Thomas and your Oratrix but the said Thomas and
your Oratrix did well knowe that the said George and John Browne could and did well
hope they or one of them would upon his or their Corporall oathes discover the
particular truth of the premisses which that they might doe and might make a perfect
and particular Answeare to all and singular the premisses And that the said Thomas
and your Oratrix might be releeved touching the same accordinge to Equity and good
conscience your Orator and Oratrix thereby prayed the ayd and assistance of this
honourable Court and procoess of this honourable Court to be directed to them the

said George Browne and John Browne accordingly which beinge granted and they the said George Browne and John <Browne> therewith accordingly served they appeared and put in their severall Answeares thereunto whereunto the said Thomas and your Oratrix replyed and thereupon yssue being ioyned severall witnesses were afterwards examined on both sides and the depositions thereupon taken were thereupon returned and duely filed in this honourable Court and afterwards the same were published according to the ancient Laudable & accustomed rules & proceedings of this honourable Court and a day was appoynted for the heareinge and determininge of the matters aforesaid before your Lordshipp in this Honourable Court again and by the said Bill Answear and Replications of witnesses & severall orders touchinge the same all remaineing of Record and in the Registry of the honourable Court Relacion thereunto beinge had and whereunto for more certainty herein your Orator and Oratrix may more plainely and att large did appeare And your Orator and Oratrix doe further showe unto your Lordshipp that before the said cause came to be heard (to witt) in or about the moneth of August in the yeare of our lord 1663 hee the said Thomas Spigurnell your Oratrix late husband dyed and by reason thereof ....te said suite abated he haveinge first constituted and made his last Will and Testament in writeinge and therein and thereby given bequeathed and left unto your said Oratrix all his right Tytle and Interest of in and to the said 1200li portion doe remaineing in the hands of the said George Browne as aforesaid together withall benefit and advantage to be had and received thereby for your Oratrix further livelyhood and subsistance of her selfe and three small children leeft by the said Thomas Spigurnell and of his said will constituted and made John Pyne of Curreymallet in the said County of Somersett Esquire And John Dryer of Long Sutton aforesaid yeoman Executors in trust for the said children to whome he gave and devised all his reall and personall estate exceptinge the said portion soe belonging unto your said Oratrix as aforesaid) And appoynted the same to be sould and equally distributed and amongst his said Children as in and by the said last will and Testament of the said Thomas Spigurnell or the true copy thereof taken and extracted out of the Registry of the prerogative Court of Canterbury where the same was proved in due forme of Lawe by the said Executors in trust or one of them ready to be produced to this honourable Court to manefest the same relacion thereunto beinge has may alsoe more plainely and att large appeare soe that the said portion soe remaineing due and unpaid as afore said by the said George Browne unto your Oratrix aforesaid withall the future lively hood and subsistance your Oratrix hath to subsist by, or to depend upon And your Orator and Oratrix doe further showe unto your Lordshipp that after the death of the said Thomas Spigurnell and whilest your Oratrix remaynd a widdow both by her selfe and severall other friends on her behalfe in all faire and friendly manner often times desired and requested the said George Browne to make payment and satisfacion of the said portion soe due and of right belonging unto your Oratrix aforesaid and gave him due notice of the contents of the said last Will and Testament of the said Thomas Spigurnell as aforesaid And that the same was all the livelyhood and subsustance your said Oratrix had to depend upon as aforesaid yet the said George Browne most unnaturally and inconscionably utterly refused and denyed soe to doe or to give any satisfaccion att all unto your Oratrix concerning the same and your Orator

88

and Oratrix doe yet further shewe that about halfe a yeare since your Oratrix inter
marryed and tooke to husband your said Orator and were Lawfully ioyned together in
Matrimony and by reason thereof they became ioyntly interessed and intituled of in
and to the said twelve hundred pounds portion and damages soe originally and of
right belonging and appeerteyninge to your Oratrix as aforesaid and thereupon your
Orator in right of your Oratrix his said wife shortly after repayred unto the said
George Browne and gave him notice of the said Marriage and hath since both by
herselfe and severall other friends and agents on <his and> his said wifes behalfe
endeavorred <and persuaded> the said George Browne in all friendly and usuall
manner to make payment and satisfaccion of the said portion which he still hath <and
doth> most unlawfully and unconscionably refuse to doe To thend therefore that the
said George Browne (who well knoweth all and every the premisses aforesaid to be
true in such a manner and forme as aforesaid Answeare all and every the premisses
and that all the said proceedings of Bill Answeares Replicacion <deposicions> and
orders may stand revived in such and the same manner to all intents and purposes as
the same were att the time of the death of the said Thomas Spigurnell as aforesaid
And that your Oratrix may be speedily releeved herein upon the whole matter
accordinge to Equity and good conscience May it please your Lordshipp the premisses
considered to grant unto your Orator and Oratrix his Majesties most gracious writt of
subpena to be directed unto the said George Browne and <John Browne> thereby
comandinge them att a certaine day and under a certaine paine therein to be lymited
personally to be and appeare before your Lordshipp in this high and honourable Court
of Chancery then and there to answeare the premisses or shewe cause to the contrary
if they can why all the matters and proceedings aforesaid should not stand and be
recited as aforesaid and further to stand to and abide such further order and decree
therein as to your Lordshipp shall seeme meet And your Orator and Oratrix as in duty
bound shall allways pray.

[*signature of*] Wm. Jennens

[END OF DOCUMENT]

13.

Description: Complaint of Edward Chard of Long Sutton in the county of Somerset gentleman and Elizabeth his wife versus George Browne, date missing
Reference: T.N.A., C 6/176/18
Note: No month is visible on the document but it is after June 1665 when Edward Chard married Elizabeth Spigurnell widow and before 18 April 1666 when George Browne gave his answer to this complaint.

.... 16 1665 Longville
To the right honourable Edward Earle of Clarendon lord high Chancellor of England. Humbly complaineing sheweth unto your Lordshipp your orator and oratrix Edward Chard of long Sutton in the county of Somersett gentleman and Elizabeth his wife the onely daughter of Robert Browne in the said County deceased and late wife of Thomas Spigurnell in his life tyme and your Oratrix his then wife about the terme of St. Michaell in the yeare 1661 exhibited their bill into this honourable Court against George Browne onely brother of your oratrix and John Browne of Frampton in the county of Dorsett thereby setting forth that the said Robert Browne in his life in the yeare 1633 did purchase of Walter then Lord Bishopp of Winton the office of Clarke of the Castell and burrough of Taunton in the said county to himselfe and the said John Browne beinge the sonne of John Browne late of Framton Esquire deceased whoe was your oratrix <fathers> elder brother for the terme of there lives and the longer liver which was an office granteable by the Bishopp of Winton for the tyme being, which said purchase was made and contracted for by and made by the said Robert Browne and the fyne paid by him your said oratrix ffather and the name of the said John Browne incerted by his oppoyntment in the pattent in trust for him and his assignes and accordingly the said Robert Browne entred into the said office and tooke upon him the rents and yearely proffitts for the terme of his life which was for six yeares duringe which tyme the said John Browne did not intermedle with the said office or receave any the rents or proffitts though the same was worth 140li per annum and the said Robert being soe seized had issue 2 children (vizt) George and your oratrix and made his last will and testament dated 2 of August in the yeare 1637 and conceiveinge that he might appoint the trust and after his death by the said pattent did amongst other things to his said wife to the use of his children and proferr them and to raise porcions and appointed that instantly after his death that the said office should be bought of the said Bishopp for annother life in trust for his wife and children and made his wife sole executrix and John Porter overseer as the said will may appeare and shortly after the said Robert Browne dyed and the said John Browne him survived and solely enstated in the said office but uppon the trust aforesaid And did farther sett forth that your oratrix said late father to her husband an estate of 200li by the yeare to the knowledge of the said Elizabeth Browne your oratrix mother and after somme treaty betweene the said Thomas Spigurnall and your oratrix mother

touching a marriage to be had betweene the said Thomas and your oratrix which was agreed on about 4 yeares before the exhibitting of the bill with the approbacion of the said George Browne your oratrix brother and that your oratrix should have 1000li to be raised out of the said office by vertue of the said trust besides the porters office and other lands to the value of 200li being in all 1200li and the said Elizabeth did charge the said office with the said 1000li parte of your oratrix porcion and to further the payment of the same did order the said John Porter whoe executed the said office to accompt and pay the said proffitts unto the said Thomas Spigurnell in his life tyme and he did pay the same without any contradicion of the said John Browne who had notice of the same appoyntment and did sett forth that after the said marriage to with[90] about the yeare 1659 the said George Browne did exhibitt into the court of Exchequer against his said mother to know what estate the said Robert[91] Spigurnell was to have with your oratrix who gave her answer that she had charged the said office with the said 1000li which beinge duly fyled he waved his proceedings and dismissed his said bill in the said Court and fyled an other in the court of Chancery against his mother and the said George Browne the party trusted to which she gave the like answer and the said John Browne in his answer that he was trusted and did entend to performe the same and they knew that there was noe other porcion or maintenance to be raised but out of the said office yett the said George allthough he kneweth that it was the will of his ffather and was privy and consentinge to the marriage agreement and the premisses aforesaid yett they combyneing togeather to defraud your oratrix husband of the said 1000li and promising that the life of the said John Browne in a newe pattent to be gained and the said George procured the same to be assigned and did not performe according to the said will he obteyned the and[92] from the present lord bishopp in his own name entendinge to defraud your oratrix said husband of the 1000li due to him and your said oratrix whereupon they did pitticion the then lord Bishopp setting forth the same whoe thereupon did issue his prohibicion to the Deane and Chapter to make stay of the confirmacion but the said George Browne made such hast that he procured the same before they could come with the same and hath made and contrived divers and sundry secrett estates unknowne to the said Thomas in his life tyme and alsoe to your oratrix and would not suffer him to receive the said 1000li out of the said office although he had an estate left him by his father and mother worth 6000li besides the said office haveing possessed himselfe with the said last will of the said Robert Browne In tender consideracion whereof and for that the said Thomas and your oratrix had noe remedy and they well hoped that they would discover the same upon their oathes the truth of all and singuler the premisses they prayed the aid of this Court and that process might be awarded and directed to them the said George Browne and John Browne which being granted and they served they appeared and put in there answers and issue being ioyned and severall witnesses examined and after sett a day appointed for hereinge and determine the same as by the severall proceedings remaineing of Record the said cause came to be heard about the moneth of August in the yeare 1663 hee the said Thomas Spigurnell your oratrix late husband dyed by reason whereof the suit abated and haveinge first made his last will and bequeathed all his interest in the said 1200li remaineing in the hands of the said George Browne as aforesaid and made and constantuted[93] John Pyne of Curreymellet in the said County and John Drier of lone Sutten aforesaid executors in trust for and to be distributed equally betweene the said Children as by the will and testament of the said Thomas Spigurnill which was proved in due forme of law by the said Executors as by the same may appeare And your orator doth further shew that after the death of the said Thomas Spigurnall and while your oratrix was a widdow your oratrix demanded the same And your oratrix further sheweth that about halfe a yeare since youre oratrix interrmaried and tooke to husband and were <u>lawfully</u> joyned togeather lawfully and by reason thereof they became joyntly interressed and intituled to the said 1200li and damages belonged unto your oratrix and thereupon your oratrix in right of his said wife shortly after repaired unto the said George Browne and gave him notice of the said marriage and hath by himselfe agents endeaverred to perswade the said George Browne in a frindly manner to make payment and satisfaccion which he still hath and refuseth to doe To the end there that the said George Browne who knoweth all the premisses to be true as aforesaid and may Answer all and singuler the premisses and that all the said proceedings of Bill Answers Replicacions deposicions may stand revived in such and the same manner and to all entents and purposes as the same were att the time of the death of the said Thomas Spigurnall as aforesaid and that your orator and oratrix may be spedially releeved herein upon the whole matter according to equity and good conscience may it please your lordshipp the premisses considered to grant unto your orator and oratrix his majesty most gracious writt of subpena to be directed unto the said George Browne and John Browne comandinge &c

Wm. Jennens

[END OF DOCUMENT]

14.

Description: The answer of George Browne to the complaint of Edward and
Elizabeth Chard, 18 April 1666
Reference: T.N.A., C 6/176/18

[*annotated*] Wilkinson

The severall answere of George Browne gentleman defendant to the bill of Complaint
of Edward Chard and Elizabeth his wife Complainants
The saide defendant now and at all time hereafter saving to himselfe the benefitt and
advantage of excepcion to the incertaintyes insufficiencyes and imperfecins of the said
bill of Complaint and the matters therein contained, for answere thereunto sayeth that
the Complainant Elizabeth is daughter of Robert Browne esquire deceased in the saide
bill of Complaint named and is the relict and was sometymes the wife of Thomas
Spigurnell in the saide bill of Complaint <alsoe> named but whether shee bee now
the wife of the Complainant Edward Chard this defendant doth not know But doth
confesse it to bee true that the saide Thomas Spigurnell and the Complainant
Elizabeth did in the life tyme of him the saide Thomas Spigurnell in or about the yeare
one thousand six hundred sixty and one exhibite severall bills of Complaint into this
honourable Courte against the defendent and one bill of Complaint against the
defendant and against John Browne esquire in the Complainants bill of Complaint in
that behalfe named but whether the saide bill were in effect and substance such and
the same as in and by the Complainants now bill of Complaint is in that behalfe sett
forth this defendant doth not know nor remember but for the certaintie thereof
referrs himselfe to the same bill of Complaint remaininge as this defendant doth
beleive of Recorde in this honourable Courte but ths defendant doth beleive that hee
the defendant and the said John Browne did put in severall answeres to the same bill
which were fyled uppon which yssue was joyned and severall witnesses were examined
but whether theire deposicions were returned and duly files in this honourable Courte
and afterwards published and a day for hearinge of the cause was appointed as in and
by the Complainants bill of Complaint is in that behalfe sett forth this defendant
sayeth hee not know but for the certaintie thereof referres himelfe to the Records
rules and orders of this honourable Courte relating thereunto But this defendant doth
beleive that before the saide cause was heard or determined to witt about the time in
the saide bill of Complaint in that behalfe meconed the saide Thomas Spigurnell dyed
but whether hee before his death made any or such a will as in and by the
Complainants saide bill of Complaint is in that behalfe sett forth this defendant sayeth
hee doth not know, nor doth this defendant know whether such or any pretended will
at all of him the saide Thomas Spigurnell hath since his death bene in due forme of
law ever proved in the Perogative Courte of Cantebury but is induced to beleive the
contrary for that hee hath bene often credibly informed that John Dryer in the saide
bill of Complaint named who is supposed to bee one of the executors of the same

will and to make probate thereof did never take any such oath relating to that supposed will as by the law and course of proceedings in that Courte in the probate of wills all persons who prove any wills there have used and ought to take: Butt this defendant doth confesse that three Hundred pounds as soe much of the porcion of the Complainant Elizabeth which was intended to her by Elizabeth Browne hers and this defendants late mother out of hers and this defendants saide late fathers estate was by an awarde in writing made by the saide John Browne to whome the saide Thomas Spigurnell in his life tyme and this defendant did by mutuall consent referr all matters in difference betweenethem appointed and awarded to bee paide by the defendant to the saide Thomas Spigurnell in full of all he claimed in or out of the estate lands tenements and offices of this defendants saide late father and mother And this defendant sayeth that at the tyme and place by the saide awarde appointed for the payment thereof hee this defendant did tender the same unto the saide Thomas Spigurnell being then and there present who counted all the moneyes soe tendered and was thereuppon or otherwise satisfyed that the same was full three hundred pounds and did put upp the same in baggs but this saide Spigurnell refusing to performe that parte of the saide awarde which by the direcion true intent and meaninge of the same he was to performe to this defendant and alsoe to deliver to this defenandt all the deeds and writings in his custody touching the same as by one parte of the same awarde ready to be produced unto this honourable Courte by this defendant for the greater certainty doth referr himselfe it will appeare and this defendant having not in his custody the bond of awarde entered into by the saide Spigurnell to this defendant to performe the same whereby to inforce the performance thereof but the saide bond being in the hands of the saide John Browne who refused to deliver upp the same to this defendant he this defendant doth confesse that hee did not at that tyme permitt the saide Spigurnell to carry away the saide three hundred pounds hee then refusing to performe that parte of the saide awarde which on his parte was to bee performed but this defenant then told him that if he would on his parte performe that parte of the saide award which on his parte was to be performed according to the true intent thereof this defendant would not at all obstruct his carriage away of the same or to that effect which he refusing to doe this defendant did retain the saide three Hundred pounds and hath the same still in this defendants hands. And this defendant sayeth that he hath at all tymes bene and is now ready to pay the saide three hundred pounds and to performe the saide awarde on this defendants parte to bee performed soe as the same on the parte of the saide Thomas Spigurnell to be performed might or yett may accordinge to the true intent and meaninge of the same awarde be observed and performed to this defendants attorney although the saide Thomas Spigurnell in his life tyme did not only refuse to performe the same but by multiplicity of vexatious suites wherein he improiled this defendant since the saide award and tender soe made as aforsaide touching the same hath putt this defendant to above two hundred pounds costs in this defendants just and necessary defence of the same suites with this that this defendant hath bene informed and doth beleive it to be true that the Complainant Elizabeth was drawne to intermarry the other Complainant uppon pretence he was a person of good quallity and greate estate which now appearing to bee otherwise and that the Complainant

Edward Charde is a person of a very meane or noe estate at all and for that it appeares by the Complainants owne bill of Complaint that the saide three hundred pounds is all the future livelyhood and maintenance which the Complainant Elizabeth hath to subsist by or depend on this defendant humbly prayes that the saide three Hundred pounds when paide may by the ayde and favor of this honourable Courte be soe setled and disposed of that the same may not be in the power of the saide Edward Charde to spend waste or consume it but that the same may remaine for the future maintenance and livelyhoode of the Complainant Elizabeth without that that any other matter or thinge clause sentence or allegacion in the saide bill of Complaint contained materiall or effectuall in the law for him this defendant to make answers unto and of herein and hereby sufficiently answered unto confessed and avoided traversed or denyed is true all which this defendant is readdy to averr jusitfy and prove as this honourable Courte shall awarde and humbly prayeth to be hence dismissed with his reasonable costs and charges in this behalfe most wrongfully and without cause sustained.

Taken at Taunton the 28th day of April in the 18th year of the reign of King Charles the Second anno domini 1666 on the day the defendant received the sacrament.

    [*signed*] Aldred Seaman
    [*signed*] Hen. Norman

[END OF DOCUMENT]

15.

Description: Complaint of Edward Chard and Elizabeth Chard, on or before
13 May 1667
Reference: T.N.A., C 6/46/77
Note: This is the case of Edward Chard and Elizabeth Chard v John Gollopp. Gollop
at this date was the joint holder of the patent of Clerk of Taunton Castle with
Elizabeth's brother George Browne.

To the right honourable Edward Earle of Clarendon lord high Chancellor of England
humbly Complaineinge sheweth unto your lordshipp your daily Orator and Oratrix
Edward Chard of longsutton in the County of Somersett gentleman and Elizabeth his
wife the onely daughter of Robert Browne late of Taunton in the County of
Somersett Esquire deceased and later wife and relict of Thomas Spigurnell of
longsutton gent deceased That whereas the said Thomas Spigurnell in his lifetyme and
your said Oratrix Elizabeth his then wife more about the tyme of St michaell was in
the yeare of our lord 1661 exhibited ther bill of Complainte into this Court against
George Browne gentleman the onely brother of your said Oratrix and John Browne
of Frampton in County Dorsett Esquire thereby settinge forth that the said Robert
Browne your Oratrix late father in his lifetyme more about the yeare of our lord 1633
did purchase of Walter then lord Bishopp of Winton the Office of Clarke of the
castle and Burrough and lordshipp of Taunton in the said County of Somerset unto
himselfe and unto the said John Browne being the sonne of John Browne late of
Frampton in the said County of Dorsett esquire deceased who was your Oratrix
fathers older Brother for the time of their lives And the life of the longest liver of
them which was an Office antiently grantable by the Bishopp of Wynton for the tyme
beinge who had power in right of his Bishopppricke to grant the same And by the
instruction itselfe under the said late Bishopps seale if it might bee produced would
more plainely appeare which said purchase was contracted and made by the said
Browne alone and the fine or consideracon therefore given was paid by the said
Robert Browne your Oratrix late father with his proper moneys and the name of the
said John Browne the younger was incerted with a patent or onstrument or grant of
the said Office by the directon and appointment of the said Robert and in trust for
him his Executors Administrators and also and accordingly hee the said Robert
Browne entred into the said Office alone and had tooke and coverted to his owne use
all the rents and yearely profitts of the said office and premisses dureinge the[94] future
terme of his life which was for six yeares and upward dureinge all which tyme the said
John Browne did not intermeddle in the said Office or receive any rents or profitts
thereof though the same was worth 140li per Annum and that the said Roberte beinge
soe of seised and haveinge issue by Elizabeth his then wife and children (vizt) George
his onely sonne and your Oratrix Elizabeth his onely then ~~Wife~~ daughter made his last
will and Testament in writeinge dated the second daye of August in the yeare of our

lord 1637 and concerneinge as the truth was and is) that hee much lymitted[95] and appoint the benefitt of the trust which after his death by the said intent[96] and Grant would rest in the said John Burrough and intendinge to settle and appoint how the truth[97] should be disposed of and imployed by his said last will did amongst other things give and appoint the said office and premisses which hee holds under the Bishopp of Wynton for his owne life and the life of the said John Browne as aforesaid to his said wife Elizabeth dureinge her widdowhood to the use of [his] Children to use in turn …ferre them and to rayse porcons on them as in her discretion should bee thought fitt with the advise of his overseers thereby further instans after his death the said Office should bee bought of the Bishopp for another life in trust for his said wife and children and after said will made his said Wife his sole Executrix and John Porter gentleman Overseer thereof as by the said will and elacion beinge thereunto had more plainely would appeare and shortly after dyed and the said John Browne became solely of late as in the said Office and your Orator further and tooke to husband your said Orators were lawfully joyned and thereupon your Orator in right of his said wife shortly after repaired unto the said George Browne and gave him notice of their said marriage and hath since both by himselfe and severall other friends and Agents on his and his said Wifes behalfe endeavored and perswaded the said Browne in a friendly manner to make payment of the said porcons which he hath and still most unconsionably and also to thend therefor and that the said George Browne who self knoweth all and every the premisses aforesaid to bee true may Answere all and every the premisses And that att the said proceedings of bill Answere Replacacion Supposicons and orders may stand revived in such and the same manner to all intents and purposes as the same Were att the tyme of the death of the said Spigurnell as aforesaid and that your Orator and Oratrix may bee speedily releived herein accordinge to equity and good conscience may it please your lordshipp to grant unto your Orator, Oratrix his majesties most gracious bill of subpeona to bee directed on the said George Browne John Gallopp and John Browne concerneinge the same

[END OF DOCUMENT]

16.

Description: Answer of John Gollop, 13 May 1667
Reference: T.N.A., C 6/46/77
Note: This is the answer to the complaint of Edward Chard and Elizabeth Chard number **14** in this volume. Gollop at this date was the joint holder of the patent of Clerk of Taunton Castle with Elizabeth's brother George Browne.

The severall Answers of John Gollop gentleman one of the defendents to the Bill of Complaint in the nature of a Bill of Revivor of Edward Chard and Elizabeth his wife Complainants

All just excepcions to the severall insufficiencies and imperfeccions of the said Bill of Complaint and the matters therein conteyned to the defendant now and alwaies reserved for answer to soe much thereof as doth concerne this defendant he sayth that he was not any party to the Bill of Complaint in the Complainants said Bill mencioned to be heretofore exhibited in to this honorable Court by Thomas Spigurnell in the Complainants said Bill of Complaint named and is advised by his Counsell that the proceedinges thereuppon hee ought not nor can be .ev.ed against as this defendant by the Complainants now Bill of Complaint however for the satisfaccon of the said Complainants and this honourabble Court touchinge the right which this defendant hath in and to the Office of Clarke of the Castle of Taunton in the County of Somerset this defendant sayth that he doth not clayme any interest in the same to the prejudise of him this defendant but doth say and confess that his name was used in the purchase of the same of Brian Lord Byshopp of Winton in trust by and for George Browne gentleman in the said Bill of Complaint named did not otherwise Without that that there is any other matter or things clause or circumstance in the said Bill of Complaint conteyned materiall or effectuall in the Law for this defendant to make answer and herein whereby not sufficiently answered unto confessed or avoyded transfer or denyed to the knowledge of this defendant is true All which matters and things this defendant is ready to aveare justifie mainteyne and prove as this honourable Court shall avear and therefore humbly prayeth to be here discharged with his reasonble costs and charges in this behalfe most wrongfully susteyned.

　　　[*signed*] John Gollop

This response was taken at Beaminster in the County of Dorset on the 13th day of May in the 19th year of the reign of King Charles the Second of England &c [1667] by his oath in our presence[98]
[*signed*] Walcot Abington　Tho. Abington

[END OF DOCUMENT]

17.

Description: Final decree in Chancery in the case of Chard versus Browne, 11 April 1668
Reference: T.N.A., C 78/728 no.8 1668
Note: It can be argued that the 'dispute' started in 1658 when Spigurnell obtained the patent and this final decree realised a judgement some ten years later.

11 April 1668
Decree - Chard versus Browne

[*m*.28] whereas heretofore that is to say in the Terme of Saint Michael the Archangell in the yeare of our lord one thousand six hundred and sixtie George Browne Esquire onely sonne and heire of Robert Browne Esquire deceased Complaynant [*m*.27] did exhibite his Bill of Compaint into this high and honourable Court of Chancery against Thomas Spigurnell gentleman since deceased and Elizabeth his wife Elizabeth Browne since deceased and others Defendants Thereby setting forth that the Complainants said ffather haveing long before his death settled all his lands of Inheritance of Twoe hundred pounds per Annum and upward upon the Defendant Elizabeth Browne his then wife the Complainants mother for her Joynture and being alsoe seized to him and his heires of a Coppyhold Tenement parcell of the mannor of Taunton Deane in the County of Somersett of about ffive pounds per Annum and alsoe interessed and possessed of the residue of a Terme of one thousand yeares of a certaine messuage and Tenement called middleton in Huish Campflower in the said County of Somersett of ffowerscore pounds per Annum and upward and likewise possessed of ready money goodes and Chattells worth three thousand pounds and upwards and haveing yssue onely the Complainant and Elizabeth his daughter both very young hee the said Complainants father intending to make provision for a reasonable mayntenance for the Complainant and his said sister dureing theire mynorityes out of his reall and personall estate not in Joynture to the Complainants said mother and to have a convenient porcion raysed out of the same after his death from the Complainants said sister and that the residue thereof should come to the Complainant And yett to leave a seeming over aweing power in the Complainants said mother touching the same the Complainants said ffather the second day of August one thousand six hundred thirtie seaven made his last will and Testament in writeing and thereby amongst other thinges did give as well his chattells reall as his other personall estate to the Complainants said mother in Trust for the Complainant and his said sister and thereby directed that shee should have them for her widdowhood and dispose of the same for the proferrment of the Complainant and his said sister as shee should thinke meete and they should merritt And further thereby declared that if the Complainants said mother married againe that then shee should content her selfe with her joynture and make over the said reall and personall estate to the Overseer of

the said will to the use of the said Children to bee distributed as hee should thinke fitt
And that the Complainants said late ffather and the Defendant John Browne the sayd
ffathers brothers sonne whose name was used onely in Trust for the Complainants
said ffather being seized for the Termes of theire naturall lives and the life of the
Survivor of them of the Office of Clerke of the Castle of Taunton in the County of
Somersett with the perquisites proffits and appurtenances thereto belonging worth one
hundred and Eighty pounds per Annum above reprizes the Complainants said ffather
did by his said will give the said Office to the Complainants said mother dureing her
widdowhood for the meyntenance of his Children and rayseing of porcions for them
And directed that after his death the said Office should bee bought for another life to
bee added to the said John Browne in Trust for his said wife and Children And of his
said will made the Complainants said mother Executrix and one John Porter
gentleman his Overseer and shortly after dyed, after whose death the Complainants
said mother proved the said will and tooke upon her the Execucion thereof and
believed shee would have performed the Trust had shee continued in health But shee
groweing sicke and weake and deprived of the exercise of her limbs by reason of the
dead Palsie and the Defendant Thomas Spigurnell haveing intermarryed the
Complainants said sister Elizabeth and designed to gayne the whole reall and personall
estate of the Complainants said ffather to himselfe hee the said Thomas Spigurnell
obteyned from the Complainants said mother in her weaknesse one or more writeing
or writings under her hand and seale prepared by him and not understood by her to
violate the said Trust and by colour thereof hee had possessed or disposed of all or
the greatest parte of the said Testators Estate and received the proffitts thereof and of
the said Office ffor releife wherein and to have a performance of the said Trust the
said Complainant humbly prayed the ayd and Assistance of this honourable Court and
processe of Subpena to bee awarded against the said Defendants to appeare and
Answere the premisses which being graunted and the said Defendants there withall
served they appeared accordingly and the said Defendants Thomas Spigurnell and
Elizabeth his wife put in theire Answeres to the said Bill, And afterward that is to say
in the Terme of Saint Michaell the Archangell in the yeare of our lord one thousand
six hundred sixtie one the said Thomas Spigurnell and Elizabeth his wife
Complainants did exhibite theire Bill of Complaynt into this hornourable Court
against the George Browne and John [m.26] Gollop Gentleman and the said John
Browne Defendants Thereby setting forth that the said Robert Browne in one
thousand six hundred thirty three did purchase of Walter lord Bishop of Winton[99] the
said Office of Clerke of the Castle of Taunton aforesaid to himselfe and unto the said
Defendants John Browne for theire lives and the longest liver of them which said
purchase was made by the said Robert Browne alone and the ffyne and consideracion
for the same payd by him and the said John Browne's name was incerted into the said
Patent in Trust for the said Robert Browne his Executors Administrators and Assignes
And the said Robert being soe thereof seized, the second day of August one thousand
six hundred thirty seaven made his last will in writeing to the effect as in the former
<said> bill is sett forth and shortly after dyed, and the said John Browne him Survived
and was solely estated in the said Office in Trust as aforesaid And that the
Complainant Thomas Spigurnell haveing an estate worth neare Twoe hundred pounds

per Annum upon a treaty had betweene him and the said Elizabeth Browne touching a marriage betweene the Complainants which afterwards tooke affect Itt was about ffower yeares before the Bill exhibited agreed betweene the Complainant Thomas Spigurnell and the said Elizabeth Browne with the consent of the said George Browne that the Complainant Thomas Spigurnell should have as a marriage porcon with his said wife One thousand pounds to bee raised out of the proffitts of the said Office by virtue of the said Trust over and besides the Porters Office and some other lands worth about Twoe hundred pounds And that in pursueance of the said marriage agreement and Trust the said Elizabeth Browne with consent of the Defendant George Browne did by Deed charge the said Office with the rayseing of one thousand pounds part of the Complainants said wifes porcon and gave order unto the said John Porter whoe executed the said Office to passe accounts with and to pay the proffitts thereof to the Complainant Thomas Spigurnell which was done accordingly without any contradiccion of the said John Browne whoe had perfect notice of the said appointment And that the said George Browne exhibited his Bill in the Court of Exchequer about the yeare one thousand six hundred ffiftie Nine against the said mother to compell her to set forth what estate shee had settled on the Complainant Thomas as a marriage porcion with the said Elizabeth to which shee Answered and Confessed shee had charged the said Office with the payment of <the said> one thousand pounds whereupon hee Dismissed that Bill and exhibited his Bill in this Court herein before recited and that the Defendant George Browne contrary to his said ffarthers will and to defraud the Complainants procured the said John Browne to deliver upp and Surrender that sayd Patent and obteyned a new Patent or graunt of the said Office from the Bishopp of Winton for the life of himselfe and one other intending thereby to defeate the Complainant of the benefitt of the said Trust whereas the said new Patent ought to bee subiect thereunto howbeit the said George Browne did refuse to permitt the Complainants to receive the said one thousand pounds and damages out of the proffitts of the said Office, ffor releife wherein the Complainants humbly prayed the ayd and Assistance of this honourable Court and processe of Subpena to bee awarded against the said Defendants to appeare and Answere the premisses, which being graunted and the said Defendants therewithall served they appeared accordingly and put in theire Answeres to the said Bill And the Defendant George Browne thereby sett forth the same matter in effect as in the said Bill before recited And further sett forth that severall Suites happening betweene the said Defendant George Browne and the Complainant Thomas Spigurnell all matters in difference betweene them were referred to the said John Browne and bonds of greate penaltyes were by them mutually entred into to stand to his Award therein which said John Browne made his Award touching the said premisses and thereby Awarded that the Defendant George Browne should pay unto the Complainant Thomas Spigurnell the summe of Three hundred pounds att a day then to come and since past And that thereupon the said Thomas Spigurnell was to deliver up unto him all the writeing in his hands concerning the said Estate and Office and relinquish all his interest therein and all suites betweene them to cease And that in obedience to the said Award the said Defendant George Browne att the day in the said Award lymitted did tender and was ready to pay to the said Thomas Spigurnell the said Three hundred pound. Soe [*m.*25] as hee would deliver upp the said writings and assigne his interest in the said estate according to the said Award and did sucease his said suite in this Court and att law But the Complainant Thomas Spigurnell refuseing to performe the said Award on his parte hee the said Defendant George Browne did not deliver the said Three hundred pounds unto him but was and had beene allwayes ready to have paid the same soe as the said Complainant Thomas Spigurnell would performe the said Award on his parte, and hoped to prove that a sufficient porcion was or might have beene raysed since his ffathers death out of the estate left in Trust by him to the Defendant George Brownes mother And Confessed that uppon surrendering upp the old Patent hee had att his owne charges obteyned a new graunt of the said Office unto him the said George Browne and the Defendant John Gollop gentleman for theire lives and the the life of the longest liver of them which graunt had beene confirmed by the <said> Deane and Chapter of Winchester And denying and avoyding the other materiall charges <of the said Bill> concluded his Answere with the gererall Traverse To which Answeres of the said Severall Defendants the Complainants in both the said Causes replyed respectively And the said partyes thereupon discending to yssue divers wittnesses were exammined in the said Causes the Deposicions of which wittnesses were duely taken retorned and published according to the Auncient and usuall rules of this Court But before the said Causes or either of the received a hearing in this Court the said Thomas Spigurnell dyed whereby the said suites abated And afterwards in the Terme of Saint Hillary in the yeare of our lord One thousand six hundred sixtie ffive Edward Chard gentleman and the Complainant Elizabeth his wife late wife and relict of the said Thomas Spigurnell Complainants did exhibite theire Bill of Revivor into the honourable Court against the said George Browne John Browne and John Gollop gentlemen Defendents Thereby reciteing the originall Bill of the said Thomas Spigurnell and Elizabeth his wife And further sett forth that the said Thomas Spigurnell before his death made his last will in writeing and had thereby given unto the Complainant Elizabeth all his interest in the said Twelve hundred pounds porcion and all benefitt to bee received thereby for the further livelyhood and subsistance of her selfe and three small children left by the said Thomas Spigurnell and of the said will made one John Pyne Esquire and John Dryer his Executors in Trust for the said Children to whom hee gave and Devised all his reall and personall estate except the said porcion belonging to the Complainant Elizabeth and appointed the same to bee sould and equally distributed amongst the said Children And that although the said porcion was all the subsistance the Complainant Elizabeth had yett the said George Browne utterly refused to give her any satisfaccion concerning the same And further sett forth that the Complainants about halfe a yeare before the Bill exhibited Intermarried and thereby became intituled to the said Twelve hundred pounds porcion and damages And thereupon the Complainant Edward Chard in the right of the said Elizabeth his wife desired the Defendant George Browne to make the payment thereof which hee refused to <doe> To the end therefore that the said Original Bill of the said Thomas Spigurnell and the Complainant Elizabeth his wife and all proceedings thereupon might stand revived in such manner as they were att the tyme of the death of the said Thomas Spigurnell the said Complainants humbly prayed the usuall processe of this Court in that behalfe to bee awarded against the said Defendants and to appeare and Answeare the premisses

102

which being graunted and the said Defendants therewithall served they appeared accordingly and <the defendants George Browne and George Gollopp> put in theire Answeres thereunto And the said George Browne by his Answere sett forth amongst other thinges the Award in his former Answere mencioned which hee was willing to performe on his parte soe as the same might bee performed on the Complainants parte And the said John Gollop by his Answere said that his name was used in the purchase of the said Office in Trust for the said George Browne and not otherwise And afterwards in the yeare of our lord One thousand six hundred sixtie six the said George Browne Complainant exhibited his Bill of Revivor into this honourable Court against the said Thomas Spigurnell Elizabeth Spigurnell and Mary Spigurnell Children of the said Thomas Spigurnell deceased John Pyne John Dryer Edward Chard and Elizabeth his wife Defendants Thereby reciteing his said Originall Bill And further sett forth that the said Thomas Spigurnell haveing in his life tyme his will and the Defendants John Pyne and John Dryer Executors thereof in Trust for the Defendants Thomas Spigurnell Elizabeth Spigurnell and Mary Spigurnell Infants his Children [*m*.24] and sett forth the content of the said will to bee as before recited And had beene informed that the said John Dryer had proved the said will And that by vertue <thereof> the Defendant made several Tytles to the personall estate lands and Offices of the Complainants said late Father To the end therefore that the said Originall Bill of the said Complainant George Browne and all proceedings thereupon stand revived against the said Defendants and bee in the same plight they were in att the time of the death of the said Thomas Spigurnell the said Complainants humbly prayed the usuall processe of this Court in that behalf to bee Awarded against the said Defendants to appeare and Answere the premisses which being graunted and the said Defendants therewithall served they appeared accordingly And the Defendants Thomas Spigurnell Elizabeth Spigurnell and Mary Spigurnell being Infants the Defendant Elizabeth Spigurnell theire mother was by the Court Assigned Gardian for the the said Defendants the Infants to defend the suite But the said Defendants did not put in any Answere to the said Bill And both the said Causes standing revived and ready for hearing Afterwards the present Eleaventh day of Aprill was by this Court appointed for the hearing of the said Causes On which day upon the hearing and debateing the matter in question betweene the said parties in the presence of Councell learned on both sides the scope of the said severall Bills and Answeres appeared to bee in effect as before recited And the Councell for the Defendant George Browne insisting that the Defendant was still ready (after much trouble and great expence hee hath beene since put unto in these suites) to performe the Award and pay the said Three hundred pounds Albeit Spigurnell and his wife had already received out of the Defendants ffathers estate sufficient to satisfye the said One thousand Two hundred pounds or att least a porcion suitable to her quallity Provided that the said Chard and his wife and the said Spigurnells Executors would deliver upp to him all the writeings which concerned the said estate and Offices and ioyne with the Executors of the said Spigurnell in a Conveyance of the premisses to the said George Browne But the Councell of the said Chard and his wife insisted that the Award was wilfully broken by the said George Browne whoe therefore ought not to have any benefitt thereby And that the said Award was made many yeares since and however the Complainants

Chard and his wife ought to have Interest for the Three hundred pounds ever since itt was payable by the Award whereupon and uppon full debate of the matter and hearing what was alleadged on either side Itt is this present Terme of Easter that is to say on Saturday the Eleaventh day of Aprill in the Twentieth yeare of the reigne of our Soveraigne lord Charles the Second by the grace of God of England Scotland ffrance and Ireland King Defender of the ffaith &c By the right honourable Sir Orlando Bridgeman Knight and Baronet lord Keeper of the greate Seale of England and by the Authority of the said high and honourable Court of Chancery Ordered Adiudged and Decreed that the said George Browne shall pay the said Three hundred pounds and seaventy pounds for the damages thereof into the hands of such person or persons and att such time and place as Sir Moundeford Gamston Knight one of the masters of this Court shall nominate and appointe in Trust for the Complainant Elizabeth But itt being alleaged by the Councell of the said Elizabeth that shee hath contracted severall debts over and besides the charges of the present suites and hath noe Estate but the said Three hundred and seaventy to satisfye the same Itt is further Ordered and Decreed by the Authority aforesaid that the said master doe Exammine how much the debts are which the said Elizabeth is lyeable to satisfye and to allowe soe much out of the <said> Three hundred and seaventy pounds as will discharge the same and to nominate some sufficient person or persons whoe <will> give good security to pay the interest of the residue of the said Three hundred < and seaventy> pounds which shall bee then left to the hands of the said Elizabeth for her livelyhood and meyntenance dureing her life and after her death to pay and distribute the said residue of the said Three hundred and Seaventy pounds soe to be served amongst her Children in such manner as shee the said Elizabeth shall by Deed under her hand and seale whether sole or being marryed lymitt and appointe And for want of such lymitacion and appointment equally amongst all her children liveing att the tyme of her death And att the payment of the said money by the said George Browne Itt is Ordered and Decreed that the Complainant Chard and his wife and the Executors the Infants and the said John Pyne and John Dryer shall deliver upp to the said George Browne all the writeings in theire hands or in the hand of any other [m.23] by the delivery or privity of them or of any or either of them which doe concerne the reall and personall estate and Offices of the said Robert Browne and Elizabeth his wife or any or either of them and shall alsoe Convey Release and Assigne over all theire Interest therein to the Defendant George Browne or to such as hee shall nominate discharged of all Incombrances done by them or any or either of them And shall in the meantyme deliver true Coppies of the same Deeds to the said George Browne hee payeing for the same to the end hee may the better prepare the said Conveyances and Assignment, And in soe doeing the said John Pyne and John Dryer shall bee protected by this present Decree, And itt is further Ordered and Decreed that the sayd Children the Infants when they shall come of age shall alsoe joyne in the said Conveyance and Assignment and that the said George Browne his heires Executors Administrators and Assignes shall alsoe have hold and enioy all the reall and personall estate of his said ffather and mother and likewise the said Offices by the Decree of this Court against the said Edward Chard Elizabeth his wife John Pyne John Dryer and Thomas Spigurnell Elizabeth Spigurnell and Mary Spigurnell the Infants and all Clayming by from or under them or any or either of them or from by or under the said Thomas Spigurnell deceased And in case the said parties shall differ touching the said Conveyances Release or Assignments the said master is to direct and settle the same.

[END OF DOCUMENT]

18.

Description: Assignment of a debt owed to George Browne, 1 April 1669
Reference: S.H.C., DD/WO/5/6/1
Note: This is the first and earliest document in this bundle of deeds, as signified by the number 1 in round brackets.

Dryer per Browne
The Assignment of my Debte to George Browne in persuance of a Decree in Chancery 1 Ap. 1669[100]

(1)

This Indenture made the First day of Aprill in the one and Twentieth yeare of the Raigne of our Soveraigne Lord Charles the Second by the grace of god of England Scotland France and Ireland King Defender [of] the faith &c and in the yeare of our Lord One Thousand six hundred sixtie and Nyne **Betweene** Edward Chard of Long Sutton in the Countie of Somersett gent and Elizabeth his wife the Relict of Thomas Spigurnell late of Long Sutton aforesaid gent deceased Thomas Spigurnell Elizabeth Spigurnell and Mary Spigurnell children of the said Thomas Spigurnell and Executors of the last will and Testament of the said Thomas Spigurnell John Pyne the elder of Curry Malet in the said Countie Esquire and John Dryer of Long Sutton aforesaid in the same Countie yeoman Executors in trust of the saide Thomas Spigurnell the father of the one parte and George Browne of Sherford within the parish of Wilton in the same Countie Esquire sonne and heire of Robert Browne late of Sherford aforesaid Esquire deceased by Elizabeth his wife of the other parte **Whereas** the saide Robert Browne was in his life tyme lawfullie interested and possessed for a long terme of yeares yet unexpired of and in a certaine messuage Tenement and Lands or certaine messuages Tenements and Lands with theire appurtenances commonlie called Middleton scituate lying and being in the parish of Huish Champflower in the said Countie of Somersett and alsoe lawfullie seized to him and his heires forever according to the Custome of the Mannor of Taunton Deane of and in certaine Lands Tenements and hereditaments sometymes in the possession of one Collins and being alsoe seized for his owne life and the lives of severall other persons or for yeares determinable by theire deathes of and in certaine Tenements and Lands with theire appurtenances scituate lying and being on Stokehill and elswhere within the parish of Stoke=Mary in the said Countie and of and in a certaine messuage or Tenement or Lands with theire appurtenances wherein the said Robert Browne and Elizabeth his wife did and the said George Browne doth now inhabite scituate lying and being att Sherford aforesaid within the said parish of Wilton being the inheritance of Sir William Portman Baronett and Knight of the Bath **And whereas** the said Robert Browne togeather with John Browne of Frampton in the Countie of Dorsett Esquire whose name was therein used onlie in trust for him the said Robert Browne were in the life tyme of him the said Robert Browne lawfullie seized for the termes of theire

106

naturall lives and the life of the longest liver of them of and in the Office of Clerke and Porter of the Castle of Taunton in the said Countie of Somersett and of the profitts benefitts and advantages of and belonging to and arising out of the same **And whereas** the said Robert Browne being of all and singular the premisses soe seized and possessed and having issue onlie the saide George Browne and Elizabeth the now wife of the said Edward Chard in and by his last will and testament in writing bearing date the second day of August in the yeare of our Lord god one Thousand six hundred thirtie and seaven amongst other Legacies therein by him given and bequeathed did give unto the said Elizabeth his wife in trust for his children his lease att Stokehill for three lives with his Coppy hold Taunton Deane land sometimes in the possession of the said Collins and his lease for a Thousand yeares of his Land called Middleton in the saide parish of Huish Champflower and his personall Chattles that she might have the use of them for her widdowes estate and dispose of them for the behoofe and proferrment of her said children as she should see cause and they should meritt and did in and by the same will give the said offices of Clerke and Porter of the said Castle in the same manner to his saide <use> during her widdowhood to the use of his said children to maintaine them and proferr them and did raise porcions for them as in her discretion with the consent of his Oveseer should be thought fitt and of his saide will made the saide Elizabeth his wife his executrix and shortlie after dyed upon whose death the said Elizabeth in due forme of law proved the said will and tooke upon her the burthen and execucion of the same **And Whereas** the said Elizabeth Browne afterwards by her deed or writing under her hand and seale bearing date the Thirtieth day of March in the yeare of our Lord god one Thousand six hundred ffiftie and eight in for and in consideracion of a marriage agreed to bee had by and betweene the saide Thomas Spigurnell the father and Elizabeth the now wife of the saide Edward Chard did give grant and bequeath unto the saide Thomas Spigurnell the father in his life tyme the saide Lands and Tenements in Huish Champflower and her several Land and Tenements in Stokehill in the said County of Somersett and all her right intrest and title to them each and everie of them and did thereby promise and agree imediatelie after the saide marriage had to make further assureance of the same **And whereas** the saide Elizabeth Browne the Executrix did alsoe in and by the said deed or writing under her hand and seale give and bequeath to the saide Thomas Spigurnell the Father the somme of one Thousand Pounds to bee raised by the profitts of the said offices of Clerke and Porter of the said Castle and did promise and agree for his better receipt of his said one Thousand pounds upon request to make him any Conveyance or assureance of the same Offices and in case her terme in the same should cease before the said one Thousand pounds should bee raised that then the saide Thomas Spigurnell the father should after her decease have to him and his heires for ever the small parcell of Land she bought of Mr Jervis and the Tenement she then lived in with the Lands belonging to it which she held of the said Sir William Portman for three lives then to bee nominated and alsoe the residue of her plate and goods not then disposed of and till payment of the said one Thousand pounds should receive the rents issues and profitts of the saide Lands and Tenements att Huish Champflower and Stokehill and of the said Offices as in and by the said deed more att large appeareth **And whereas** the said Elizabeth Browne the

Executrix afterward by her deed under her hand and seale bearing date the second day
of May in the yeare of our Lord god One Thousand six hundred ffiftie and Nyne for
the consideracione therein expressed did give grant and demise unto the said Thomas
Spigurnell the father in his life tyme all her messuages Lands Tenements and
hereditaments called Middleton scituate lying and being in Huish Champflower
aforesaid and all her messuages Lands Tenements and hereditaments on Stokehill with
the said Offices of Clerke and Porter of the saide Castle of Taunton **To have** and to
hold the saide messuages Lands Tenements and hereditaments in Huish Champflower
aforesaid with theire and everie of appurtenances unto the said Thomas Spigurnell the
father his executor administrators and assignes for and during all the rest and residue
of an estate for the terme of one Thousand yeares which she had therein there to
come and unexpired **And To have** and to hold the saide messuages Lands Tenements
and hereditaments on Stokehill aforesaid with theire and everie of theire
appurtenances unto the said Thomas Spigurnell the father his executors administrators
and assignes for and during the terme of ffourescore and Nyneteene yeares fully to
bee compleate and ended if Thomas Browne and George Browne sonnes of John
Browne Esquire or either of them should soe long live **And to have** and to hold the
said Offices of Clerke and Porter of the Said Castle with all the benefitt profitts and
advantages to the same belonging unto the said Thomas Spigurnell the father and his
assignes for the payment of the said one Thousand pounds if the saide John Browne
should soe long live in and by the saide last recited deed reference being thereunto had
it doth alsoe more at large appeare **And whereas** the saide Elizabeth Browne since
dyed intestate upon whose death Letters of Administracion of her goods and Chattles
and alsoe Letters of Administracion of the goods and Chattles of the said Robert
Browne by her unadministred with his will thereunto annexed have been in due forme
of Law granted to the saide George Browne **And whereas** divers suites and
controversies did in the life tyme of the saide Thomas Spigurnell the father arise and
were commenced and depending in his Majesties high Court of Chancery by and
betweene him and the saide Thomas Spigurnell the father and the saide George
Browne touchinge the premisses the finall ending and determining of which was by
the saide Thomas Spigurnell the father in his life tyme and the saide George Browne
mutuallie referred unto John Browne the elder of Frampton in the Countie of Dorsett
Esquire who by writing under his hand and seale dated the sixteenth day of May in the
yeare of our Lord one Thousand Six hundred sixtie and one made an award touching
the same and did thereby amongst other things order and award that the said George
Browne should att or before the foure and Twentieth day of June then next following
pay to the said Thomas Spigurnell the father the somme of Three hundred pounds
and that the said Thomas Spigurnell the father should on payment of the same deliver
to the saide George Browne all such deeds writings and evidencies as hee ever had
concerning the severall estates and offices of the saide Robert Browne and Elizabeth
his wife and relinquish and release any clayme or title thereunto as in and by the said
award reference being thereunto had at large appeareth **And whereas** the saide
Thomas Spigurnell the father not acquiesceing in the said award exhibited his bill in
the said high Court of Chancery against the saide George Browne and others to have
the said Offices made lyable to the raising and Satisfaccion of the said one Thousand

pounds and thereupon the said George Browne proceeded in a suite by him before that tyme commenced in the same Court against the said Thomas Spigurnell the father but before either of the said suites received a hearinge the said Thomas Spigurnell the father dyed having in his life tyme made his will and amongst other Legacies thereby given left unto the said Elizabeth his then wife her porcion in the said George Brownes hands and of his said will made saide Thomas Spigurnell his sonne Elizabeth Spigurnell and Mary Spigurnell all infants his Executors and the saide John Pyne and John Dryer his executors in trust upon whose death both the saide suits in the saide high Court of Chancery abated **And whereas** the said John Dryer hath in due forme of Law proved the said will and tooke upon him the burthen of the execucion thereof and of the said trust in him and in the said John Pyne in and by the same will resposed **And whereas** the said Edward Chard and Elizabeth his wife since theire said intermarriage exhibited theire Bill against the said George Browne and others in the said high Court of Chancery to revive the said bill formerlie there exhibited against him and others as aforesaid by the said Thomas Spigurnell the father as aforesaid and all the proceedings thereupon had which were accordinglie revived **And whereas** the said George Browne since the death of the saide Thomas Spigurnell the father alsoe exhibited his bill into the said high Court of Chancery against the said Edward Chard Elizabeth his wife Thomas Spigurnell the sonne Elizabeth Spigurnell Mary Spigurnell John Pyne the elder and John Dryer to revive the saide former bill by him heretofore exhibited in the same Court against the said Thomas Spigurnell the father Elizabeth his wife and others and all his proceedings thereupon had which were accordinglie revived **And whereas** the causes upon both the said bills of Revivor were heard in his Majesties said high Court of Chancery upon Satterday the eleventh day of Aprill last past when it was amongst other things ordered and decreed that the saide George Browne should pay the said Three hundred pounds and Threescore and tenn pounds for the damages of the same into the hands of such person or persons and at such tyme and place as Sir Mondiford Bramston knight one of the Masters of the said Court should nominate in trust that out of and with the same such debts as the said Elizabeth the wife of the said Edward Chard is lyable to satisfye should bee paid and that the interest of the residue of the saide Three hundred and seaventie pounds which should bee then left should bee paide to the hands of the said Elizabeth Chard during her life for her mayntenance and that after her death the said residue of the saide Three hundred and seaventie pounds whereof she was soe to have the interest should bee divided amongst her children in such a manner as she by her deed under her hand and seale should Lymite and for want of such Lymitacion equallie amongst all her children att her death and that the saide Edward Chard and Elizabeth his wife John Pyne and John Dryer should att the same tyme convey release and assigne all theire interest in the reall and personall estate and Offices late of the said Robert Browne and Elizabeth his wife or of either of them to the saide George Browne discharged of all incumbrances done by them to which conveyances the saide Thomas Spigurnell the sonne Elizabeth Spigurnell and Mary Spigurnell the infants were to bee parties and to joyne in the same when of age as in and by the saide decree amongst other things more att large appeareth **wittnesse** nor these presents that the saide Edward Chard and Elizabeth his wife Thomas Spigurnell the sonne Elizabeth

Spigurnell and Mary Spigurnell the infants and the said John Pyne and John Dryer aswell for and in consideracion that the saide George Browne hath paid the saide Three hundred and seaventie pounds according to the direccions of the said Master pursueant to the said Decree as alsoe in obedience to and performance of the same Decree they the said Edward Chard Elizabeth his wife Thomas Spigurnell the sonne Elizabeth Spigurnell Mary Spigurnell John Pyne John Dryer **have** granted assigned sett over and for ever released and confirmed and by these presents doe and everie and either of them doth grante assigne sett over and for ever release and consigne unto the said George Browne his heires executors administrators and assignes the said messuages Tenements and Lands messuage Tenement and Lands with theire and everie of theire appurtenances commonlie called Middleton scituate lying and being in the parish of Huish Champflower aforesaid and the said Lands Tenements and hereditaments sometimes in the possession of one Collins and the saide Tenement and Lands with theire appurtenances scituate lying and being on Stokehill and elsewhere within the saide parish of Stoke Mary and the said messuage or Tenement and lands with theire appurtenances wherein the saide Robert Browne and Elizabeth his wife did and the said George Browne doth now inhabite scituate lying and being att Sherford within the saide parish of Wilton and the said Offices of Clerke and Porter of the said Castle of Taunton and all other the messuages Lands Tenements hereditaments Offices and reall and personall estate whatsoever late of them the saide Robert Browne and Elizabeth his wife or of either of them and all the estate and estates rights titles interests claymes profitts properties comodities advantages and demannds whatsoever of them the said Edward Chard Elizabeth his wife Thomas Spigurnell the sonne Elizabeth Spigurnell Mary Spigurnell John Pyne John Dryer and of everie or of any or either of them of in to or out of the premisses or or any or either of them or of in or to any parte or parcell of them or of any or either of them **To have and to hold** the same and everie parte and parcell thereof with all singular theire appurtenances profitts privilidges and advantages whatsoever unto the said George Browne his heires executors administrators and assignes for and during all the residue and Remainders of the saide severall estates and termes in and by the saide recited deeds or either of them or by any other way or meanes whatsoever given granted bequeathed or conveyed or meant mencioned Covenanted agreed or intended to bee granted or conveyed to the saide Thomas Spigurnell the father by the saide Elizabeth Browne deceased in her life tyme and that in as large ample and beneficiall manner and forme to all intents and purposes as they the said Edward Chard Elizabeth his wife Thomas Spigurnell the sonne Elizabeth Spigurnell Mary Spigurnell John Pyne and John Dryer any or either of them may might should or ought to enjoy the same by vertue of the said recited deeds and last will and Testament of the saide Thomas Spigurnell the father or by any other way or meanes whatsoever **And** the saide Edward Chard Thomas Spigurnell the sonne Elizabeth Spigurnell Mary Spigurnell John Pyne and John Dryer each and everie of them severallie respectively and apart for himselfe and herselfe and for his and her owne heires executors and administrators and for his and her owne act and acts onlie and severallie and for the act and acts of his and her owne heires and executors and administrators that is to say the saide Edward Chard for himselfe and the said Elizabeth his wife and for his and

her owne heires executors and administrators and for his her and theire owne
respective act and acts onlie and severallie And the saide Thomas Spigurnell the sonne
for himselfe and his owne herires executors and administrators and for his her and
theire owne respective act and acts onlie and severallie And the saide John Dryer for
himsellfe and the saide Elizabeth Spigurnell for herselfe and her owne heires executors
and administrators and for her his and theire owne respective act and acts onlie and
severallie And the saide Mary Spigurnell for herselfe and her owne heires executors
and administrators and for her his and theire owne respective act and acts onlie and
severallie And the said John Pyne for himselfe and his owne heires executors and
administrators and for his her and theire owne respective act and acts onlie and
severallie And the saide John Dryer for himselfe and his owne heires executors and
administrators and for his her and theire owne respective act and acts onlie and
severallie and not joyntlie or one of them for the other or for the act or acts of the
other or for the heires executors or administrators of the other doe severallie
Covenant promise and grant to and with the saide George Browne his heires
executors administrators and assignes shall or lawfullie may from tyme to tyme and att
all tymes hereafter quietlie and peaceablie have hold and enioy all and singular the
saide messuages Lands Tenements Offices and hereditaments and other the reall and
personall estate whatsoever late of the saide Robert Browne and Elizabeth his wife
deceased or of either of them and all and singular other the premisses with theire and
everie of theire appurtenances according to the true intent and meaning of these
Presents without any manner of lawfull lett suite trouble entry interrupcion clayme
denyall disturbance or eviccion whatsoever to be had or made by them the saide
Edward Chard Elizabeth his wife Thomas Spigurnell the sonne Elizabeth Spigurnell
Mary Spigurnell John Pyne and John Dryer or of any or either of them respectivelie
or of theire or any or either of theire respective heires executors administrators or
assignes or any of them or of any other person or persons whatsoever lawfullie
clayming or to clayme from by or under them any or either of them respectivelie And
that free and cleare and freely and clearelie acquitted exonerated and discharged of
and from all former and other guifts grants bargaines sales leases estates assignments
forfeitures morgages surrenders judgments extents Annuities rents arrearages of rent
titles troubles charges incumbrances and demannds whatsoever had made committed
done left undone or suffered to bee done by them the saide Edward Chard Elizabeth
his wife Thomas Spigurnell the sonne Elizabeth Spigurnell Mary Spigurnell John Pyne
and John Dryer or by any or either of them or by any other person or persons
whatsoever lawfullie <clayming or to> clayme from by or under them or any or either
of them respectively or from by and under theire or any or either of theire respective
rights titles interests acts or estates or by theire or any or either of theire respective
meanes assent privitie or procurement **In wittnesse** whereof the parties to these
presents have hereunto Interchangeablie sett theire hands and seales the day and yeare
first above written.
[*signed*] Edward Chard Elizabeth Chard John Dryar

Sealed and delivered by the withinnamed John Dryer in presence of Jos: King John
Lockyer Ed: Davis

Sealed and delivered by the within named Edward Chard and Elizabeth his wife in the presence of

Aldred Seaman

Edm: Dawe

Jos: King

Tho: Harvey

Aldred Seaman Junior

Jes: Norman

In pursuance of an Order of the Eleaventh day of Aprill *Anno Regni Carolus Secondi regis xx⁰* I have perused and Considered of the within written Conveyance, and doe thinke fit and directe the parties within named (whoe have not allready signed and executed the within written Conveyance) to Seale and execute the same unto the within named George Browne as by the said Order they are directed to doe Given under my hand this Tenth day of November 1669

      [*signed*] Mo: Bramston

This deede was showed to John Dryer at the time of his examinacion taken in Chancery on ~~the behalf of~~ a Contempt supposed to be by him committed at the suite of George Browne Esqʳ Complainant

      [*signed*] Ni Strode

This dede was showed to Joseph King and Edmund Dawe at the time of theis examinacions taken in Chancery on the behalf of George Browne Esqʳ Complainant against John Dryer and others Defendants to proove a Contempt

      [*signed*] N. Strode

[END OF DOCUMENT]

19.

Description: Mrs Ann Browne's lease of the Middleton estate, 24 September 1680
Reference: S.H.C., DD/WO 6/5/2
Note: This is the second document in the bundle.

Anno 1680
Mrs Anne Brownes lease of the remainder of the terme of 1000 yeres of Middletons in Huish she beinge Administratrix to her husband Geo Browne

(2)[101]

This Indenture made the ffower and Twentyeth day of September in the Two and Thirtyeth yeare of the Raigne of our Soveraigne Lord Charles the second by the grace of God of England Scotland ffrance and Ireland King Defender of the ffayth &c Anno domini 1680. **Betweene** Anne Browne of Sherford in the Parish of Wilton in the County of Somersett Widow, the Relict and Administratrix of all and singular the Goods and Chattles Rights and Creditts which were of George Browne of Wilton aforesaid Esquire her late Husband, now deceased of the one parte And John Beresford of Taunton Castle in the said County of Somersett Gentleman of the other parte **Whereas** Robert Browne late of Sherford aforesaid in the sayd Parish of Wilton and County of Somersett Esquire, deceased, was, in his life time, lawfully interessed and possessed for a Long Terme of yeares, then and yet unexpired, of and in a certayne Messuage; Tenement and Lands, or certayne Messuages Tenements and Lands with their Appurtenances, commonly called Middleton, scituate lying and being in the Parish of Huish Champflower in the sayd County of Somersett **And whereas** the sayd Robert Browne, (being soe intressed and possessed of and in all and singular the premisses, and having issue, only the sayd George Browne, and Elizabeth Browne (who was the wife of Thomas Spigurnell, late deceased, and is now the wife of One Edward Chard late of Long Sutton in the County aforesayd Gent) did in and by his last Will and Testament in writing bearing date the Second day of August in the yeare of our Lord God One Thousand Six Hundred thirty and Seaven (amongst other Legacies by him therein given and bequeathed) give and bequeath unto Elizabeth his wife in trust for his Children, his Lease for One Thousand yeares which he had of and in certrayne Lands, called Middleton, in the sayd Parish of Huish Champflower, in trust and to the intent and purpose that the same Elizabeth should dispose of the same Lands for the behoofe and preferrement of her sayd Children, as shee should see cause, and they should meritt; And of the same Will, made the sayd Elizabeth his wife, Executrix; After the death of the sayd Robert Browne, the same Elizabeth his wife, did in due forme of Law prove the sayd Will of him the sayd Robert Browne, and take uppon her the Burthen and Execucion of the same Will **And whereas** the sayd Elizabeth Browne, the mother, afterwards by her deed or Writing, under her hand and seale, bearing date the Thirtyeth day of March in the yeare of our Lord God One

Thousand Six Hundred Fifty and Eight, for and in consideracion of a Marriage then to be had and solemnized by and betweene the sayd Thomas Spigurnell, and the sayd Elizabeth, the daughter of the sayd Robert Browne, **did** give grant and bequeath unto the sayd Thomas Spigurnell in his life time **The** sayd Lands and Tenements in Huish Champflower aforesayd, And all her Right, interest and Title to them and to receive the Rents, Issues and profits of the same Lands and Tenements in Huish Champflower As in and by the same deed, more att large appeareth **And whereas** the sayd Elizabeth Browne (being Executrix of the Will of the sayd Robert Browne) did afterwards by her deed under her hand and seale bearing date the second day of May in the yeare of our Lord God One Thousand Six Hundred ffifty and Nyne, for the consideracions therein expressed, give grant and demise unto the sayd Thomas Spigurnell in his life time **All** her Messuages and Lands, Tenements and Hereditaments called Middleton, scituate, lying and being in the sayd Parish of Huish Champflower and County of Somersett, with their and every of their appurtenances unto the sayd Thomas Spigurnell his Executors Administrators and Assignes for and during all the rest and residue of an Estate for the terme of One Thousand yeares which he had then therein to come and unexpired, As in and by the deed or writing herein last before recited more at large it doth and may appeare. **And whereas** the sayd Thomas Spigurnell (being soe possessed of the sayd Messuages Tenements Lands and premisses for the Remaynder of the sayd Terme of One Thousand yeares as is herein aforesayd) did make his last Will and Testament in writing And did thereby make his sonne and daughters, Thomas Spigurnell Elizabeth Spigurnell and Mary Spigurnell (who were all Infants at the time of the death of the sayd Thomas Spigurnell, the ffather) Executors of the same Will of him the sayd Thomas Spigurnell the ffather **And** did alsoe in and by the same Will nominate, consititute and appoynt John Pyne Esquire, and one John Dryar to be Executors in Trust of the same Will of him the sayd Thomas Spigurnell, the Father, And shortly thereafter he the sayd Thomas Spigurnell the ffather, dyed, And after the death of him the sayd Thomas Spigurnell the ffather, the sayd John Dryer (uppon the refusall or relinquishement of the sayd John Pyne) did alone (in due forme of Law) prove the same Will of him the sayd Thomas Spigurnell the ffather **And** after the same Will of the sayd Thomas Spigurnell the ffather was soe proved, the sayd Edward Chard and Elizabeth his wife (who was the Relict of the sayd Thomas Spigurnell) did exhibite a Bill of Revivor into his Majesties High Court of Chancery agaynst the sayd George Browne **And** the sayd George Browne did alsoe Exhibit a Bill of Revivor into the same High Court of Chancery, agaynst the sayd Edward Chard and Elizabeth his wife, and the sayd Three Children of the sayd Thomas Spigurnell, the ffather, **And** upon a full and due hearing and consideracion of both the sayd Bills, and of the Matters and Causes which in and by each of the same Bills were expressed, set forth and complayned of, it was ordered and decreed in and by the same High Court of Chancery That the sayd George Browne should pay the summe of Three Hundred Threescore and Tenne pounds of law full English money at such time and to such persons as Sir Mondiford Brampston Knight (one of the Masters in the same High Court of Chancery) should appoynt, in trust to pay the debts of the same Elizabeth **And** that she the same Elizabeth should have the Interest of the Residue which should be remayning of the sayd summe of Three Hundred Threescore and Tenne pounds after the debts of the same Elizabeth should (of the same summe of money) be payd, for and towards the mayntenance of her the same Elizabeth during the time of her naturall life **And** that after the decease of the same Elizabeth, the Residue which at the time of the death of the same Elizabeth, should be remayning of the sayd Summe of Three Hundred Three Score and Tenne pounds, should be divided amongst the sayd Children of her the same Elizabeth in such manner as shee the same Elizabeth, by deed, in her life time, should appoynt, **And** that if the same Elizabeth should not in her life time, by deed make any appoyntment to whom and in what manner the said residue of the sayd Three Hundred Threescore and Tenne pounds should be payd, That then the same residue of the sayd Three Hundred Threescore and Tenne pownds should be payd unto and equally divided amongst all the Children of her the same Elizabeth **And** that the sayd Edward Chard and Elizabeth his wife, and the sayd John Pyne and John Dryer should at the same time, convey their interest in that reall and personall Estate of the sayd Robert Browne and Elizabeth his wife unto the sayd George Browne, discharged of all Incumbrances whatsoever done by them the sayd Edward Chard and Elizabeth his wife **And whereas** the sayd Edward Chard and Elizabeth his wife and the sayd John Dryer (The sayd John Pyne not accepting of nor intermeddling with the sayd Trust, nor anything concerning the same) by their deed Indented bearing date the ffirst day of Aprill in the one and Twentyeth yeare of the Raigne of our sayd now soveraigne Lord King Charles the Second (in which last mencioned deed the sayd Three Children of the sayd Thomas Spigurnell the ffather, and alsoe the sayd John Pyne were all named as Parties to the same deed) **did** (for and uppon the payment and receipt of the summe of Three Hundred Threescore and Tenne pownds of lawfull English money grant (amongst other things, according unto and in performance of the sayd Decree) unto the sayd George Browne the sayd Messuage Tenement and Lands or Messuages Tenement and Lands and other the premisses whatsoever with thappurtenances, commonly called Middleton scituate, lying and being in the sayd Parish of Huish Champflower and County of Somersett, And all other the Reall and personal Estate of the sayd Robert Browne and Elizabeth his wife and of either of them **To have** and to hold the same Messuage Tenement and Lands or Messuages Tenements and Lands and premisses for the severall Remaynders of the said severall Termes therein mencioned As in and by the sayd Last recited deed indented more at large it doth and may appeare **And whereas** the sayd George Browne (being lawfully possessed and interessed of and in all and singular the premisses) did dy intestate on or about the Twentyeth day of January in the yeare of our Lord God One Thousand Six Hundred Seaventy and Eight **And** (after the death of the sayd George Browne) Administracion of all and singular the Goods and Chattells, Rights and Credits of him the same George Browne were (in due forme of law) granted and committed unto the sayd Anne Browne **And** shee the same Anne Browne did afterwards enter into, and become lawfully possessed and interressed of and in all and singular the sayd premisses and every part and parcell thereof with thappurtenances for and during all the rest and residue of the sayd terme and termes of yeares which he the sayd Robert Browne ever had of and in the premisses or any part or parcell thereof and which was or were in the same premisses or any part thereof to come and unexpired at the time of the death of him the sayd George Browne **Now** this Indenture **witnesseth** that the sayd Anne Browne for and in consideracion of the summe of Three Hundred pownds of lawfull money of England to her in hand payd by the said John Beresford, att and before thensealing and delivery hereof the Receipt Whereof shee the sayd Anne Browne doth hereby acknowledge, and thereof and therewith shee doth hereby declare that shee is fully satisfied and payd and therefore of and from the same summe of money and of and from every part and parcell thereof shee the sayd Anne Browne doth cleerely acquit exonerate, release and absolutely free and discharged the sayd John Beresford his Executor and Administrators and every of them for ever by these presents And for other good and valuable causes and consideracions her the sayd Anne Browne hereunto especially moving **hath given**, granted, demised, transferred assigned and sett over, and by these presents doth give, grant, demise, transferre, assigne and sett over unto the sayd John Beresford <his Executors Administrators and Assignes> **All that** the sayd Messuage Tenement Lands and premisses or Messuages Tenements Lands and premisses with their and every of their appurtenances scituate lying and being in the sayd Parish of Huish Champflower in the sayd County of Somersett, And all and singular the Estate, Right, Title, interest, Terme and Termes of yeares Remaynder, property, clayme and demand whatsoever which shee the sayd Anne Browne now hath, may, might, should or in any wise ought to have or clayme of in or to the same Messuage Tenement Lands and premisses, or Messuages <Tenements> Lands and premisses or any part and parcell thereof with thappurtenances in or by any lawfull way, meanes or manner whatsoever **And the said** Anne Browne for herselfe her Executors and Administrators and for every of them doth covenant promise and grant to and with the sayd John Beresford his Executors and Administrators and to and with every and either of them by these presents That he the sayd John Beresford his Executors Administrators and Assignes shall and lawfully may peaceably and quietly from time to time and at all times hereafter from henceforth for and during all the rest, residue and remaynder of the sayd Terme of One Thousand yeares which is now to come and unexpired, have, hold, use, occupy, posses and enioy all and singular the sayd Messuage Tenement, Lands and premisses or Messuages, Tenements Lands and premisses and every part and parcel thereof with thappurtenances, And that free and cleere and freely and cleerly acquitted exonerated freed and discharged by the sayd <Anne> Browne her Executors and Administrators of and from all manner of former and other Guifts Grants, Leases, Assignments, Morgages, fforfeitures, Arearages of Rents, Titles, troubles, charges and incumbrances whatsoever, had, made, committed, omitted, permitted, suffered or done, or to be had, made, committed, omitted, permitted, suffered or done by the sayd Anne Browne her Executors Administrators or Assignes or any or either of them. **And** that the sayd Anne Browne her Executors and Administrators shall and will at any time or times hereafter when shee or they or any of them shall be thereunto requested by the sayd John Beresford his Executors Administrators or Assignes make, doe, acknowledge, suffer and execute, or cause to be made, done, acknowledged suffered and executed all and every such further and other lawfull and reasonable Act and Acts deed and deeds Thing and Things devise and devises Assurance and Assurances in the Law whatsoever for the further, better, and more perfect granting conveying, assuring and

confirming of the sayd Messuage or Messuages, Tenement or Tenements and Lands
and other the premisses and every part and parcell thereof with thappurtenances unto
the sayd John Beresford his Executors, Administrators and Assignes from henceforth
for and during all the rest, residue and Remaynder of the sayd Terme of One
Thousand yeares which is now there in to come and unexpired, as by the sayd John
Beresford his Executors Administrators or Assignes, or by his or their Councill
learned in the Law shall be reasonably devised advised and required **In witnesse**
whereof the parties to these presents their hands and seales interchangably have put
even the day and yeare abovewritten

[signed] Anne Browne[102]

the ffour and twentieth day of September 1680 Received then of the within mencioned
John Beresford the within mencioned Summe of Three hundred pounds in full of the
purchase mony within named I say received

By me	Anne Browne
test	Jo. Rawlingson
	Nathaniell Jessop
	Peter Diggons
	Walter Cole[103]

Sealed and delivered in the presence of us
Jo Rawllingson of Hestercombe
Nathaniell Jessop of Quantockshead
Peter Diggons of Dodington
Walter Cole of Taunton

[END OF DOCUMENT]

Appendices

1. A list of the principal manuscripts

2. Petition of Thomas Spigurnell to the Commissioners for Compounding, January 1651/2

3. Entry Book decree in the Exchequer Court in the case of Spigurnell versus the Attorney General *et al*, 28 June 1658

4. Interlocutory order in the Exchequer Court in the case of Spigurnell versus the Attorney General *et al*, 30 January 1660/1

5. Interlocutory order in the Exchequer Court in the case of Spigurnell versus the Attorney General *et al*, 6 February 1660/1

6. Final decree in Grigg versus Spigurnell, May 1663

7. Thomas Spigurnell's estate rent roll, 1664-1666

8. Inventory of Thomas Spigurnell's goods, 9 June 1666

Appendix 1

The principal manuscripts

The principal manuscript, held at The National Archives under the reference C 22/767/33, included in this volume is a roll consisting of nine membranes recording the depositions taken at Taunton in 1663. All the membranes apart from numbers two, seven and nine are written on both sides with detailed depositions. The last membrane, number nine, is used as the wrapper and has been annotated with details of the case and the reference number. There are two series of contemporary numbering on the membranes and I have used the numbers that appear at the head of each membrane. The size of the membranes varies from one length to the other and there was no standard size. The approximate sizes of the membranes are given below:

The other manuscripts which have been transcribed and included in this volume are of varying sizes. The type of documents that were common in the High Court of Chancery proceedings consist of the following documents:

Membrane number	Size in cms (width by length)	Membrane number	Size in cms (width by length)	Membrane number	Size in cms (width by length)
1	37 x 73	4	28 x 66	7	32 x 66
2	49 x 66	5	29 x 65	8	35 x 75
3	29 x 61	6	32 x 76	9	35 x 41

Bill of Complaint by the plaintiff (also referred to as the *complainant* or *orator*) which states his name, quality or occupation and residence as well as the nature of the complaint. Alternatively the proceedings could start with a *Bill of Information* by the crown. Either would be addressed to the Lord Chancellor or the Lord Keeper of the Great Seal. These bills are very long and full of legal jargon but end with a citation of the names of those complained against. In over 20% of cases the filing of a bill resulted in an informal settlement perhaps by arbitration, and maybe with a financial settlement, and no more records for the case are found. Of those which went further into the pleadings stages (below) some 70% did not result in a decree, but were abandoned for the same reasons but which are not recorded because they took place out of court.

Writ of Subpoena ordering the defendant to appear in court. Not a lot of these have survived.

Answer by the Defendant, which is the defendant's version of the facts, or a *Plea to Reject the Bill* on legal grounds.

Replication, or *Exception*, by the plaintiff which further protracts the case.

Rejoinder by the defendant.

Rebuttal may be given by the plaintiff.

Surebuttal may be given by the defendant.

Interrogatories which are lists of questions to be put to the parties, drawn up by counsels for both parties.

Depositions by witnesses, which give their name, age, residence and occupation. Those termed 'Country depositions', covering the period 1558-1714, were taken outside London or abroad by a commission set up for that purpose. In some instances there are two sets of depositions, one for the plaintiff and one for the defendant.

A Bill of Revival, if one of the parties died before the case was heard.[104]

Appendix 2

Petition of Thomas Spigurnell to the Commissioners for Compounding, January 1651/2

To the Honourable the Commissioners for Compounding

The humble petition of Thomas Spigurnell of Taunton in the County of Somersett gentleman

Sheweth

That since Allexander Middleton of Drayton in the said County of Somersett yeoman compounded with your Honours for delinquency, the Commissioners for Sequestations in the said County of Somersett, have (uppon your petitioner discovery) seized and secured an estate of Sixty Two pounds and Eight pence per annum belonging to the said Mr Middleton which hee undervalued in the particuler of his estate on his composition with your Honours; for which said discovery, a ffift parte of the profitts of the said 62li 0s 8d per annum (accrewing unto the Commonwealth by reason thereof) beeing given unto your petitioner by the resolve of parliament made on that behalfe.

Your petitioner humbly praieth your order unto the said Commissioners of Somersett to pay the said ffifts unto your petitioner for his said discovery accordingly

And your petitioner shall every pray &c

[*signed and in the hand of*] Thomas Spigurnell

[*annotated*] 14 Jan 1651

The Commissioners to certify when the first discovery was made

Reference: T.N.A., SP 23/118 f.1131

Appendix 3

Entry Book decree in the Exchequer Court in the case of Spigurnell versus the Attorney General *et al*, 28 June 1658

Monday the xxviii[th] day of June [1658]

Somersett[105]

Whereas Thomas Spigurnell gent in Easter terme 1657 did exhibite his English bill into this Court against his Highnes Attorney Generall William Hill Lawrence Saunders and Henry Whipple Thereby setting forth that the right honourable William Steele Lord Chauncellor of Ireland late Lord cheife Baron of this Court Sir John Thorowgood knight George Cooper Richard Younge John Pocock Ralph Hall Richard Sydenham Edward Hopkyns John Humfry and Edward Cressett Esquires or five or more of them were seized in ffee by vertue of severall Acts of Parliament And an Ordinance of the Lord Protector and his Counsell of and in all tenths and tythes of Corne and Grayne yearely groweing ariseing encreaseing and renewing within the parish of Wyvelscombe and Fitzhead in the County of Somersett And being soe seized they by their Indenture of Lease bearing date the seaventeenth day of June in the yeare of our Lord 1656 did demise unto the said plainant his Executors administrators and assignes all the said tenths and tythes of Corne and Grayne together with all other tenths and tythes whatsoever to the said parsonage of Wyvelscombe and Fitzhead belonging or in any wise apperteyning with all and singuler their appurtenances To have and to hold from the five and twentith day of March then last past before the date of the said Indenture for and during the terme of two yeares from thence nexte ensueing att the yearely rent or somme of one hundred and fifty pounds By vertue whereof the said plainant became interessed in and lawfully intituled to have and receive the said Tythe And that the said defendants William Hill Jane Hill Lawrence Saunders and Henry Whippell pretending tytle unto the said Tythes would not suffer the said Complainant quietly to take and receive the same and had ever since the five and twentith day of March then last past collected and received and att the said tyme of the exhibiteing of the said Bill did collect and receive all the aforesaid tythes And therefore to the intent the said defendants might discover what tytle they had unto the said tythes and whether if any Lease were obteyned from his Highnes of the same, the same Lease were not obteyned by misinforming the said plainant prayed that his Highnes Attorney Generall might answere the said bill and hee like wise prayed proces against the other defendants. And the said defendants being served with proces appeared and the said Henry Whipple and Lawrence Saunders putt in their joint and severall answeare thereunto and in their answeres said that they did not knowe that the said Lord Chancellor of Ireland and the other persons before named were seized in ffee of and in the said tythes or that they demised the same unto the said plaintiff and disclaymed any estate unto the tythes of Wyvelscombe And further said that the Rectory of Fitzhead being as they have heard and believe sequestred for the Delinquency of[106] Sir John Stowell knight of the Bath and John Gorges Esquire haveing (as hee affirmed) power to demise the same the said John Gorges the twelveth day of July 1655 demised the said Parsonage of Fitzhead to the Defendant Henry Whipple for one yeare from xxiiii[th] day of June 1655 att the yearely rent of fifty five pounds and after that the said Gorges had soe demised the same to the said Defendant Whipple and Thomas Saunders Esquire affirming that hee had power to [f.251v] demise the same The said Saunders demised the said parsonage of Fitzhead to the said Defendants untill the five and twentith day of March then last past and that during the tymes they held the same parsonage of Fitzhead to the five and twentith day of March then last past ~~and~~ they did receive the profitts thereof but since the five and twentith day of March then last past they did not clayme any interest or estate therein nor have they received any profitts thereof and they believe the said Parsonage of Fitzhead and the Tythes thereof are of the yearely value of three score pounds And the said Jane Hill did alsoe putt in her answere wherein shee saith that she doth not knowe that the said Trustees were seized in Fee of the premisses or that they made any Lease thereof unto the said plaintiffs And that about Aprill 1656 [blank] Saunders Esquire Comissioner for Sequestracions for the County of Somersett and especially interessed and appointed by his Highness for the setting of sequestred Lands in that County and amongst others the said Rectory of Wyvelscombe did demise the same to the said Defendant for one yeare from the xxiiii[th] day of June 1656 and the said Defendant was to pay the yearely rent of one hundred pounds for the same By vertue whereof shee received and tooke all the tenths and tythes of Corne and Grayne within the said Rectory of Wyvelscombe And that shee had a Graunt thereof from the said Mr. Saunders for the yeare nexte ensueing and hoped shee might quietly enjoy the same accordingly And Edmond Prideaux Esquire his Highness Attorney Generall did alsoe putt in his answere on the behalfe of his Highness wherein hee saith that hee knoweth not that the said Trustees were seized in Fee of the said Tythes or made any Lease thereof unto the said plaintiffs and that hee hath heard that the Impropriate Rectory of Wyvelscombe and Fitzhead aforesaid was heretofore parcell of the possessions and estate of Sir John Stowell a Deliquent and the estate of the said Sir John Stowell whereof the said Rectorie were parcell were by Act of Parliament vested and settled in William Skynner and others and their heires and the rents and profitts thereof ought to bee received by the Receivor Generall of his Highnes Receiver in the said County for the use of his Highness soe as it may be true the said defendants <did receive the profitts of the said Rectorie> by vertue of some demise or contract thereof which ~~the~~ some or all or any of them made by the Receivor Generall for the yeare ended the five and twentith of March 1657 but for what tyme or terme <hee knewe not> whereunto the said plaintiffs replyed therein denyeing that the Lord Protector in Aprill 1656 or any tyme before was intitled to the severall Rectories of Wyvelscombe and Fitzhead or either of them in the bill and answeres mencioned or that Mr Saunders mencioned in the answere of the said Jane Hill was intrusted or appointed by his Highnes for the letting of the said Rectory of Wyvelscombe or that hee did lease the same to the said Jane Hill or that John Gorges or the said Saunders did lett the said Rectory of Fitzhead to the Defendant Wipple or had any authority soe to doe As by the said bill answeres and[107] Replicacion more att large appeare Whereupon the said Defendant being served with Proces appeared and joyned in Comission which being executed and Deposicions thereupon taken on both sides and the Deposicions published The said cause was appointed to bee heard this day Now upon full and deliberate hearing of the said cause and of Mr. Atkins and others of counsell with the [*f.252r*] said plaintiffs and of [*blank*] on the behalfe of the Lord Protector and of [*blank*] on the behalfe of the said other defendants and upon opening of the said bill answere and Replicacion and upon reading of diverse proofes on both sides This Court is of opinion that a Tryall shalbe had att the Common Lawe concerning the tytle of the said Tythes before the said cause receive a determinacion in Equitie in this Court And therefore itt is this day ordered by the Court that the said plaintiffs shall forthwith bring a feigned accion against the said Henry Whipple Lawrence Saunders and Jane Hill wherein the said plaintiffs shall declare that in consideracion of the somme of twelve pence payd by him unto the said Defendants they did assume and promisse That if the said plaintiffs should prove that William Steele Lord Chauncellor of Ireland late Lord cheife Baron of this Court Sir John Thorowgood of Kensington knight George Cooper Richard Younge John Pococke Ralph Hall Richard Sydenham Edward Hopkyns John Humfrey and Edward Cressett Esquires five or more of them on the seaventeeth day of June in the yeare of our Lord 1656 were seized in ffee by the vertue of severall Acts of Parliament and Ordinances of his Hignes the then Lord Protector and his Counsell of and in all tenths and tythes of Corne and Grayne yearely groweing encreaseing and renewing within the said parish of Wyvelscombe and Fitzhead in the County of Somersett and being soe seized they by their Indenture of Lease bearing date the said day and yeare did demise sett and to farme lett to the said plaintif his Executors administrators and assignes all the said tenthes and tythes of Corne and Grayne together with all other tenths and tythes whatsoever to the said Parsonage of Wyvelscombe aforesaid and Fitzhead belonging or in anywise apperteyning with all and singuler the appurtenances To have and to hold from the five and twentith day of March then last past before the date of the said Indenture for and dureing the terme of two yeares from thence nexte ensueing <that then the said defendants would pay unto the said plaintiff the summe of five shillings> Unto which Accion the said Defendants shall forthwith appeare gratis and plead to yssue and the said yssue joyned shal be tryed att the nexte Assizes to bee holden for the County of Somersett in Lent nexte following and att the said tryall both parties admitting all circumstances shall insist onely upon the tytle to the Tythes aforesaid and nothing else and the deposicions of such witnesses as shalbe either dead or not able to travayle shal be used and given in Evidence on both sides att the said Tryall And the Equitie of the said cause is reserved to this Court.

By the Remembrancer
tryall for the plaintiff

Reference: T.N.A., E 126 number 6 f.251r Entry Book decree, 28 June 1658

Appendix 4

Interlocutory order in the Exchequer Court in the case of Spigurnell versus the Attorney General *et al*, 30 January 1660/1

Somersettshire[108]

Wheras in the cause here depending by English bill betweene Thomas Spigurnell gentleman plaintiff and the Attorney Generall William Hill Jane Hill Lawrence Saunders and Henry Whipple defendants upon Monday the eight and twentith day of June 1658 upon hearing of the cause and counsell learned on both sides Itt was ordered by the Court that the said plaintiff should bring a feegned Accion in the office of Pleas of this Court against the said Henry Whipple Lawrence Saunders and Jane ~~Whipple~~ Hill wherin the said plaintiff should declare as by the said order was directed Unto which Accion the said defendant should forthwith appeare gratis and plead to yssue and the yssue ioyned should bee tryed att the Assizes to bee holden for the County of Somersett in Lent then next following and upon Saturday the xviii[th] day of June last the Court being informed that the said Tryall was not then had It was then ordered by the Court that the said plaintiff should declare and the said defendant should plead and a tryall should bee had thereupon at the next Assizes to bee holden for the said County of Somersett in such manner and fforme as was directed by the said former order And afterwards upon Monday the xiiii[th] day of November last the said cause being continued in the paper of causes and the late Attorney Generall of the Comonweath being dead Itt was ordered by the Court [*f.135v*] that the said cause should bee continued in the paper untill there should bee an Attorney Generall appointed for the Commonwealth Now upon hearing Mr. Atkins of Counsell with the said plaintiff informing this Court that according to the aforesaid orders the said plaintiff hath long since filed a Declaracion in the Office of pleas of this Court but the said defendants have not yet appeared thereunto and therefore desired that a Decree might bee made in the said cause for the plaintiff in regaurd the yssue appointed to bee tryed by the said orders cannot bee tryed through the fault of the said defendants and upon reading of the said order upon hearing made the xviii[th] day of June last and upon hearing Mr. Smyth on the behalfe of Mr Attorney Generall Itt is this day ordered by the Court that the said cause shalbe continued in the paper of causes for this day sennight and unlesse the said defendants shall in the meane tyme plead in the Office of Pleas according to the said former order the Court will then proceed to the hearing of the said cause.

Reference: T.N.A., E 126 No. 7 f.135r 30 January 1660/1

Appendix 5

Interlocutory order in the Exchequer Court in the case of Spigurnell versus the Attorney General *et al*, 6 February 1660/1

Somerset[109]

Monday the sixth day of February

Whereas in the Cause here depending by English bill betweene Thomas Spigurnell gentleman plaintiff and the Attorney Generall William Hill Jane Hill Laurence ~~Hill~~ Saunders and Henry Whipple defendants upon Monday the xxviii[th] day of June 1658 upon hearing of the cause and of counsell on both sides Itt was ordered by the Court that the said plaintiff should bring a feigned Accion in the Office of Pleas of the Court against the said Henry Whiple Laurence Saunders and Jane Hill wherein the said plaintiff should declare as by the said order was directed unto which Accion the said Defendants should forthwith appeare gratis and plead to yssue and the same should bee tryed att the Assizes to bee holden for the County of Somersett in Lent then next following which order was renewed by another order made the xviiith day of June last and upon Monday the thirtieth day of January this Terme Itt was ordered by the Court That the said cause should bee continued in the paper of causes for this day and unlesse the said Defendants should in the meanetyme appeare and plead in the said Office of pleas according to the said former order, the Court would then proceed to the hearing of the said cause Now upon opening of the bill by Mr Atkyns and hearing of Mr Stephens of counsell with the said plaintiff and that Mr Stroud for the defendants William Hill and Jane Hill and of Mr Smyth on the behalfe of Mr Attorney Generall and upon reading of the said order of the thirtieth of January last after long debate of the matter ffor as much as the defendants Counsell tooke some excepcions to the yssue directed to bee tryed by the said former order Itt is this day ordered by the Court that the Counsell on both sides shall agree upon the yssue to bee tryed or if they cannot agree concerning the same then counsell on both sides are to bee heard on Saturday next Unlesse the said Defendants shall appeare and plead soe as a tryall may bee had concerning the matter in question this next Assizes[110] then an Attachment shalbe awarded against them.

Hall for the plaintiffs

T.N.A., E 126 no7 f.137v an interlocutory order, 6 February 1660/1

Appendix 6

Final decree in Grigg versus Spigurnell, May 1663

[*m*.44] Decree Grigg and Spigurnell[111]
Whereas heretofore that is to say on the twelveth day of July in the yeare of our lord one thousand six hundred and sixty Richard Grigg Complainante did exhibite his Bill of Complainte into this high and honourable Court of Chancery against Thomas Spigurnell gentleman and another defendant Thereby setting forth that about the yeares one thousand six hundred forty and seaven and one thousand six hundred forty and eight in the late warrs the estate of Sir John Stowell Knight of the Bath in the County of Somersett was was either sold or given away for his loyalty to the late King unto the souldiers and sufferinge people within the Towne of Taunton and County aforesaid that were in Armes for the then Parliament and in particuler the Revercion in fee simple of one tenement and threescore Acres of land in Quantocks=hills in the said County in the possession of the Complainant who had then and att the tyme of the Bill exhibited an estate therein unexpired was sold and given away to the said soldiers and sufferinge people of Taunton which estate in Revercion of the said tenement and premisses beinge since purchased by one George Treagle att a very lowe rate he the said George Treagle together with the Trustees for the said souldiers and sufferinge people By their Deeds dated the seaven and twentieth day of August one thousand six hundred fifty nyne Conveyed the Revercion in fee of the said Tenement and sixty Acres of land unto one Roger Hurley named a defendant in the said Bill and his heires for ever in trust for the use of the said defendant Thomas Spigurnell as the defendant Hurley by some deed or writeing under his hand and seale has since deceased And the defendants haveinge soe purchased the said premisses and makeing little question but to have enioyed the same though they well knewe the Inheritance thereof to bee the said Sir John Stowells hee the said defendant Thomas Spigurnell about October one thousand sixe hundred fifty nyne pretendinge himselfe to bee lawfull owner of the said premisses contracted with the Complainant for the fee simple thereof after the determinacion of his estate therein for threescore and tenn pounds and gave Bonds unto the defendant Thomas Spigurnell and seavenscore pounds for payment thereof thirty pounds whereof the Complainant had paid unto the defendant Thomas Spigurnell as by twoe Acquittances under his hand appeared upon payment whereof the defendant Thomas Spigurnell promised that if ever the said Sir John Stowell enioyed his estate againe hee the said defendant would repay unto the said Complainant the said thirty pounds with interest thereof And further promised that if the Complainant had not a good estate in fee simple in the said premisses accordinge to the contract aforesaid That then the defendant Thomas Spigurnell would also not onely repay unto the Complainant the said thirty pounds with interest but alsoe the residue of the said threescore and tenn pounds with the interest thereof from the tyme received the same from the Complainant And the Complainant further shewed that the said Sir John Stowell being restored to his said estate the defendant Thomas Spigurnell could not performe his said Contract neither would hee

repay unto the said Complainant the[112] said thirty pounds interest according to his said Contract And denyed to deliver upp the Bond for payment of the said threescore and tenn pounds though often thereunto entreated and threatened to put the same in suite against the Complainant and to recover the penalty thereof ffor releefe wherein and that the defendant might Answere the premisses the Complainant humbly prayed the ayde and assistance of this honourable Court and proces of subpena to bee awarded against the said defendant to appeare and Answere the premisses which being granted and served the said defendant Thomas Spigurnell appeared accordingly and put in his Answere to the said Bill And thereby amongst other things confessed that hee had a Bond for payment of seaventy pounds in the Bill mencioned whereof hee had received thirty pounds But denyed hee ever made any promise to the Complainant to restore the seaventy pounds if the said Sir John Stowell came to his land as in the said Bill was sett forth And said hee expected to have the said forty pounds behinde on the said Bond with damages and Costs as hee hoped was lawfull for him to have and that hee had beene much dampnified for what thereof And denying and avoideing the other materiall charges of the said Bill concluded his said Answere with the generall traverse To which Answeare the Complainant Replyed and the said parties thereupon discending to issue divers wittnesses were examined in the said cause the Deposicions of which wittnesses were duely taken retorned and published according to the ancient and usuall rules of this Court As by the said severall pleadeings of Bill Answeres Replicacion Examiinacions of wittnesses and other proceedings remaineing of Record in this honourable Court more att large appeareth And the said Cause soe standing in Court and ready for heareing this present eighteenth day of may was by this Court appointed for the heareing thereof On which day upon the heareing and debateing of the matter in question betweene the said parties in the presence of Councell learned on both sides the scope of the Complainants Bills and defendants Answere being in effect as is before recited whereupon and upon debate of the matter and reading some proofes in the cause Itt is this present Terme of Easter that is to say on Monday the eighteenth day of May in the fifteenth yeare of the Raigne of our Soveraigne lord Charles the Second by the grace of god of England Scotland France and Ireland King Defender of the Faith &c By the right honourable Edward Earle of Clarendon lord high Chancellor of England and by the authority of the said high and honouraable Court of Chancery Ordered Adjudged and Decreed that the said Complainante shall pay unto the defendant Spigurnell the summe of forty pounds without damages or Cost att the defendants dwelling house in long Sutton on Michaelmas day next And thereupon itt is likewise Decreed that the said defendant shall deliver upp the said Bond to the Complainant to bee Cancelled.

Reference: T.N.A., C 78/722 no.22 Grigg and Spigurnell, May 1663

Appendix 7

Long Sutton Court rent roll, 1664-1666

Name	Source of income	Amount	
1664			
Edward Clasey and Edward Hill	For the Foresheere of 9 acres of meadow in the Westerne Hamocks	£7	7s
Edward Clawsey	For hay grown in the little field closes		5s
Henry Clawsey	Foreshare of 5 acres of meadow in Westerne Hamocks	£4	5s
John Barker [?]	The other meadow at Ablack 6 acres	£5	
John Bull	For arable land	£3	
John Bull	Withy Bed Close and 6 acres of arable	£1	15s
Joseph Bull	7 acres of meadow in Higher Ablack	£1	15s
Lawrance Barnard	For arable land	£1	
Robert Barnard	After grass of 14 acres meadow in Western Hamocks	£1	10s
Widow Roberts and John Westlake	'Foresheere' of 7 acres of meadow at Ablack next the river	£5	5s
1665			
John Bull	Horse pitts		20s
Lawrence Barnard	20 acres of arable in the common fields	£5	4s
Lawrence Barnard	Horseacre		8s
Nicholas Dryer	Little Field closes	£3	
Nicholas Dryer	Lypeyuts	£1	10s
Robert Creason	Shrouds of some Withy trees grown in Ablacke		5s
Robert Richards	Meadow called Paddocke	£5	
Robert Thomas	4 acres of arable		16s
Robert Thomas	Landmore and Haymore	£11	
Thomas Dryer	5½ acres of arable	£1	3s
William Gee	Close called Venshade		20s
William Gee and Robert Baunton	Eastern Hamocks and Leases in Whetmore	£22	
William Wallis	8 acres	£2	17s
William Wallis and Robert Barnard	Orchards and grounds called Broadehay and Sherrells	£4	10s
William Wallis	Pigeon dunge		5s
William Wallis and Lawrance Barnard	Orchard and Broadehay and Sherhills	£6	

1666		
Henry Classey	Heigher A Black	£7
Jane Linterne	For the moiety of Lower Ablack	£2 10s
Jane Linterne	For the other moiety of Lower Ablack	£2 10s
John Bull	Colds Oasten	£1
John Bull	Horsepitts	£1 6s 8d
John Creason	19 acres of arable in East field	10s
Lawrance Barnard	Hangland	£2
Lawrance Barnard	Horse acre and 4½ acres of arable	£1
Nicholas Dryar	Lypeyates	£2
Nicholas Dryar	Several closes of pasture	£3
Robert Baunton and William Gee	Close of meadow Eastern Hamocks and close Enshade	£22
Robert Creason	Withybed Close	£1
Robert Richards	Paddock	£5
Robert Thomas	Leases and grounds in Landmore and Heymore	£15 5s 2d
William Chambers	Western Hamocks and leases in Wetmoore	£19
William Wallis	Pigeon dunge	5s
William Wallis and Lawrance Barnard	Orchard and Broadehay and Sherhills	£6

Note: Note the amounts were collected at the year ending Lady Day. It is possible that some payments may be missing for a particular person in a year, as the above is only a record of what was received and not what was outstanding. The data above was extracted and tabulated from a Chancery proceeding.

Reference: T.N.A., C 6/180/48

Appendix 8

Inventory of Thomas Spigurnell's goods, 9 June 1666

9 June 1666

'The severall answere of John Dryer one of the defendants to the Bill of Complaynt of Thomas Spigurnell and Elizabeth and Mary Spigurnell infants, sonne and daughters of Thomas Spigurnell gentleman late deceased, by Elizabeth their mother and supposed gardian Complainant'

... (vizt) of Two Tableboards Two Chayres one Livery Cupboard one payre of Andirons one fyer pan and Tongues, then being in the Hall of the said Farme howse prised by Judicious persons at Three pounds, In the Buttery of the said House Two quarter Barrells Three Tubbs, and one Silting Trow prized by the said persons at Ten shillinges In the milkhowse Two halfe hogsheads one quarter Barrell Two little Tubbs, a Byn and one dressing board prized as aforesaid at fifteene shillings In the Ketchin one Table board Two Joyne Stooles one Firme one Cupboard, a paire of Iron doggs, one fyerpan and Tongues one fender, Two payre of Crookes Three Iron spitts Three payre of Pothookes one chopping knife, one cleaver one Jack Three Brass Kittles Three Crookes, fower Skillots one warming pan, one Gridiron, one driping pan Five pewter platters Two pye plates Two skymmers Two Basing Ladles, Two Candlestickes and Ten Latten Implements of Howshold stuffe Fower pounds, In the Brewhouse one Furnace one Tubb Two pounds and Ten shillings, In the Gallery one presse Ten shillings In the Kitchin Chamber Two Beddsteedes, one Bedd one Blanckett and a Coverlett Ten shillings In the Long Chamber one Standing Beddsteed, one little Coverlett and one litle Box Ten shillings In the Hall Chamber Three Bedsteeds Two Bedds Two Coverleds one Ruge Three fether Bolsters, Three payre of Blancketts one litle payre of Andirons, one Chayre, one Desk, Seaven paire of Canvas Sheets Fower Board Clothes one Dozen of Table Huung Fower pounds, one foole and some other smale harnes belonging to plowinge Twentie shillings one Stone Colt Eight pounds, one old lame Mare Two Saddles and Bridles Fiftie shillings The Hay fower pounds The wheat sold in Market per Bushell at the highest value according to markett prizes in all fower pounds Eighteene shillings and Seaven pence The Reed Twentie shillings All the Barley sold for fower poundes Ten shillings and Eight pence, The wood and Boards Lumber and other smale thinges Twentie shillings. At Drayton wood Ten dozen of Hurdells Three poundes Six shillings and Eight pence Hardwood faggotts Seaven shillings one Thowsand of Wallett faggotts Sixteene shillings and Eight pence Fiftie Six oakes filled Eighteene pounds Thirteene shillings and fower pence one hundred of Oake Poles Three shillings and fower pence, In London in the howse of the defendant Cotten and in his Studdey his Bookes Fiftie shillings one Dyaper Table Cloth Seaven shillings Six Dyaper Table napkins Three shillings one one Dyaper side board Cloth fower shillings one other dyaper Table Cloth Seaven shillings Nyne other Table napkins Seaven shillings Six pence, one paire of Callacow Sheets Fowerteene shillings one paire of Dowlas Sheets Eighteene shillings Two other dowlas Sheets Twelve shillinges Five bands Two payre of Cuffes Five shillings Fower pence Three paire of Stockins and halfe Sheete Seaven shillings One Stuff Cloake Sixteene shillings one Stuff Coate Sixteene shillings Three payre of Shewes fower shillings one old Wastcoate Two Hatts, one Cloth dublet and britches and Cloake and one paire of Boothose Topps (all old and decayed Twentie shillings, mathematicall Instruments Fifteene shillings, all which goods mencioned to be in London were prized by Judicious persons to amount in value unto Ten pounds Five shillings and Ten pence or neere thereabouts ...

[London £10 5s 10d]
[Total £65 9s 3d]

Note: This information was given in a court case some years after Thomas Spigurnell died. However, it is undubtedly accurate and is likely to have been copied from an inventory made shortly after he died.
Reference: T.N.A., C 6/180/47 Spigurnell v Pyne

---

1 Followed by three words crossed through.
2 Followed by six or seven words crossed through.
3 Followed by five or six words crossed through.
4 One word is illegible.
5 Possibly one or two words are illegible.
6 Translated as 'This response was taken on the first day of February in the second year of the reign of King Charles the Second in Wilton in Somerset, was committed by the above named defendant before us'.
7 One word being illegible.
8 The rest of the line is very worn with more than one word being illegible.
9 The rest of the line is very worn with more than one word being illegible.
10 The rest of the line is very worn with more than one word being illegible.
11 The rest of the line is very worn with more than one word being illegible.
12 These two words are almost illegible.
13 Possibly three illgible words.
14 The rest of the line is very worn with more than one word being illegible.
15 Two words are illegible.
16 The rest of the line is very worn with more than three or four words being illegible.
17 The rest of the line is very worn with more than one word being illegible.
18 The rest of the line is very worn with more than three or four words being illegible.
19 The rest of the line is very worn with more than three or four words being illegible.
20 The rest of the line is very worn with more than three or four words being illegible.
21 The rest of the line is very worn with more than three or four words being illegible.
22 The rest of the line is very worn with more than one word being illegible.
23 The rest of the line is very worn with more than one word being illegible.
24 The rest of the line is very worn with more than one word being illegible.

25 The rest of the line is very worn with one or two words being illegible.

26 The rest of the line is very worn with more than one word being illegible.

27 The rest of the line is very worn with more than one word being illegible.

28 The rest of the line is very worn with more than one word being illegible.

29 The rest of the line is very worn with more than one word being illegible.

30 The rest of the line is very worn with more than one word being illegible.

31 The rest of the line is very worn with more than one word being illegible.

32 This last word appears to be 'did' but is badly worn.

33 These last three words are very worn and the common form is given here in square brackets.

34 Interlined above the word *use*.

35 The word 'by' is repeated.

36 The word 'unto' is repeated.

37 The word 'foure' has been crossed out.

38 Followed by the word 'of' crossed through.

39 Followed by one word crossed through.

40 The capitalisation in this document is totally erratic and has been standardised for the ease of reading.

41 The signature of John Browne.

42 These two signatures are at the foot of the document.

43 The clerk must have made an error in writing the Chritian name George instead of Thomas.

44 These three lines are endorsed on Thomas Spigurnell's reply.

45 The top right hand corner of this document is tied at this point.

46 One word is illegible.

47 Lissante and Whetcombe both signed.

48 Annotated at the top of the document in a different hand.

49 The signature of John Browne.

50 The number '1' appears at the head of the membrane rather than the foot.

51 dare not.

52 Three or four letters are illegible.

53 Followed by two or possibly three illegible words.

54 Followed by four or possibly five illegible words.

55 These last two words are unclear.

56 Interlined over one word crossed through.

57 'of the said' is unclear.

58 Followed by at least one illegible word.

59 The scribe inserted the letter 'z' four times over a word, or words, that had been rubbed out.

60 Two illegible words.

61 Long Sutton.

62 Two illegible words.

63 Two illegible words.

64 Two illegible words.

65 Three illegible words.

66 One illegible word.

67 One or two illegible words.

68   Two or three illegible words.

69   At least five illegible words.

70   Possibly one or two words in the bottom left corner of the manuscript that are not visible due to the membranes being tightly sewn together.

71   Possibly one or two words in the bottom left corner of the manuscript that are not visible due to the membranes being tightly sewn together.

72   Followed by 'and'.

73   The end of membrane is signed by the commissioners 'Tho: Dyke HPlucknett Will: Doble'.

74   Interlined above two words rubbed out.

75   The word 'take' is repeated.

76   Followed by one word rubbed out.

77   The end of membrane is signed as before by the three commissioners.

78   A mis-spelling of surveyor.

79   Followed by 'and' repeated.

80   A term used for a kinsman who was usually a first cousin.

81   Followed by one word rubbed out.

82   The end of membrane is signed as before by the three commissioners.

83   Followed by one word crossed through.

84   One word is illegible.

85   Of a confused or disorderly nature.

86   Burton Bradstock.

87   The end of membrane is signed as before by the three commissioners.

88   'C22' is written in pencil in a recent hand.

89   Unfortunately there are relatively few surviving commissions and documents generated by the commissioners for the period 1661-1667; see the introduction to PROB 5 at https://discovery.nationalarchives.gov.uk/details/r/C12116, accessed 1 August 2021. A search of PROB 3, 5, 28, 31, 32 and 36 revealed nothing under 'Browne' or 'Spigurnell'.

90   'to with' in the manuscript is correct. It is one of several errors in this complaint.

91   This incorrect word is one of several errors in this complaint.

92   This incorrect word is one of several errors in this complaint.

93   This incorrect word is one of several errors in this complaint.

94   The word 'the' is repeated.

95   This word is very worn and unclear.

96   This word is very worn and unclear.

97   This word should be *trust*.

98   This sentence is in Latin and has been translated into English.

99   Winchester.

100   Endorsed on the outside of a folded indenture.

101   The number '(2)' has been added at a later date and signifies the second document in the bundle.

102   Seal a flower.

103   The last six are signatures.

104   P. Christensen, 'England Overview of Chancery Court (National Institute)' in *The National Institute for Genealogical Studies* (2012), 1.

105   Heading entered in the margin.

[106] Followed by one word crossed through.

[107] Followed by five or six words crossed through.

[108] Heading appears in the margin.

[109] Heading appears in the margin.

[110] The Western Circuit Assize order book contains no mention of Spigurnell or Browne during the period 1660-1663 (T.N.A., ASSI 24/22 Western Circuit Assize order book, 1652-1677). I am exceptionally grateful to Susan Moore for providing copies of the order book.

[111] Heading appears in the margin.

[112] 'the' is repeated.

PERSONAL NAMES

PLACE NAMES

SUBJECTS

Lightning Source UK Ltd.
Milton Keynes UK
UKHW051041260123
415923UK00011BA/59